BEDAZZLED SAINTS

Studies in Early Modern German History

H. C. Erik Midelfort, Editor

BEDAZZLED SAINTS

Catacomb Relics in Early Modern Bavaria

Noria K. Litaker

University of Virginia Press • *Charlottesville and London*

University of Virginia Press

Printed in the United States of America on acid-free paper

First published 2023

9 8 7 6 5 4 3 2 1

Library of Congress Cataloging-in-Publication Data

Names: Litaker, Noria K., author.
Title: Bedazzled saints : catacomb relics in early modern Bavaria / Noria K. Litaker.
Description: Charlottesville : University of Virginia Press, 2023. | Series: Studies in early modern German history | Includes bibliographical references and index.
Identifiers: LCCN 2023003659 (print) | LCCN 2023003660 (ebook) | ISBN 9780813949949 (hardcover) | ISBN 9780813949956 (ebook)
Subjects: LCSH: Relics—Germany—Bavaria—History. | Christian saints—Cult—Germany—Bavaria. | Catacombs—Germany—Bavaria. | Catholic Church—Germany—Bavaria—History. | Bavaria (Germany)—Religious life and customs.
Classification: LCC BX2333 .L58 2023 (print) | LCC BX2333 (ebook) | DDC 235/.209433—dc23/eng/20230407
LC record available at https://lccn.loc.gov/2023003659
LC ebook record available at https://lccn.loc.gov/2023003660

Cover art: Front, Holy body of St. Felix in Marienberg pilgrimage church, Raitenhaslach, 1761 (photograph by Uta Ludwig; courtesy of Pfarrverband Burghausen); back, Saint Victoria's body before restoration, St. Nikolaus parish church, Rosenheim, 1675 (photograph by Uta Ludwig; courtesy of the Archdiocese of Munich and Freising)

For my family and in memory of my friend Anne Fleming

CONTENTS

ILLUSTRATIONS

Figures

Maps

ACKNOWLEDGMENTS

One of my favorite Dürer etchings is *Saint Jerome in His Study.* Alone, the saint hunches over his desk while his faithful lion rests in the foreground. Saint Jerome's pose is one that is familiar to me from many hours in the archives, yet the research and writing of this book has been anything but a solitary pursuit. Along the way, I have benefited from the teaching, expertise, and support of so many people. This acknowledgment is a small gesture of appreciation for each person's contribution to my growth as a scholar and as a person.

My path to studying the history of early modern Europe began at Ithaca College, though this was certainly not what I had planned when I arrived on campus as an aspiring sports journalist. At Ithaca, the Park Scholar Program generously provided the opportunity for me to spend two semesters abroad—in Vienna and Dublin—during my sophomore and junior years in college. I roamed around Europe exploring as many cities, churches, and art museums as possible and encountered the early modern era firsthand through objects, artwork, and architecture. Back in Upstate New York, my undergraduate mentors, Wendy Hyman and Ellen Staurowsky, encouraged my intellectual curiosity and challenged me to think critically about topics ranging from Title IX to the role of ghosts in Shakespeare plays. Together with my time in Europe, Wendy's marvelous classes on Renaissance literature—and her patient and kind support—convinced me to pursue graduate studies in history.

It was during my graduate studies at the University of Pennsylvania that my research on catacomb saints began to take shape as a dissertation. I would like to thank Antonio Feros, Tom Safley, Larry Silver, and Lee Palmer Wandel for their dedication to training me as an interdisciplinary scholar and for their insightful feedback—over many years—on the many iterations of this book. When I arrived at the University of Nevada, Las Vegas, in 2017, I found new friends and colleagues who helped usher this project to completion by providing moral and intellectual support. Over the last six years, Elizabeth Nelson has become a wonderful friend and mentor. She and her family have warmly welcomed me into their home, fed me delicious meals, and provided a home away from home in Las Vegas. Other colleagues in the history department at UNLV, including Greg Brown, John Curry, Austin Dean, Mike Green, Jeff Schauer, and Paul Werth, provided thoughtful critiques and suggestions on my work during our faculty seminars.

Over the course of the last decade many institutions provided financial support for the research and writing of this book. I would like to thank the University of Pennsylvania history department, the University of Pennsylvania's School of Arts and Sciences, Penn's Graduate and Professional Student Assembly, the German Academic Exchange Service (DAAD), the German Historical Institute Washington, the Lemmermann Fondazione, the Central European History Society, and the Doris J. Quinn Foundation. At UNLV, I have benefited from grants from the History Department, the College of Liberal Arts, and the University Faculty Travel Committee.

This book has received the Weiss-Brown Publication Subvention Award from the Newberry Library. The award supports the publication of outstanding works of scholarship that cover European civilization before 1700 in the areas of music, theater, French or Italian literature, or cultural studies. It is made to commemorate the career of Howard Mayer Brown.

I also owe thanks to the many archivists and librarians who facilitated my research and brought my attention to important sources in their collections. The staffs at the Bavarian State Archives and the Bavarian State Library were extremely helpful throughout my two years of archive work. They frequently made suggestions about where to find useful sources and patiently pulled stacks and stacks of archival materials and books for me. I was also warmly welcomed and assisted at the Archiv des Erzbistums München und Freising (Dr. Christoph Sterzenbach), the Klosterbibliothek der Redemptoristen–Gars (Franz Wenhardt), the Pfarrachiv St. Peter in Munich (Johannes Haidn), the Museum Dingolfing (Georg Rettenbeck and Dr. Thomas Kieslinger), the Fürstlich Oettingen-Wallersteinsche Archiv Harburg (Hartmut Steger), the Bayerisches Landesamt für Denkmalpflege (Dr. Stefan Pongratz), the Staatliche Graphische Sammlung München (Dr. Achim Riether), the Stadtarchiv München (Dr. Brigitte Huber), Wasserschloss Taufkirchen (Bodo Gsedl), and the Archivio storico del Vicariato di Roma (Domenico Rocciolo).

I owe a special debt of gratitude to Uta Ludwig, catacomb saint restorer extraordinaire. Uta invited me to her home, shared her expertise on the construction of catacomb saint bodies, and provided access to her entire photo archive. Because of her generosity, I gained a much better understanding of the intense labor required to build and decorate "holy bodies," an insight that greatly influenced this book's arguments about the significance of this relic presentation in early modern Bavaria. I will always be thankful for her help as well as her enthusiasm for the project.

Throughout the course of my research and writing, many scholars, including Simon Ditchfield, Massimiliano Ghilardi, Tony Grafton, Heidi Hausse,

Bridget Heal, Jan Machielsen, Walter Melion, Emily Michelson, Katrina Olds, Nadja Pentzlin, Caroline Pfeiffer, and Dieter Weiß provided reading suggestions and archival guidance and generously shared their work. Their insights, feedback, and probing questions have improved this book immensely. Participants in the 2017 Lovis Corinth Colloquium at Emory University, the Christian Time in Early Modern Europe Workshop at Princeton, as well as fellow panelists and audience members at Renaissance Society of America and Sixteenth Century Studies conferences also pushed me to consider the significance of holy bodies in new ways. I also appreciate the anonymous reviewers for the University of Virginia Press, who carefully read my manuscript and helped sharpen my writing and enrich my thinking about catacomb saints. Additionally, I am most grateful to Erik Midelfort for including this book in the Studies in Early Modern German History series as well as for the guidance of my wonderful editor at UVAP, Nadine Zimmerli. Nadine has patiently fielded many questions from this first-time author and expertly shepherded the book to publication.

Dear friends have provided invaluable intellectual and emotional support as I worked on my doctoral dissertation and then on my book. The love, wit, and wisdom of Elizabeth Della Zazzera, Kim Hoffman, Janine Knedlik, Katie Lacz, Zoe Litaker, Liz Maltby, Hope McGrath, Heather Nepa, and Lyndsey Runaas has sustained me over the years, and I am immensely grateful for their friendship. Many other friends have provided advice and help over the decade it has taken to finish this book. I especially want to acknowledge Tomie Akin-Olugbade, Christina Bollo, Octavia Carr, Sophie Choukas-Bradley, Lori Daggar, Jack Dwiggins, Samantha Falk, Sabriya Fisher, Anne Fleming, Jamie and Andi Graefe, Heidi Hausse, Alex and Emma Hazonov, Carla Heelan, Molly Taylor-Poleskey, Jennifer Rodgers, Kate Sheppard, and the members of my Philly kickball team.

I do not have the words to properly thank my family for their support and love throughout this very long journey. They have never stopped cheering for me or believing in me, even when I started bringing home pictures of sparkly saints. Thank you to my parents, Wayne Litaker, Dianne McQueen, Susan Manring, and Ed Sutton; my grandmother, Anne Litaker; my sister, Zoe Litaker; and my puppy, Lucy, who provided much-needed companionship during the isolation of the COVID pandemic. Thank you for everything, I could not have done this without you all.

PORTIONS OF chapter 3 were first published in Noria Litaker, "*Hoc est corpus meum:* Whole-Body Catacomb Saints and Eucharistic Doctrine in Baroque Bavaria," in *Quid est sacramentum? On the Visual Representation of Sacred*

Mysteries in Early Modern Europe, 1500–1700, ed. Walter Melion, Elizabeth Carson Paston, and Lee Palmer Wandel, 154–83 (Leiden/Boston: Brill, 2019). Portions of chapter 4 were first published in Noria Litaker, “Lost in Translation? Constructing Ancient Roman Martyrs in Baroque Bavaria,” *Church History* 89, no. 4 (2020): 801–28.

BEDAZZLED SAINTS

INTRODUCTION

> We have seen a new heaven above from which the saints have
> descended
> as if the earth should become their heaven.
> —Johannes Baptist Querck, SJ, 1698

WHEN JOHANNES BAPTIST QUERCK delivered these words to the congregation gathered at Raitenhaslach cloister on August 20, 1689, he was not speaking metaphorically. Three days earlier, the relics of Saints Ausanius, Concordia, and Fortunatus had arrived at the church with great fanfare, as a crowd of thousands watched. The long procession brought the saintly relics—posed as intact skeletons and covered in gleaming jewels—into the newly renovated baroque church and installed them on three side altars. Ausanius, Concordia, and Fortunatus were hardly the only holy bodies to arrive in the Electorate of Bavaria[1]—and other Catholic territories—in the early modern period. They were part of the mass export of more than thirty-five thousand relics from the Roman catacombs to all corners of the Catholic world during the sixteenth through eighteenth centuries.[2] The ability to export relics on such a scale stemmed from the accidental "rediscovery" of the Roman catacombs in 1578 and the declarations of Catholic archaeologists who asserted that the vast majority of those buried in the labyrinthine passages had been ancient Roman martyrs.[3] Almost overnight, the church had a new and seemingly unending source of saintly relics at its disposal, an especially valuable resource for an institution eager to defend the cult of saints and relics against Protestant attacks. Over the next three centuries, the church, along with many smugglers, distributed thousands of Roman catacomb relics from Poland to Portugal to Peru. Though the church labeled some of the exported remains as "holy bodies," in most cases the small wooden boxes sent out to the faithful did not contain intact skeletons.

In the years after 1648, early modern Catholics in the Alpine regions of southern Germany, Switzerland, and northern Italy developed a relic presentation for catacomb saint remains that matched the label given to some of them by the church in Rome: "holy bodies." These relics were presented, not in fragments, as was traditional during the medieval period, but as lavishly

FIGURE 1. Saint Hyacinth, Fürstenfeld cloister, 1672. (Photograph by author)

decorated whole bodies in glass shrines—an innovative presentation, unique to the early modern period (fig. 1). The display of these relics as a whole body was a very intentional act—one which required an immense amount of time, effort, and money to execute. No decree from Rome required that the relics be staged in this manner. Rather, communities chose to acquire and then materialize the bodies of these ancient martyrs in human form.

This book examines the acquisition, distribution, construction, and display of the nearly four hundred bodies of early Christian martyrs that arrived in Bavaria from 1648 to 1803 to illuminate current debates about the negotiated nature of early modern sanctity—and confessional identity more broadly—in the period after the Thirty Years' War. It specifically analyzes the reliquary form of the holy body and how it functioned in ways distinct from fragmentary relics. Although Christian theologians had long asserted that saints were present in even a single relic particle, catacomb saints—dressed in clothing and staring out at viewers from bejeweled eyes—appeared fully human. When discussing fragmented medieval relics, Julia Smith has noted how these relics "were prone to slide into the interstices of identity and anonymity. Shorn of their labels, these objects became merely 'things,' indeterminate, ambiguous, unspecified, and devoid of relationship to those who encountered them."[4]

Whole-body catacomb saints, in contrast, were not in danger of being perceived as "things"; instead, they were *people.* At the local level, the presence of these holy bodies—and their human form—had a significant impact on the ritual of the saints' arrival (*adventus*), their role as local patrons (*patronus*), and how they were presented within the church (*domus*). At the same time, the form of the intact body enabled early modern Bavarians to concretely demonstrate their connection to and belief in important movements and doctrines promoted by the universal Roman Catholic Church, including the paleo-Christian revival and the transubstantiation of the Eucharist.

Though whole-body catacomb saints represented an innovative way to present relics, early modern Bavarian's determination to make the holy tangible and locally accessible was part of a trend within the region's piety, and baroque Catholicism more broadly.[5] This desire was not limited to creating holy bodies; it was part of a larger movement that led to the elaboration of the sacred landscape in Bavaria; across the duchy, replicas of holy sites such as Mt. Calvary, the Holy House of Loreto, and the Holy Sepulcher proliferated, as did lavish baroque churches whose interiors attempted to make heaven present on earth.[6] During this period, Bavarians built an increasing number of wayside shrines, and roadside crosses dotted the landscape in response to a "widespread desire for more holy sites and places to worship."[7] All of these physical structures gave Catholics in the region direct access to the sacred within their immediate environment. Some of the impetus for this emphasis on making the holy present can be traced to the influence of the Jesuits, who had long emphasized the importance of making religious figures, sites, and narratives visually and materially apprehensible in their churches and devotional literature.[8]

The presentation of catacomb saints as whole bodies is part of this larger phenomenon of making the holy present in the local environment, with one important qualitative difference. These saints were not artistic or architectural "replicas" of the Holy Grave, Calvary, or House of Loreto. They were the actual bodies of early Christian martyrs—singular, individual, and unable to be replicated at will. Unlike medieval saints who were "materialized by being divided up and distributed," catacomb saints were materialized by being put together.[9] The assembly process itself and the attendant outlay of labor and money provide insight into how early modern Catholics shaped their religious experience at the local level and "forged their own path within a universal church."[10] Although catacomb saints came from the very heart of the universal church in Rome—and visually reinforced certain Tridentine doctrines—their presence in one location and the humanity engendered by their skeletal display helped generate new forms of Catholic relic piety at the local level.

Previous scholarship has frequently interpreted the distribution and use of catacomb saint relics as part of the Counter-Reformation movement to defend the cult of saints and relics against Protestant attacks. In certain regions of Europe, including areas of the Low Countries, northern Italy, France, and Switzerland, the relics were sometimes acquired for explicitly anti-Protestant reasons and clustered along confessional borders.[11] In these cases, the act of acquiring and displaying relics was inherently a defensive statement of continued belief in the efficacy of the saints as intercessors and the power of their relics, something rejected by all Protestant confessions. However, both the timing and geographical distribution of the holy bodies in Bavaria and Europe point to another important dimension of the use of these relics: as an affirmative expression of Catholic identity. The majority of catacomb saint relics were exported from Rome *after* the end of the major European religious wars (1648), when confessional boundaries had largely stabilized. Furthermore, Italy, where churches had acquired more than half of the catacomb relics, had remained Catholic after the outbreak of the Protestant Reformation.[12] These trends signal that these saints did not simply play an "external role . . . as guardians of Catholic territory" but an important "internal role, binding together the faithful."[13]

Catacomb saints embodied both the outward- and inward-facing roles saints and relics played in early modern Catholicism. For the institutional church and its Catholic archaeologists, the saints' remains were material proof of the continuous practice and orthodoxy of relic veneration throughout Christian history.[14] Once the remains left Rome, however, it was up to local Catholics in towns and cities across the world—lay and clerical—to decide how to welcome, honor, and display the ancient bones. Closely examining the acquisition and distribution patterns of the relics as well as their display provides important insights into how early modern believers balanced universal Catholic doctrine with the desire to materially express their faith in a local environment.

Relics, themselves, offer a particularly useful lens through which to explore the nature of Catholic piety and the construction of early modern sanctity because "material remains have no intrinsic status as relics. . . . The symbolic and semiotic value of such objects is a reflection of the subjectivity of the society that honors and prizes them. The manner in which relics are discovered, identified, preserved, displayed, and used by particular communities is thus singularly revealing about the attitudes and assumptions that structure their outlook."[15] Given the critical role of saints in early modern Catholicism, examining the remains of catacomb saints—perhaps the most circulated holy relics of the era—from the perspective of material culture offers a new vantage point from which to evaluate the development of confessional culture in seventeenth- and eighteenth-century Catholic communities.

With the outbreak of the Protestant Reformation, the related issues of saints, sanctity, and relics became pressing concerns for the institutional church in Rome. Protestant theologians of all kinds—Lutheran, Reformed, and radical—rejected the veneration of holy relics, vigorously attacking the traditions surrounding the practice as idol worship and a waste of precious community resources. They argued that traditions such as indulgences, pilgrimages, and the exhumation of human bodies had no basis in Scripture and directed the faithful's attention and prayers away from Christ.[16] Furthermore, Protestant theologians contended that the landscape of Europe was riddled with fake and duplicate relics.[17] The Catholic Church responded to these critiques in the final session of the Council of Trent (1545–63) by unequivocally affirming the theological orthodoxy and historicity of the veneration of saints and relics. The Council wrote: "The holy bodies of the blessed martyrs . . . are to be venerated by the faithful, and that through them many blessings are given to us by God."[18] At the same time, the church conceded that certain "abuses" had crept into rituals honoring the relics and images of saints and admonished its clerics that "all superstition must be removed from invocation of the saints, veneration of relics and use of sacred images; all aiming at base profit must be eliminated; . . . and people are not to abuse the celebration for the saints and visits to their relics for the purpose of drunken feasting, as if feast days in honor of the saints were to be celebrated with sensual luxury."[19] With these instructions in hand, church officials attempted to reform and enforce boundaries around who and what qualified as holy and to eliminate any abuses related to the cult of saints. These reform efforts included creating new and stringent procedures for canonization, researching the history and validity of established local cults, revising and rewriting hagiographies to purge them of inaccurate information, and setting standards for the depiction of saints in artwork and the authentication of relics.

In the last several decades, historians and art historians have studied the myriad ways the institutional Roman church worked to define, regulate, and portray sanctity and saintly figures in early modern Catholicism.[20] Pierre Delooz and Peter Burke began this work by examining the categories and nationalities of people canonized by the church in the early modern period, and Simon Ditchfield has explored the impact that the post-Tridentine strictures on the cult of saints had on stimulating historical writing, as cities and towns attempted to prove the longevity of their local cults and associated liturgies.[21] Historians have also analyzed the criteria and methods used by the Congregation of Rites in early modern canonization processes as well as the guidelines for authenticating relics and holy bodies.[22] Studies of unsuccessful attempts at canonization as well as the study of those deemed heretical by the Catholic Church have also provided important insights into Rome's efforts to circumscribe and control the boundaries of sanctity in the period after the Reformation.[23]

Though the church worked to determine, verify, and control manifestations of sanctity in people and the environment, scholars have begun to emphasize the critical role church followers played in the development and success of the cult of saints in the early modern period.[24] It was often the faithful—not the institutional church in Rome—whose enthusiasm for a particular holy person and the religious sites, objects, and miracles associated with them that determined whether or not a cult persisted. Saints and their holy remains were experienced and used in local environments, and their veneration continued to play an integral part in the day-to-day lives of early modern Catholics the world over. Parents baptized children with saints' names. Saints' feasts marked time throughout the year, and holy relics drew pilgrims to churches across the continent. Saints' images appeared in media of all kinds from magnificent painted altarpieces to wonder-working statues to cheap engravings and woodcuts. In times of difficulty, believers prayed to saints for intercession and protection from the accidents, illness, and unexplained tragedies that occurred frequently in early modern life.

Whereas many aspects of early modern sainthood have received scholarly attention, relics—including the ways in which the remains of saints were housed, displayed, and used in ritual from the sixteenth through the eighteenth centuries—have been the subject of comparatively little systematic research. This is striking given that scholars have recognized the degree to which, in "baroque Catholicism, sanctity was embodied, and not a matter of souls or spirits only" and argued that the Catholic Reformation represented the "triumph of the material."[25] Art historian Helen Hills has even contended, when discussing visual depictions of Counter-Reformation saints in Italy, that the "production of first a body and face was fundamental to the formation of baroque holiness."[26] The lack of research on early modern relics and holy bodies, noted a decade ago by several early modern historians, is particularly apparent when compared to the extensive research on relics and reliquaries in the medieval period.[27] This situation has begun to change in the last several years as scholars of early modern history and art history have begun to focus some attention on the circulation and uses of relics in the post-Reformation period; however, there is still no survey of relics and their use in the Catholic Reformation.[28]

Despite this lack of a broad overview of the topic, recent articles and edited volumes have begun to shed light on the variety of ways relics were used for religious, political, and economic ends in the early modern era.[29] Historians have examined how relics could play important roles in state conversion efforts in the Atlantic world as well as in re-Catholicization efforts on the continent, provide tangible ties to the old faith in recusant Catholic communities in England, or bolster royal prestige through their collection in palaces like El Escorial in Spain.[30] Art historians have begun the task of examining the housing of relics in the early modern period with focus on case studies of particular churches or chapels.[31]

The distribution and circulation of catacomb saint relics has also begun to draw more attention in the last decade, although few studies have focused specifically on the materiality of holy bodies and the significance of this type of relic display. A group of scholars at l'École française de Rome recently published the most comprehensive study to date on the extraction and global circulation of catacomb saint relics by the Catholic Church.[32] This edited collection provides critical information on the number of relics sent from the cardinal vicar and papal sacristan's offices through the early modern period and traces relic distribution from eastern Europe to the Atlantic world. Regional studies by Hansjacob Achermann and José Luis Bouza Álvarez, which focus on catacomb saints in the Swiss part of the diocese of Constance and Galicia (Spain) respectively, remain the only book-length investigations into the distribution and reception of catacomb saint relics in a regional context. In the German literature, catacomb saints have most often been the focus of folklorists (*Volkskundler*) rather than religious historians. Articles on catacomb saints in Germany have largely appeared in regional journals and *Heimatschriften.* Like other works of *Lokalgeschichte,* these articles usually focus on a single church or saint rather than examining the importation, decoration, and presentation of catacomb saints across a larger region or state.[33] The same is true of the limited Anglophone research on catacomb saints, which has used case studies of small areas or single saints to explore re-Catholicization efforts, the impact of strict enclosure of nuns after the Council of Trent, and hagiographical writing.[34]

This study comprehensively examines the acquisition, distribution, construction, and display of catacomb saint relics across Bavaria over the course of two centuries. This approach reveals patterns that would not be apparent in the study of a single town, church, or saint over a shorter period and places the focus on the materiality of the relics themselves. Closely attending to the distribution patterns as well as the physical display of catacomb saint bodies provides a new lens through which to examine the development and material expression of Catholic confessional culture in early modern Bavaria, especially after 1648.

Recent research on Catholic piety and practice has demonstrated that confessional culture—like the definition of sanctity—developed as the result of negotiation between church authorities and everyday believers.[35] Narratives of top-down religious reforms implemented by the state using the tactics of "social disciplining" emphasized by the "confessionalization thesis" have largely given way to a more nuanced picture that grants agency to multiple actors at various levels of society in the formation of confessional identity. This thesis, which was particularly influential in shaping the study of the German Reformation in the late 1970s and 1980s, emphasized the role of the state in regulating and enforcing religious conformity in close cooperation with church authorities.[36] In the last several decades, studies of southwest Germany, Westphalia, the Upper Palatinate, and Augsburg have reinforced the importance of local actors—at various levels of society—in shaping religious culture and confessional identity in the Holy Roman Empire and beyond.[37] The periodization for the "Age of Confessionalism" has also received scrutiny and reevaluation, particularly in Catholic areas. Rather than ending in 1648 after the Thirty Years' War, it appears the process of Catholic identity formation often lasted far into the eighteenth century.[38] Despite these trends, the history of the Catholic Counter-Reformation religion in the Bavaria has—in many ways—remained largely unchallenged by this reassessment of the process of confessional identity formation. Bavaria is often presented by scholars as the archetypal "confessional state," in which church and state worked hand in hand to successfully implement Tridentine Catholicism on the populace in a top-down manner, a process that was successfully completed by 1648.[39]

There is certainly no doubt that the ruling dynasty of the duchy (later Electorate), the Wittelsbachs, played a critical role in the adherence of the state to the Catholic Church in Rome. From the beginning of the sixteenth century, the dukes of Bavaria ruled over one of the largest and most territorially consolidated states in the Holy Roman Empire (map 1). When the Protestant Reformation began in 1517, the Wittelsbach corulers, Wilhelm IV (r. 1508–50) and Ludwig X (r. 1516–45), were among the earliest and most important defenders of Catholicism in the empire and worked to maintain Catholicism as the dominant religion in their state. They published and enforced the Edict of Worms (1521), which banned Martin Luther from the empire, prohibited the circulation of Protestant books, and outlawed evangelical preaching. Despite their strong support for the Catholic Church, the dukes did not have the resources to enforce these anti-Protestant laws, and in the first fifty years after the Reformation, Lutheranism grew in the duchy. The evangelical movement was especially popular with the nobility, who managed to extract a concession from Duke Albrecht V (r. 1550–79) that allowed them to receive the consecrated bread and wine of the Eucharist—rather than having the wine reserved

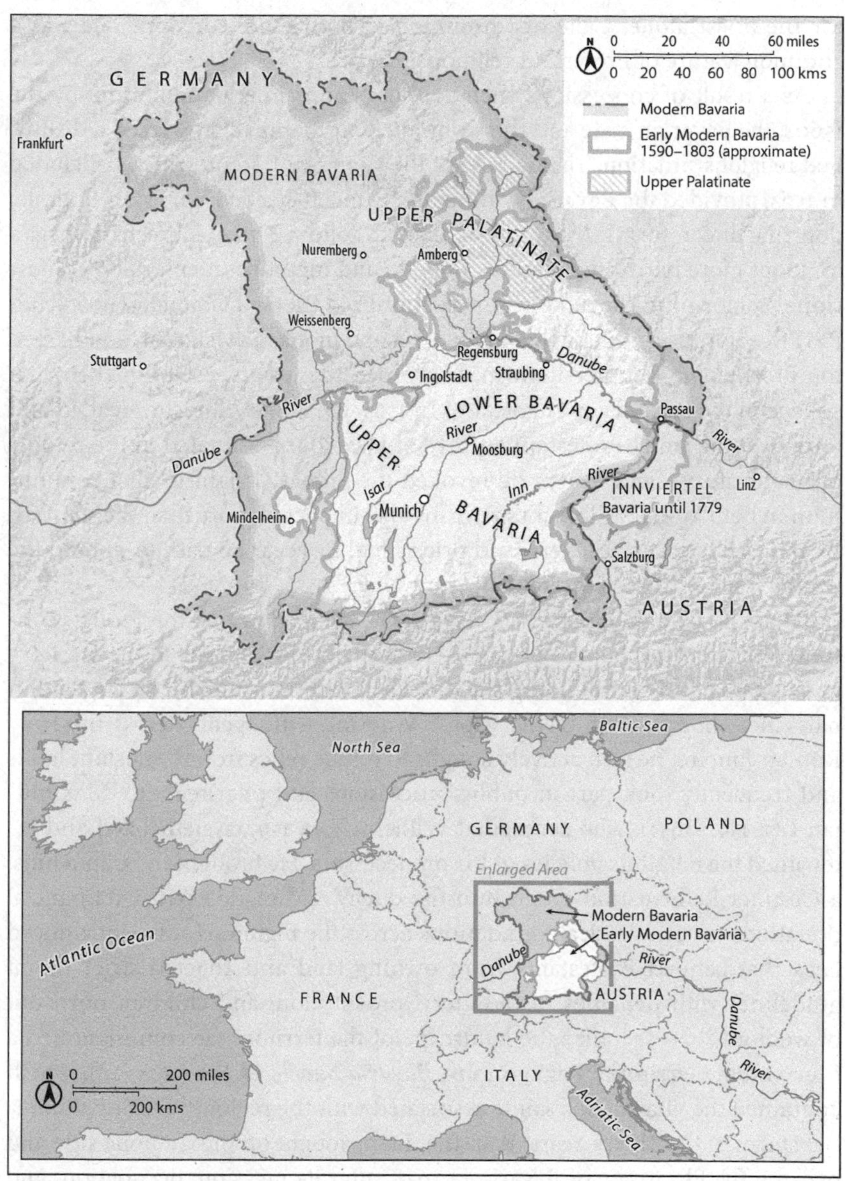

MAP 1. Bavaria in the early modern period. (Map by Ben Pease)

for the priest alone. Called communion in both kinds, this practice was a common feature of Protestant religious practice.

As a result of concessions such as those concerning communion, by the 1560s, the Bavarian state and the Counter-Reformation clergy faced a disunified religious situation. The decrees of the Council of Trent, which concluded in 1563, provided the Bavarian ruling family much-needed clarity on Catholic doctrine and reform. With a clear path to follow, Duke Albrecht V began to adopt more hard-line religious policies and methods of enforcing confessional conformity. The duke set up a centralized Clerical Council (Geistlicher Rat) to enforce orthodoxy through parish and monastic visitation and helped the preeminent Counter-Reformation order, the Jesuits, establish their first college in the territory in Ingolstadt. In 1563–64, Duke Albrecht invaded and took over the small Protestant enclave of Ortenburg—situated in the middle of his territory—and in 1571 he revoked the nobility's right to take communion in both kinds.[40] Albrecht's reforms also impacted more than the nobility. By 1569, all officials, teachers, and priests had to swear an oath to uphold the decrees of the Council of Trent.[41]

Albrecht's son, Wilhelm V (r. 1579–97)—later known as the Pious—continued many of his father's policies. He brought more Jesuits to the territory and spent lavishly on building the order's church in Munich, the largest Renaissance church north of the Alps.[42] Working with agents across the Holy Roman Empire, he also actively sought to rescue relics from Protestant lands and frequently took part in public processions and pilgrimages.[43] Maximilian I (r. 1597–1651), who succeeded Wilhelm V in 1597, systematized and intensified the religious policies of his predecessors. He brought the Capuchins, a Counter-Reformation order, into the duchy and made extensive financial donations to ecclesiastical foundations across the region. He also introduced laws that banned Protestants from owning land and enacted strict moral guidelines with penalties for adultery, prostitution, and children born out of wedlock.[44] To sacralize the landscape of the territory, he commissioned a four-volume territorial hagiography, *Bavaria Sancta et Pia* (1615–28), which contained the vitae of 203 saints associated with the region.[45] During the initial stages of the Thirty Years' War, the duchy fought on the Catholic side and became the Electorate of Bavaria in 1628, after its invasion, occupation, and annexation of the Calvinist Upper Palatinate (map 1). After taking over this territory, the Wittelsbach government and its clerical allies began the forced re-Catholicization of this area.[46]

In addition to punitive actions, the Wittelsbachs actively sought to cultivate a Catholic confessional culture in their territory. Duke Wilhelm V (r. 1579–97) created and implemented a particular brand of Wittelsbach piety that included actively and publicly demonstrating the family's Catholic faith. The defining characteristics of this so-called *pietas Bavarica* were Eucharistic devotion (especially evident in lavish Corpus Christi processions), Marian piety, revitalization of pilgrimages, and the founding of and participation in confraternities.[47] The Wittelsbach ruler and his family participated publicly in observing these religious rites by joining confraternities, making pilgrimages to Altötting, Wessobrunn, and Ettal, and erecting Marian columns in public squares across the territory. This public display of religiosity was an important part of the Wittelsbach monarchical program meant to provide an example to the duchy's inhabitants and to promote religious uniformity between the monarch and his subjects.[48] The official exercise of religious rites became part of the family's devotional style, passed from generation to generation, and resulted in a state, church, and prince that, according to Gerhard Woeckel, were "a unified whole."[49]

This view has been echoed in other scholars' research on the duchy, much of which has focused on the role of the ruling family as well as on the Counter-Reformation orders of the Jesuits and Capuchins in shaping the nature of Bavarian piety. According to Alois Schmid, "the court set the direction in religious life, and it spread to the entire duchy and all areas of life. The religious culture of the time was led and carried by the court."[50] Similarly, Peter Steiner, in an article on Maximilian I, asserts that it was the duke himself who founded baroque Bavarian culture.[51] As evidenced in these statements, the actions of the Wittelsbachs—whether it was bringing the Jesuits to the area or participating in lavish displays of Catholic pilgrimages and festivals or enacting strict anti-Protestant laws—have often been credited with defining almost every contour of Catholic piety in early modern Bavaria.

Although the region was a centralized, unitary state, its confessional culture was not set in stone by 1648, nor was it completely determined by the ruling family and its agents. As this examination of catacomb saints and their whole-body presentation reveals, during the period from 1648 to 1803, a flourishing baroque Catholicism developed in the duchy that arose from the interaction and combination of local and universal Catholic ideas. To date, Trevor Johnson's study on the reconversion of the Upper Palatinate and Nadja Pentzlin's research on Corpus Christi processions in the duchy remain the only works that emphasize the important role the local populace had—along with secular and ecclesiastical authorities—in shaping Catholic piety in the area.[52]

This book begins by tracing the importation of whole-body catacomb saints to Bavaria in the post-Reformation period (chapter 1). It examines how and why early modern Bavarians chose to acquire catacomb saint relics from Rome and analyzes the temporal and geographic distribution of the holy bodies across the territory. Using GIS mapping in combination with written sources, the chapter demonstrates that the effort to bring saints to the region was not principally motivated by anti-Protestant animus nor was it directed by the Catholic ruling family. Instead, a diverse group of actors, using their own initiative and agency, brought the saints to Bavaria as an affirmative expression of their Catholic identity and piety. Chapter 2 focuses on the bodies of the saints themselves, exploring the large investment of time, money, and labor early modern Bavarians expended to construct incomplete, jumbled Roman relics into "holy bodies" and decorate them in dazzling style. The process involved the skills of a wide variety of local community members—from doctors to nuns to carpenters. The extensive resources dedicated to the project reflect the great importance Bavarian Catholics placed on presenting catacomb saints as whole-body relics rather than in fragments.

The remaining chapters of the book examine how this new type of whole-body relic functioned in ways distinct from the fragmentary relics common before 1648. Chapters 3 and 4 analyze how the form of the whole body enabled early modern Bavarians to participate in important doctrinal and intellectual debates at the heart of post-Reformation Roman Catholicism. Chapter 3 specifically demonstrates how the martyred bodies of the ancient saints—who often held vials of sacrificial blood—physically embodied Roman doctrine on the Eucharist, a key confessional marker that set Catholics apart from Protestants after the Reformation. Chapter 4 provides an in-depth examination of how early modern Bavarians used the bodies of catacomb saints to participate in an important confessional debate around the sacred history of the early church. Closely examining the costumes and attributes donned by saints as well as the vitae written for them shows that local Bavarian craftsmen, artists, relic decorators, priests, and nuns—along with erudite scholars in Rome—participated in the paleo-Christian revival as practitioners and creative scholars in their own right.

In contrast to the preceding two chapters, chapters 5 and 6 explore how the whole-body presentation of catacomb saints facilitated and hastened their integration into local Bavarian religious environments. Chapter 5 investigates the large processions and festivals organized to welcome and integrate Roman catacomb saints into Bavarian communities and how such rituals were modified due to the presence of the holy bodies. Chapter 6 examines how the presentation of catacomb saint relics as intact skeletons, in conjunction with their permanent display in glass shrines on side altars, fostered an exclusive and highly localized patronage relationship between Bavarian communities and the Roman martyrs in their midst. With their bodies wholly present and accessible in a single location, catacomb saints provided protection and intercession to the inhabitants of a very particular area.

Tracing catacomb saint relics from the Eternal City to their final resting places on altars across Bavaria provides a new perspective on the process of Catholic identity formation in the period after the Peace of Westphalia. Rather than a defensive reaction to Protestant attacks on relics, the acquisition, construction, and display of whole-body catacomb saints by early modern Bavarians was a material expression of an affirmative Catholic faith that at once embraced universal church doctrine and allowed space for creativity and accommodation of local spiritual needs. The interplay between the Roman center and the Catholic periphery was materialized in the bodies of the saints themselves, which visually invoked their status as ancient Roman martyrs and allowed them to serve as local patrons and intercessors.

PART I

ACQUISITION AND CONSTRUCTION

1

Creating Bavaria sancta from the Ground Up

THE FRONTISPIECE of *Bavaria Sancta et Pia*—a four-volume territorial hagiography of Bavarian saints published between 1615 and 1628—depicts the Archangel Michael presenting a map of the duchy to the Virgin Mary and the Christ child (fig. 2). Christ raises a hand in blessing over the state while his mother gazes attentively at the map. Commissioned and closely supervised by Duke Maximillian I, the execution of this large project spanned the course of twenty-five years (1603–28). The work sought to portray the entire Bavarian landscape as a *terra sancta*—a holy land especially blessed even among Catholic territories because of its connection with hundreds of holy men and women. In the introduction, the author, Jesuit Matthäus Rader, wrote: "When you see *Bavaria Sancta* on the title page . . . you will easily see how this title fits the subject. For if you examine all the corners of Bavaria, you will scarcely find one place where you do not stumble upon the glowing tracks of holiness and religion: cities, towns, villages, fields, forests, mountains and hills all breathe and exhibit the old Catholic faith in Bavaria. Everywhere one finds holy houses, fine monasteries, new schools, illustrious relics."[1]

Rader's 1615 depiction of Bavaria, however, was not an analysis or even a description. Rather, it was the projection of a pious wish conceived by the Bavarian Catholic ruling family to demonstrate the deep and unbroken roots of the Roman faith in its realm.[2] *Bavaria Sancta* was one part of a much larger public campaign undertaken by the Wittelsbachs to demonstrate their staunch loyalty to the Catholic cause in the wake of the Protestant Reformation. This effort included "rescuing" relics from areas where they were in danger of iconoclasm at the hands of reformers as well as bringing the first catacomb saint relics to the duchy from Rome in 1590.[3]

Though the Wittelsbachs were initially responsible for maintaining the territory's allegiance to Rome, the creation of the Bavarian sacred landscape was *not*—as has been argued by other historians—carried out solely by the secular and clerical elites as part of a Counter-Reformation program of top-down confessionalization aimed at attacking Protestant beliefs. In the years between

FIGURE 2. Engraving of the Virgin Mary, the Christ child, and the Archangel Michael in Rader, *Bavaria Sancta*, Raphael Sadeler, 1615. (Henry Charles Lea Rare Book Collection, Kislak Center for Special Collections, Rare Books and Manuscripts, University of Pennsylvania)

1648 and 1803 Bavarians themselves—through the acquisition and decoration of hundreds of whole-body Roman catacomb saints—played a vital and heretofore overlooked role in the creation of the sacralized landscape first envisioned by their rulers. As they learned about the catacombs and the trove of martyrs' relics buried therein, early modern Bavarians—both urban and rural and ranging in estate from powerful abbots to humble pilgrims—began creating their own Bavaria sancta by importing whole-body Roman saints to destinations across the entire Electorate. Based on their own initiative and agency, this group of disparate actors established a dense network of holy bodies across the region, helping to create the Bavaria sancta that had once only been a devout projection on the pages of Maximilian's great hagiography.

Mapping the temporal and geographic distribution of whole-body catacomb saints combined with analysis of translation sermons, accounts of relic acquisitions, and town and cloister chronicles also reveals that the acquisition of catacomb saint relics by Bavarian communities was not primarily motivated by anti-Protestant sentiment, nor was it driven by the dukes or their agents. The vast majority of catacomb saints (95 percent) arrived in the duchy after 1648, following the end of the Thirty Years' War and the so-called "Age of Confessionalism," when the veneration of saints and relics remained at its most religiously controversial. Furthermore, in the period between 1648 and 1803, churches in Upper and Lower Bavaria, areas that had remained Catholic throughout the Reformation, obtained far more holy bodies than the region of the Upper Palatinate, which had been taken over by the Bavarians in 1628 and forcibly re-Catholicized. These temporal and geographic distribution patterns indicate that the acquisition of catacomb relics was not a reactionary, Counter-Reformation phenomenon linked to the Wittelsbachs' efforts to ensure that their subjects remained—or were reconverted to—Catholicism. Rather, it was a manifestation of a broad-based baroque piety in which early modern Bavarians made active affirmative choices about how to express their Catholic faith.

The wide geographic distribution of the saintly bodies across the duchy further underscores that this was not a phenomenon initiated at the center, but one that relied on the agency of individual actors across Bavaria and beyond. The process of acquiring a holy body from Rome, usually undertaken on an ad hoc basis in local clerical or town communities, stemmed from a variety of motives ranging from the desire to obtain a local patron saint to wanting to decorate a new baroque church with holy remains. By the end of the eighteenth century, ordinary Bavarians had brought whole-body catacomb saint relics to all corners of the Electorate in monastery, parish, pilgrimage, and noble churches and helped fill the territory with the "illustrious relics" Rader had described in *Bavaria Sancta.*

The Wittelsbachs and Relics

During the late sixteenth and early seventeenth centuries, the Wittelsbach defense and acquisition of relics was aimed squarely at condemning and contradicting Protestant rejection of the cult of saints. The ducal family's public support for the cult of relics began in earnest shortly after the Council of Trent issued its official decree "On the Invocation, Veneration, and Relics, of Saints, and on Sacred Images" in 1563, which affirmed the orthodoxy of venerating saints and relics. The Wittelsbachs quickly began to implement and amplify the Roman church's policy in their lands in a variety of ways. Just a year after the Tridentine directive, Martin Eisengrein, a Jesuit theologian and counselor to Duke Albrecht V (r. 1550–79), delivered a sermon entitled *A Christian Sermon Concerning the Reasons Relics are Held in such High Esteem.* In this sermon,

Eisengrein defended the cult of saints and relics, stating that God had continuously worked wonders through saints' relics. He contended that relics served as powerful memorials that reminded people of saints' holiness. The Jesuit cited numerous church fathers as well as biblical verses to support the antiquity of such veneration, effectively countering the Protestant claim that the practice was a later invention not based in Scripture.[4] With support from the duke, Eisengrein's sermon was printed and circulated throughout duchy as a way to promote the ruler's position on the matter of relics. Ten years later, Johann Nas (1534–1590), a gifted Franciscan preacher active in the area, echoed Eisengrein's full-throated defense of holy remains, stating that their veneration was based both on biblical verses as well as more than a thousand years of tradition.[5] In sum, Nas asserted: "God works with and in [relics] and confirms this biblical doctrine with many miraculous signs and miracles so that we justly venerate [saints] and should look at their relics with wonder and praise God, since to this day He has not completely stopped working miracles through them."[6]

As preachers enumerated the reasons for the veneration of saints' relics, the Wittelsbachs' effort to acquire relics began to intensify, with much of the focus dedicated to "rescuing" endangered relics from Protestant areas.[7] Wilhelm V, as well as his successor, Maximilian I (r. 1597–1651), saw themselves as defenders of saintly remains and made a pointed effort to bring these embattled holy objects back to Bavaria and safeguard them from iconoclasm.[8] The dynasty's largest coup in its post-Trent relic collection efforts was the acquisition of the relics of Saint Benno. In 1523, Pope Adrian VI canonized Benno, the bishop of Meissen from 1106 to 1116 CE. Though the decision represented success for the Catholic Saxon dynasty, it also occurred in the heartland of the Protestant movement just six years after Martin Luther posted his *Ninety-Five Theses.* Luther reacted to Benno's canonization with scorn, writing a pamphlet entitled *Against the New Idol and the old Devil soon to be Resurrected at Meissen* (*Wider den neuwen Abgott und allten Teuffel, der zuo Meyssen soll erhaben werden*), which criticized the planned excavation of Benno's relics, the unhistorical presentation of his vita, and the Catholic relic cult more generally.[9] Despite Luther's opposition, Benno's relics were elevated to the high altar in Meissen Cathedral in 1524.

When the duchy of Saxony became Protestant in 1539, the town's inhabitants destroyed Benno's shrine; fearing this eventuality, Meissen's bishop had removed Benno's relics years earlier and taken them to safety in a nearby Catholic town. After protracted negotiations, the retired Duke Albrecht V and his agents convinced Bishop Johann IX of Meissen (1524–1595) to send Benno's relics to Catholic Bavaria, where they would be safe and receive their proper veneration. In 1580, the bishop's remains were translated to Munich's

Our Lady Cathedral in a festive procession with Duke Wilhelm and his court in attendance. The acquisition of the very relics Luther had so vigorously criticized was a great symbolic victory for the ruling family and helped cement their role as defenders of the Catholic faith and the cult of relics.[10]

Despite this significant accomplishment, Wilhelm V's desire for relics was not sated by the arrival of Benno's remains. He continued to acquire relics from both Catholic and Protestant areas, and over the course of his reign, he managed to accumulate more than one thousand relics.[11] Though the duke avidly collected relics, the duchy's churches and monasteries rarely benefited from the influx of these new treasures. In fact, most of the relics Wilhelm amassed during his reign were set aside for two destinations—his private Holy Cross Chapel in the ducal palace (Residenz) and the new and very large Jesuit church of St. Michael's in Munich.[12] The Holy Cross Chapel, along with the two other chapels in the Wittelsbach palace, were richly endowed with precious relics and reliquaries; access to them, however, remained extremely limited.[13] On the other hand, the relics destined for St. Michael's—a Counter-Reformation showpiece—featured prominently in the newly built church as well as a commemorative book published on the occasion of the church's consecration and dedicated to Wilhelm.[14]

The creation of a relic collection for the newly built St. Michael's was the impetus for Wilhelm and his sons to acquire the first catacomb saint relics to arrive in Bavaria from Rome. The ducal family obtained four whole-body saints as well as smaller relic particles between 1590 and 1593 for the church, including several gifted directly to Princes Maximilian and Philipp from Pope Clement VII during a visit to the Eternal City.[15] With the completion of St. Michael's in 1597, the Wittelsbachs' commitment to collecting catacomb saint relics diminished.[16] In 1610, the family welcomed the holy body of Saint Modestus to their private chapel in the Herzog Max Palace in Munich, which occurred with little fanfare.[17] Of the eleven other catacomb saints that arrived in the duchy before 1648, eight were obtained by Sebastian von Füll, who served Maximillian I as war commissioner and later head of the clerical council (Geistlicher Rat) on a trip to Rome. He and his wife subsequently donated the bodies to the Munich Augustinians as well as the cloisters at Polling and Benediktbeuren.[18]

Though the Wittelsbachs and their close associates were responsible for bringing many of the first catacomb saint bodies to the duchy, the distribution of these relics—and relics more generally—did not become a centerpiece of the ruling family's public-facing Counter-Reformation activities. The catacomb saint relic donations made by the Wittelsbach and von Füll families all went to locations in Upper and Lower Bavaria, which had remained continuously Catholic since the beginning of the Reformation (map 2). This is

MAP 2. Towns and villages receiving catacomb saints, 1590–1700. (Map by Ben Pease)

particularly notable given that in 1628, after victories in the Thirty Years' War, Bavaria annexed the Protestant territory of the Upper Palatinate and almost immediately began a program of re-Catholicization.[19] Though the area was in need of new relics to reconsecrate altars and physically demonstrate adherence to the Catholic faith, *none* of the sixteen whole-body catacomb saints imported from Rome prior to 1648 ended up in the re-Catholicized Upper Palatinate. Instead of distributing all available saints to a recently converted area to reinforce Catholic orthodoxy, the saints found homes in churches that were all located in the Catholic region of Upper Bavaria. Mapping the saints' locations also reveals that they are not clustered, as other scholars have asserted, along the territory's confessional borders with Protestant areas to the north and west. This indicates that the relics were not being expressly used as a way to demonstrate to their neighbors the continued veneration of saints and relics in Catholic Bavaria.[20] This limited distribution area also meant that in the half century before 1648, the vast majority of the population in Bavaria did not personally witness the translation ceremonies of the relics imported by the ducal family, nor did they see Roman catacomb saint relics for themselves. This limited the impact and exemplary power of such ceremonies primarily to Munich and the surrounding area.

Acquisition and Distribution Patterns after 1648

Only after the end of the Thirty Years' War did the importation of whole-body catacomb saints shift from a trickle to a flood. In the years between 1648 and 1803, parish and monastic communities as well as individuals across the Electorate transferred 368 holy bodies from the Roman catacombs to church altars across the entire territory. The broad-based effort to acquire the remains of early Christian martyrs also coincided with a great elaboration of their transfer festivals as well as the presentation of the remains in the form of intact skeletons. These new features of catacomb saint veneration, absent from the earlier festivities coordinated by the ruling family and its associates, marked a new phase in the cult of catacomb saints in Bavaria. This phase—driven by the Catholic faithful of various ranks—did not simply "mimic" the anti-Protestant motivations or ritual precedents set by the Wittelsbachs when acquiring and welcoming these Roman relics to the capital in Munich.[21] Examining the overall temporal and geographical distribution of the saints in the years between 1648 and 1803 provides important insights into how the motivations for the acquisition of catacomb saint relics differed from the period before 1648.

In the century and half after the end of the Thirty Years' War, the influx of whole-body saints into the Electorate of Bavaria occurred in several waves. Two early peaks occurred in the decades between 1671 and 1680 and 1691 and 1700, as the populations of sixteen and nineteen different cities and towns experienced the translation of at least one whole-body catacomb saint. Despite the challenges posed by the War of Spanish Succession (1701–14) and the War of Austrian Succession (1740–48), Bavarian churches continued to bring catacomb saints to the region at a steady pace, with 112 holy bodies arriving between 1700 and 1749. A final peak in acquisition occurred between 1751 and 1770 as parish, pilgrimage, and monastic churches in forty-one distinct locations added holy bodies to their altars. After this point, demand for the saints declined, particularly among cloisters, though translations occurred all the way until 1803.

The geographical distribution of the saints is also quite revealing when it comes to the development of confessional identity in the Electorate. Despite the forced re-Catholicization of the Upper Palatinate—which began in 1628—the region did not experience a surge of catacomb saint arrivals either before or after the end of the Thirty Years' War. Between 1648 and the outbreak of the War of Spanish Succession, cloister and parish churches in Bavaria's Catholic heartland of Upper and Lower Bavaria continued acquisitions at a pace that far outstripped their counterparts in the Upper Palatinate (map 2). This is the case in terms of the raw number of saints acquired, with eighty-two of ninety-two arriving in Upper and Lower Bavaria, as well as in the number of distinct locations (towns, villages, etc.) where catacomb saints were present across the duchy (41/47). Despite the ongoing process of re-Catholicization in the Upper Palatinate, the area did not draw an unusually large or even proportionate number of catacomb saints based on its size.

Similar trends persisted in the eighteenth century, as cloister, parish, and pilgrimage churches across the duchy continued to bring holy bodies from the Eternal City. Maps of the distribution of saints from 1701 to 1803 demonstrate that towns and cities across Upper and Lower Bavaria consistently imported more catacomb saint bodies than did their formerly Protestant counterparts in the Upper Palatinate (maps 2 and 3). The saints are widely scattered across the areas that had remained true to the Roman church throughout the sixteenth and early seventeenth centuries. The largest of the three regions, Upper Bavaria continued to lead the way with seventy-six saints in thirty-four locations between 1700 and 1750, and forty-one saints in twenty-eight locations from 1750 to 1803. Towns and villages in Lower Bavaria welcomed twenty saints to ten different locations between 1700 to 1750, and ten saints to seven locations from 1750 to 1803. Interestingly, the largest number of catacomb saint translations to the Upper Palatinate occurred between 1750 and 1803, more than one hundred years after its re-Catholicization and integration into the Electorate of Bavaria. During this period, communities in the

MAP 3. Towns and villages receiving catacomb saints, 1701–1803. (Map by Ben Pease)

Upper Palatinate acquired almost twice as many holy bodies as Lower Bavarians did. The delayed demand for the saints in the Upper Palatinate until a century after its reconversion suggests the acquisition of such holy bodies was a broad-based expression of Catholic piety rather than a program of the centralized government to reimpose orthodoxy on a formerly Protestant area.

By 1803, when most of Bavaria's monasteries were dissolved and secularized, at least 384 whole-body saints had reached the duchy (map 4). In the final analysis, the areas of Lower Bavaria and the Upper Palatinate—each of similar size—had forty-one towns or cities with whole-body catacomb saints, respectively. The major difference: one had remained Catholic throughout the entire early modern period, whereas the other was subject to concerted re-Catholicization efforts from the ruling household, especially in the decades immediately after its integration into the duchy. The fact that each of these subregions had catacomb saints in a similar number of places demonstrates that the distribution of saints was not significantly different in areas with divergent confessional histories.

The types of monastic orders in Bavaria acquiring catacomb saints further supports the conclusion that catacomb saints were not primarily used as tools to defend and enforce Catholic orthodoxy in the territory. During the course of the early Reformation, Bavarian dukes brought several specifically Counter-Reformation orders—particularly the Jesuits and the Capuchins—to help promote and teach Tridentine doctrine in the face of Protestant challenges.[22] Yet these orders—which often had very close ties to the institutional church and the papacy—were not the most active participants in acquiring, distributing, and displaying catacomb relics in their churches in Bavaria.[23] Instead, old order cloisters led the charge when it came to securing whole-body saints. The Benedictines, Augustinian Canons, Cistercians, and Franciscans collected 61 percent of the 252 total catacomb saint bodies obtained by Bavarian cloisters. Over two-thirds of the thirty-five Benedictine houses—the largest order in the duchy by number of cloisters—possessed saints, while sixteen of nineteen Augustinian houses had at least one holy body on display. The Franciscans, though less enthusiastic, still boasted bedazzled saints at thirteen of their thirty-one locations in the duchy.

In stark contrast, the two most prominent orders brought to the duchy to promote Catholic Reformation ideals barely acquired any holy bodies at all. Only one of the fifteen Capuchin houses in Bavaria had a saint while only two of ten Jesuit churches did. Female reforming orders like the English Ladies and Ursulines were more interested in obtaining catacomb saints; however, they represented a much smaller number of houses compared to their male counterparts. Three of the four English Ladies convents had saints, and all three

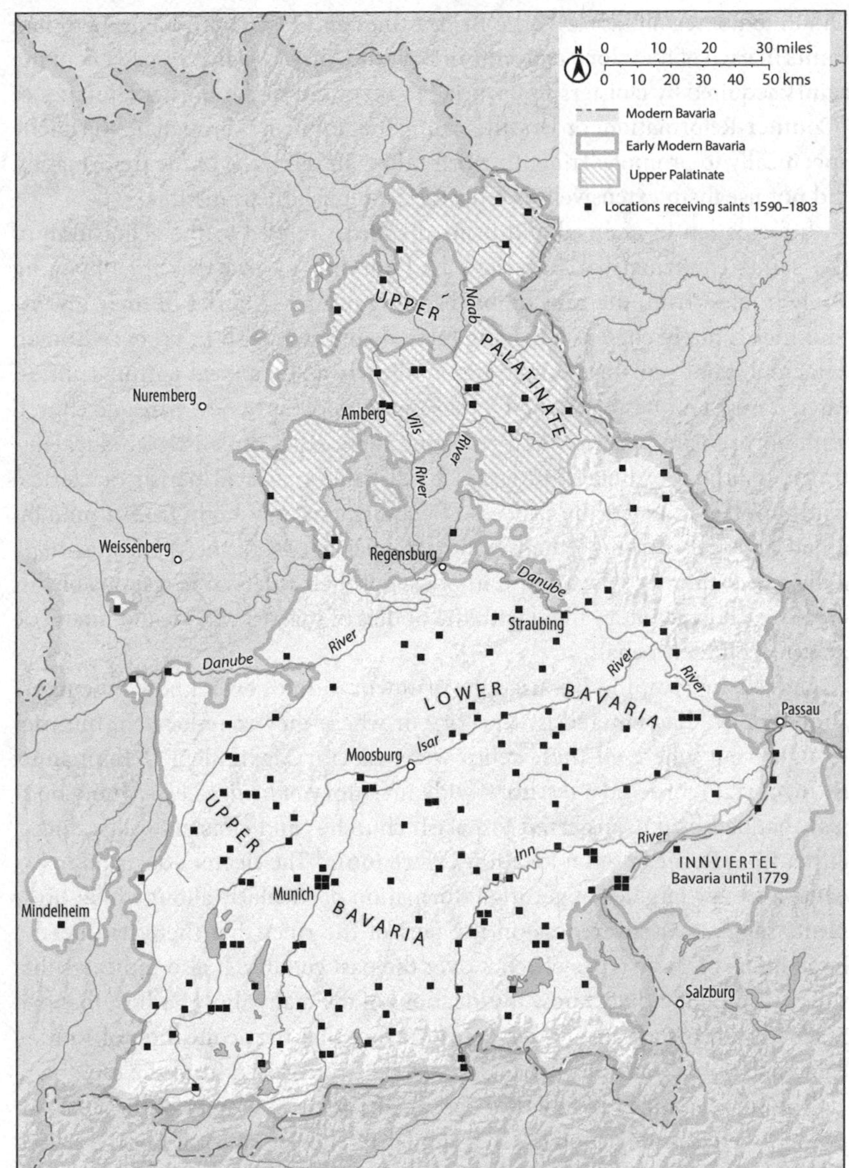

MAP 4. All towns and villages in Bavaria receiving catacomb saints, 1590–1803. (Map by Ben Pease)

Ursuline houses did as well. The Bridgettines and Sisters of St. Elizabeth had saints in each of their lone convents in Bavaria. All told, only 12.3 percent of the saints acquired by cloisters in Bavaria (31/252) went to the cloister churches of "Counter-Reformation" orders, indicating that the orders brought to the duchy specifically to promote Tridentine orthodoxy in the wake of the Reformation did not use them extensively as tools to accomplish their mission.

Information in archival and printed sources related to the acquisition of the saints confirms that Bavarians had varying motivations for obtaining "holy bodies" from the catacombs. Fending off the critiques of their Protestant foes is rarely cited as a driving force behind the wish to procure Roman catacomb saint remains. Sometimes a village wanted a local patron saint. In other cases, a monastery hoped for a saint to decorate a new baroque church with holy remains. Rather than receiving these relics directly from ducal authorities in a coordinated program of distribution, local parish or clerical communities initiated the process of acquiring a holy body from Rome on an ad hoc basis based on their own particular needs. In the years after 1648, a diverse coalition of Bavarian Catholics, not their rulers, was responsible for creating a holy territory filled with the bodies of martyrs who could intercede and heal on their behalf.

Indeed, by 1701, the Bavarian government did not even know how many "holy bodies" had entered its territory or where they were located. In order to figure out where all these relics were, Elector Maximilian II Emmanuel (r. 1679–1726), ordered a territory-wide inventory of *heilige Leiber* (holy bodies) that had been transferred to parish churches and cloisters in his duchy, either from Rome or other locations, since 1601.[24] The elector's decision to execute a survey targeted at getting information particularly about whole-body saints suggests an awareness on the part of the ruler that there had been a large influx of these types of relics over the past century. It also indicates that the government did *not* know the locations of the many "holy bodies" that had reached its territory and underscores the fact that the acquisition of Roman catacomb saints was not a process directed or supervised from the top down.

The survey is also notable for its specific focus on "holy bodies," as opposed to relics more generally. In a similar territorial inventory of the sacred conducted in 1601, Duke Maximilian I (r. 1597–1651) ordered cloisters and churches in his territory to provide an "orderly list of each and every relic" held in their collections.[25] In this letter, there is no specific mention of holy bodies as opposed to other types of fragmented relics. A century later, however, the government was interested specifically in "holy bodies," rather than an enumeration of all the smaller relics in a church's collection. This distinction highlights the increased circulation of and demand for a very specific type of relic from the labyrinthine passages under the Eternal City. After 1648, more and more churches in Bavaria wanted an entire holy body and pursued a variety of channels through which to obtain them from Rome.

The Process of Acquisition

The Bavarian dukes were not the only ones to recognize the unique nature of the whole-body relics being excavated from the catacombs and to categorize them as distinct from smaller, fragmentary relics. In a description of the relics at the cloister of Ranshofen, the author writes that the cloister had "many large and noble relics" that were housed in luxurious reliquaries of different shapes and sizes. "But," the writer laments, "there were no whole holy bodies. Therefore, the cloister applied to Rome with a most humble petition [for a holy body]."[26] The demand for intact bodies represents a marked shift in the kind of relic most common during the late medieval period. The term "holy body" had been used to differentiate between whole-body relics and smaller corporeal relics since the period of the early church and was closely related to the concept of the *corpus incorruptum*. However, by the twelfth century even miraculously preserved saintly bodies routinely fell prey to the rapid increase in the fragmentation of holy remains, making intact "holy bodies" somewhat of a rarity by the sixteenth century. With the rediscovery of the Roman catacombs, the term "holy body" reemerged and referred almost exclusively to catacomb saints being excavated from the cemeteries outside of Rome.[27]

Contemporary clerics and scholars in Rome reiterated the unique character of these whole bodies, while theologians asserted that they should be afforded greater respect and veneration than other relics. In his 1610 treatise *Reliquiarum sive de reliquiis, et veneratione sanctorum* (1610), the Augustinian Canon Giovanni Battista Segni wrote that complete bodies of saints should enjoy enhanced prestige and noted that solemn offices for complete holy bodies could be celebrated not just in the relic's home church but throughout an entire diocese.[28] Canon law also emphasized the difference between small particles and intact skeletons and stated that whole-body relics were considered first-class, or notable, relics.[29]

Though an individual, monastic, or parish community might want a "holy body" from the Roman catacombs, obtaining such a significant relic was not a simple process. Securing a whole-body catacomb saint required the involvement of a variety of individuals both in Bavaria and in Rome who used their personal networks to procure the bodies. Each acquisition had to be brokered on a case-by-case basis and required interactions and negotiations between Bavarian individuals or communities with a variety of different agents and donors both in Rome and at home. As a result, "holy bodies" arrived in the duchy through multiple channels, none of which were sponsored or supervised directly by the Bavarian state.

The most straightforward path to obtaining a coveted "holy body" was for a community or individual to identify an agent or personal contact in Rome who had connections within the Catholic Church and who could facilitate the acquisition. This type of relationship was particularly important as the complex bureaucracy responsible for the excavation, authentication, and distribution of holy bodies continued to evolve over the course of the early modern period, largely due to the church's—often unsuccessful—efforts to prevent illegal relic excavation and smuggling.[30] For around one hundred years after the "rediscovery" of the catacombs, the cardinal vicar of Rome and his associates were solely responsible for supervising the excavation and distribution of relics from the catacombs. In 1672, Pope Clement X issued a bull making structural reforms concerning the oversight of catacomb saint relic distribution.[31] The bull reaffirmed the jurisdiction of the cardinal vicar over the catacombs and created the position of the custodian of sacred relics. Appointed by and reporting to the cardinal vicar, the custodian was responsible for monitoring the sacred cemeteries and ensuring they were not profaned or violated in any way.[32] In addition to the office of the cardinal vicar, the bull named the papal sacristan as the only other legitimate source of authenticated catacomb saint relics. After 1672, clerics, pilgrims, and anyone else desiring a saint could appeal to either of these offices for a holy body or smaller relic particles. The cardinal vicar and the papal sacristan tended to attract different groups of supplicants in search of catacomb relics. The papal sacristan's office largely catered to people of higher rank, including guests and other distinguished ecclesiastical visitors who had direct connections within the Curia. The custodian of sacred relics, on the other hand, fielded requests for relics from a larger and more diverse range of petitioners including humble lay pilgrims and other visitors to Rome.[33]

In order to request a saint, a petitioner needed to prepare or commission a third party to write a request, or *memoriale,* to either the cardinal vicar or the papal sacristan.[34] Though it was illegal according to canon law to sell relics, "donations" or "tributes" of money often accompanied these letters.[35] Surviving *memoriale* reveal that Bavarians—along with supplicants from across the Catholic world—specified in their letters whether or not they wanted a "holy body" (*corpus sanctus*) or merely a box of smaller relics (*scatola*), which usually included four relic particles from four different saints.[36] On January 18, 1782, Francesco Saverio Morthl, a curate from Landshut, wrote to the custodian to express "the fervent reverence and devotion of the people of his parish and their ardent desire to have the body of any holy martyr."[37] In contrast, when pilgrims Father Giuseppe König and his companion Antonio Wipenberger, both from Bavaria, were about the leave Rome, they petitioned the custodian of sacred relics for "a box of relics" of martyrs' bones to "take back to their parish church in their homeland of Germany where they will be venerated by the faithful."[38] The two pilgrims specifically asked for a box of relics, whereas Morthl requested an entire body, indicating that those who approached the custodian, even though they might be visitors to Rome, knew the distinction between each kind of relic and the appropriate terminology to use to indicate their preferences.

Some *memoriale* contained even more detailed information on the type of "holy body" the petitioning individual or institution might want. Some preferred a male or female saint, a saint found with grave goods, or a saint with a *nomen proper* rather than a "baptized saint." During the excavation process, quarrymen found the graves of these ancient Christian martyrs with and without names. Saints whose names were found on their gravestones were classified as having a *nomen proper* and stored separately from anonymous remains.[39] If a grave had been identified as that of a martyr through symbols (dove, palm leaf, Chi Rho, etc.) but no name was present, the cardinal vicar or the papal sacristan "baptized" the remains with names from a list held in each respective office. The names were usually Latin words for attributes possessed by martyrs—Felix (happy, blessed), Fortunatus (lucky, fortunate), Placidus (gentle, peaceful), Victor/Victoria (victory)—and provided the relics with an identity.[40] The number of saints whose names were not known greatly outnumbered those found with a *nomen proper.* In the year 1672, the custodian of sacred relics, Marc' Antonio Boldetti, recorded that 394 of the 428 holy bodies excavated by his office did not have names but could be identified as martyrs through other signs or grave goods.[41] Certain petitioners requested saints with a *nomen proper,* presumably due to a desire to have a saint with a more verifiable provenance and historical identity. For others, the lack of a name provided an opportunity to ask for the saint to be named in their own honor.[42]

With either a *nomen proper* or baptized name established, the cardinal vicar or the papal sacristan enclosed the remains in a sealed wooden box and provided each set of relics with an authentication certificate. The certificate described the nature of the relics—whole body (*corporis sancti Christi Martyris*) or fragmented—and included the name of the saint, the date and site of their excavation, and the designated recipient's name.[43] Initially the certificates were written out by hand, but the scale of export quickly grew so great that by the 1660s the offices began using printed fill-in-the-blank authentication forms where these details could be quickly noted.[44]

The necessity of having a knowledgeable agent on the ground in Rome who understood which offices to approach with requests for holy bodies, as well how to write an appropriate *memoriale,* gave Bavarian monastic orders an early advantage over parish churches in acquiring catacomb saints. All the religious orders had headquarters and connections in Rome and at the Vatican. It was also not uncommon for their members or provincials to travel to Rome for meetings, negotiations, education, or training. This gave them the opportunity to pursue a holy body during their stay and to use any existing contacts to lobby for such an acquisition. As a result, in the second half of the seventeenth century, monasteries and convents in Bavaria far outpaced parish churches in numbers of catacomb saints acquired, obtaining seventy-two of the ninety-five bodies that arrived in the territory. Despite these lopsided numbers, which are largely due to monasteries' ability to acquire more than one holy body at a time, Bavarian laypeople were eager to bring holy bodies to churches they could easily access. In the second half of the seventeenth century, the saints were geographically distributed to more than fifty locations across the Electorate, including nineteen parish and pilgrimage churches. In fact, between 1671 and 1680, more towns and villages (nine) acquired catacomb saints for parish or pilgrimage churches frequented by laypeople than monastery churches (seven).

If a church or individual wanted to obtain a catacomb saint but could not travel to Rome to personally lobby for one, they could hire an agent or ask relatives or friends who lived in the Eternal City for help. Intermediaries played an especially important role for Bavarian female monastic communities that wished to procure a Roman catacomb saint for their churches. The strict enclosure of nuns required by Trent meant the sisters could not travel to Rome themselves to get a whole-body saint. Instead, nuns used their connection to male church members, who could travel more freely, to accomplish this objective. Like nuns, laypeople who could not travel to Rome also took advantage of family or community networks in their pursuit of a holy body for their local churches.[45]

There were also plenty of cases where churches received the bodies of catacomb saints as gifts from a benefactor who had connections in or had visited Rome. This could be a member of a local parish who had gone on pilgrimage, a diocesan bishop, the leader of monastic congregation, or a merchant who had acquired bodies while in the Eternal City. In these cases, the individual Bavarian church or cloister did not play the primary role in petitioning for a saint in Rome but rather was the grateful recipient of third-party initiative and beneficence. For instance, in 1667 Joachim Empacher—a Munich merchant—wanted to obtain a catacomb saint to donate to his daughter's convent at Landshut-Seligenthal. He approached the local procurator of the Discalced Carmelites, Father Aloysius á S. Andrea, and asked him to contact his fellow procurator in Rome to arrange for the acquisition of a catacomb saint. The merchant said he would take care of all the costs incurred in Rome for the acquisition. Empacher's use of the clerical network to acquire a saint was quite successful as Saint Antoninus arrived from Rome later that year.[46] Familial donors like Empacher, in addition to clerical agents, proved invaluable as convents worked to increase their collection of holy bodies. The three additional catacomb saint bodies received by the sisters at Landshut-Seligenthal were all gifts from relatives.[47]

Individual Bavarian pilgrims, especially those who traveled to Rome during Jubilee years, also succeeded in bringing back holy bodies for their churches and confraternities. In 1725, a group of Miesbach citizens journeyed to Rome and returned with the body of Saint Maurus for their parish church, and in 1750, members of the Marian Congregation of Our Beloved Lady of the Annunciation in Munich brought Saint Maximus back from the pilgrimage and installed him in the society's oratory.[48] At the next Jubilee in 1775, three pilgrims from Oberaudorf managed to obtain the body of Saint Donatus for their parish church.[49] Sometimes monks in Rome took the opportunity to send holy bodies back to their hometown churches rather than their cloisters, as did Father Matthäus Ludwig in 1760. Ludwig, who lived for many years in Rome as a representative of the Bridgettine order, obtained the body of Saint Innocent and gave it as a gift to his native village of Mammendorf.[50]

Though some catacomb saints' bodies traveled in a direct line from supplicant or donor to their intended final destination, often their paths were a bit more circuitous. Though the cardinal vicar and the papal sacristan were the only legitimate sources of relics, once these authorities turned over the box containing a holy body to a petitioner, it did not always remain with them indefinitely. The authentication certificates that accompanied the saints allowed the relics' new owner to "keep the holy relics [for themselves], to give them to others, to transfer them out of Rome to be installed and exposed for the veneration of the faithful in some public church or chapel."[51] As a result, donors or agents in Rome and beyond could obtain these holy bodies from a third party, rather than directly from church authorities, and it was not unusual at all for a saint to pass through multiple hands before reaching its final destination in Bavaria.

This was certainly the case for Saint Honoratus, who eventually ended up at the parish church of St. Peter's in Munich in 1654. In October 1646, the cardinal vicar granted the holy body to Thomas Candidus of Venice for his help with the excavation. In addition to the relics of Honoratus, Candidus received three other whole-body saints and the relics of twelve other martyrs.[52] At some point in the next four years, a Bavarian state treasury official, Stephan Höck—whose son, Wilhelm, was a Capuchin lay brother in Rome—acquired the relics of Honoratus.[53] In 1650, Wilhelm took Honoratus's relics back to Munich, where his father donated them to St. Peter's parish church.[54] Such indirect routes were not at all uncommon. In fact, both the cloisters at Geisenfeld and Raitenhaslach received saints initially intended for other locations, Naples and the kingdom of Poland respectively, while Landshut-Seligenthal had to return the relics of one Saint Theophist, whom the papal sacristan had sent to them by mistake.[55]

A final option for those who desired catacomb relics was to turn to the thriving black market. Merchants and smugglers would sneak into the catacombs, remove relics, and then sell them to eager clerical and lay buyers. On October 2, 1599, Pope Clement VIII (r. 1592–1605) issued the first in a long line of edicts prohibiting unauthorized persons from removing relics from the catacombs or even visiting the passages without the permission of the cardinal vicar.[56] This edict, as well as the many others issued over the course of the next two centuries, proved largely ineffective in curbing the illegal trade in catacomb saint relics. In 1656, papal sacristan Ambrosio Landucci wrote that the street value for stolen catacomb relics was "three or four *giulii* for an arm bone; four or five *testoni* for a rib or shin bone; for a head, four or five *scudi;* a whole body is thirty, fifty or one hundred *scudi.*" He added that relic merchants were even selling animal bones.[57] Relic sellers also provided fake authentication certificates for their wares to increase their value and desirability on the open market.[58] Given that requests for holy bodies from the cardinal vicar or papal sacristan were often not successful, it seems likely that at least some of the holy bodies that reached Bavaria bypassed the officially sanctioned channels set up by the papacy.

As indicated by the 1701 survey of holy bodies initiated by Duke Maximilian II Emanuel, this multichannel process of acquiring saints was not directed by the ducal family or their agents, nor were they always aware of how and when catacomb saints arrived in their duchy. In some cases, the saints were even acquired in direct opposition to orders from clerical authorities, some of whom had been put in place by the Wittelsbachs themselves. This was the case at the Pütrich cloister, which was located directly across from the Wittelsbachs' residential palace in Munich and relied heavily on contributions from the royal family. After their strict enclosure, which was mandated by the Council of Trent, the convent had also been put under the supervision of the Reformed Franciscan brothers, whom Duke Maximillian had brought from Italy to implement Tridentine reform in Bavaria's Franciscan houses.[59] Despite the close oversight of their supervisor, Modestus Reichert, the nuns at the Pütrich cloister in Munich managed to independently arrange the acquisition of a whole-body saint from the Roman catacombs.

The plot to bring a holy body to the convent began when Sister Caecilia Reischlin learned that her close acquaintance Gregorius, a lay Capuchin brother, would be traveling to Rome for a general chapter meeting. Gregorius, who had helped the sisters procure relics in the past, was an ideal intermediary given his connection to the clerical network in Rome and his ability to physically travel to the city itself. Once there, Gregorius managed to acquire the bones of Saint Dorothea, which were then shipped from Rome, to Bologna, to Venice, to Bolzano, and finally to Munich.[60] When supervisor Reichert discovered that the sisters had arranged such a transfer right under his nose, he was furious. The sisters had circumvented his authority, looked for help from another monastic order, and managed to participate in activities beyond the cloister walls when they were supposed to be cut off completely from the outside world.[61] Reichert attempted to keep the sisters from displaying Saint Dorothea's remains publicly in their church but was ultimately unsuccessful. After protracted negotiations and a good bit of squabbling, the saint, whose body the nuns had worked so hard to acquire, was translated into their church in a public procession in September 1663.[62] Even in the Wittelsbach capital, under the supervision of men brought in by the ruling family, cloistered nuns were able to exercise their agency and procure the body of a saint from Rome.

Cloistered nuns were not the only ones to resist clerical authority when it came to obtaining a holy body from Rome. In 1766, Matthias Weigenthaler and Sebastian Seebacher, both masons in the small village of Dingolfing, decided they wanted to acquire a catacomb saint for their chapel at the parish church. Weigenthaler, who kept a diary of each step in the acquisition process, notes that the pair began their efforts by reaching out to the mayor, whose son, Desiderius Ehrlpauer, was a Franciscan monk living at St. John Lateran in Rome.[63] The two men sent multiple letters to Ehrlpauer asking him to assist them in getting a holy body. The Franciscan wrote back that before he could move forward, he would need a letter from the town priest approving the request for a saint.

With their marching orders in hand, Weigenthaler and Seebacher approached the town priest. They believed the timing was especially auspicious as several townsmen from Dingolfing—the hospitaller and a mason—were preparing to travel to Rome. They did not want to miss the opportunity to have these men deliver the priest's letter directly to Father Desiderius at St. John Lateran. Yet, when the two men approached the parish priest to ask permission to get a body for their chapel in the church, the priest refused. Not to be dissuaded, the men decided to go back early the next morning and once again ask for the letter since they had such a great opportunity to send it personally to Rome. When they met the priest again, they reminded him that a Christian is obligated not only to honor God but also his saints and to see to the propagation of their honor. The priest replied that getting the saint would cost a lot of money and they would have to pay for it themselves. He also added that if they had so much extra money, they should give it to the parish church. As a final counterargument, the priest asserted that there was no room in the chapel to put a new saint. The men replied that they were masons and carpenters and that they could build an altar for the saint. The priest was not moved.

Still not deterred, Weigenthaler noted that he and Seebacher vowed to continue their work in honor of the saints and not to give up until they could bring a body to Dingolfing. Several days after their last encounter with the priest, Seebacher went to the parsonage at eight in the morning. Initially refused entry, he waited until one in the afternoon, at which point he made his way in by force. He proceeded to tell the priest that he would not leave until the priest signed the letter needed to acquire a saint. Finally, the priest relented, and the traveling party left Dingolfing with the priest's letter and a petition for a holy body in hand.[64] All Weigenthaler and Seebacher's efforts were ultimately rewarded. In 1769, Saint Faustina arrived from Rome and, after her decoration, was translated into the parish church the following year.[65]

Both the examples of the craftsmen in Dingolfing and the sisters in the Pütrich cloister in Munich demonstrate that the initiative to acquire catacomb saints came from individual actors on the ground and was not imposed as a program of top-down Catholicization. In Dingolfing, it was the masons who reminded the priest of the Catholic Church's support for the veneration of saints and relics. In both cases, these actors were willing to openly defy clerical authorities in their cloister or town in order to obtain a whole-body saint for their own church and to express their faith in the manner they saw fit. Whether it was resorting to clandestine meetings with a relic agent or breaking into the parish priest's home, early modern Bavarians found paths to obtain catacomb saints.

The dogged determination demonstrated by Reischlin—a cloistered nun—and the two masons in Dingolfing to bring catacomb saints back to their respective churches illustrates the value different types of early modern Bavarians placed on these holy bodies. The reasons, however, for acquiring a catacomb saint from Rome varied greatly depending on the type of church (cloister, noble, parish, or pilgrimage) and how the church intended to use the saint. Religious considerations certainly played an important role in the decision. This spiritual motivation, however, was generally expressed by Bavarians as an affirmative and enthusiastic belief in the power of saints and their relics rather than a defensive reaction to Protestant criticism of holy remains. The tone of translation sermons—which introduced these saints to their new communities—bears this out. These occasions were rarely opportunities to rail against the Protestant dismissal of relics. Their language is seldom belligerent; rather, preachers sought to educate their Catholic flocks about the imported relics and to reinforce the power and benefits of the veneration of the saints. The few exceptions to this largely nonconfessional approach emerge in Munich not long after the Thirty Years' War and in the formerly Protestant Upper Palatinate. As mentioned previously, in 1654, Saint Honoratus arrived in Munich and was translated into the parish church of St. Peter. This was the first large festival after a decades-long war that had wreaked havoc on the Electorate, and it is perhaps not surprising that the song of praise written for the martyr includes several references to the Lutheran "heretics." In the sixteenth verse, the singer asks Honoratus to "take us under your protection and defend us from all heresy," and later he states that "Munich no longer needs to fear false teachings. Because of St. Honoratus's light, religious errors must flee and darkness [will] also be driven out."[66] Twenty-one years later, however, when St. Peter's obtained the body of Saint Munditia from Rome, a printed description of the festivities made no mention of Protestants at all.[67]

Confessional concerns also played a role in the acquisition and placement of Saint Crescentianus in 1669 in St. Martin's church in Amberg in the Upper Palatinate. When a dispute over the relics broke out between the parish church and the Jesuit community in Amberg, the local archdeacon, Gedeon Forster, noted that he had wanted catacomb saint for St. Martin's since, due to earlier iconoclasm, it currently looked "more like a Calvinist than a Roman Catholic Church."[68] The town council of Amberg, writing in support of St. Martin's claim on the saint, also noted that since the church was in the middle of town, it hosted many visitors, both Protestant and Catholic.[69] The relics of Crescentianus, it is implied, would make the town's Catholicism visible to outsiders, and perhaps even help to reconvert Protestants. Yet even in the Upper Palatinate, the confessional tenor surrounding catacomb saint acquisitions faded as time passed. In 1753, at the translation of Saints Clemens and Constantius, Jesuit Ernst Geppert observed that the once-Protestant Amberg "must now rightfully be counted as among the most fervently Catholic of cities."[70]

With confessional concerns quickly receding into the background, alternative religious motivations for the acquisition of catacomb saints sprang into the foreground. One of the major reasons churches sought catacomb saints was their potential to act as new patrons and protectors who could intercede on behalf of town's citizens, their church, and the community at large during a wide range of difficulties. The late seventeenth and eighteenth centuries were still times of great uncertainty where war, disease, and weather could make basic subsistence challenging. The acquisition of a saint held the promise of protection from life's exigencies and the possibility of miraculous healing and intercession. Frontenhausen parish priest Melchior Thumb worked for years to obtain a saint from Rome because he "wanted to give his parishioners a patron saint for all time, whom they should turn to with all their hardships."[71] Similarly, in 1754 the citizens in town of Pfreimd petitioned Pope Benedikt XIV for a patron "against fire" as the town had recently suffered from several devastating blazes.[72]

The role of patron or protector was especially important for parish churches. Many cloisters focused on acquiring multiple saints—often as part of a renovation or decorative scheme—while 76 percent of the parish churches that obtained catacomb saints had only one holy body. Though this certainly has something to do with the cost of acquiring and decorating a Roman saint, it also allowed parishioners to focus their devotion on a single new patron. In some cases, catacomb saints even became the patron saints of towns (Erding—Saint Prosper; Pfarrkirchen—Saint Theodora; Hirschau—Saints Pius and Placidus); churches (Amberg—St. Martin's church); guilds (Miesbach, guild of butchers and cooks); and groups of people (Saint Munditia—St. Peter's church, Munich, patron saint of single women). Though parish churches might not have been able to acquire as many whole-body saints as did cloisters, their presence in devotional spaces dedicated to public lay worship was quite important. Over the course of 150 years, parish and pilgrimage churches in seventy different locations welcomed holy bodies. After 1750, these types of churches consistently surpassed the number of cloister locations receiving saints, indicating their continued importance to lay Catholics across the electorate into the early nineteenth century and beyond.[73]

Though the role of patron or intercessor was a powerful motivation for parish churches to acquire a catacomb saint, more prosaic reasons such as the desire to decorate a newly renovated church, compete with neighboring churches, or to draw lucrative pilgrimage traffic could also spur individuals to turn to Rome for a whole-body relic. For Bavarian cloisters, catacomb saints were not solely potential patrons but sacred treasures that could enhance the prestige of their relic collections and serve as decorative objects necessary for the remodeling of cloister churches in the baroque style. With their more abundant financial resources and direct connections to Rome, cloisters frequently obtained multiple saints for their renovation projects or for the celebration of anniversaries. Of the convents in the duchy with catacomb saints, 72 percent had more than one catacomb saint, while 62 percent of monasteries acquired more than one holy body. The demand for holy bodies in Bavarian cloisters remained quite consistent between 1650 and 1770, later than other scholars have speculated.[74] Demand peaked among cloisters in the decades 1671–80 and 1751–60, when institutions in nine and sixteen different locations, respectively, acquired holy bodies for their churches.

In translation sermons given at monasteries during this period, the saints are frequently referred to as "treasures" (*Schätze*) or "gems" (*Kleinods*) and discussed alongside other luxury items. In a sermon for the translation of three catacomb saints to the Cistercian cloister at Gotteszell in 1729, Father Joseph Silberman, a Premonstratensian from Osterhofen, praised the cloister's abbot for improving the decoration of the church. Silberman writes that during Abbot Wilhelm II's fourteen-year reign he had overseen the complete renovation of the church, and it now boasted new frescoes and stucco work, new altars and confessionals, two organs, silver busts and candlesticks, three luxuriously decorated holy bodies, splendid monstrances, chalices and other beautiful church furnishings.[75] Here, the three catacomb saints are listed among the "church furnishings," indicating that they, too, were considered part of the church decoration in a way comparable to a new monstrance or altar.

As time passed, catacomb saints became essential adornments when cloisters were rebuilt or redecorated. This was especially true among the cloisters of the older, pre-Reformation monastic orders such as the Augustinian Canons, Benedictines, Cistercians, Premonstratensians, and collegiate foundations, the majority of which undertook large building projects in the baroque period and acquired at least one catacomb saint for their new houses of worship.[76] In many cases, such as at the cloisters of Andechs, Gars, Kühbach, Rottenbuch, Neumarkt–St. Veit, and Steingaden, these renovations were undertaken due to damage to their churches during the Thirty Years' War. In other cases, renovations were not completed out of necessity. Often cloisters chose to celebrate an important anniversary—most frequently the foundation of the cloister—with a complete interior renovation in the contemporary baroque and rococo styles.[77] The Augustinian Canons at Rottenbuch began a major renovation of the interior of the church in the early 1720s, adding two new altars to the existing seven. Since these two altars in the nave of the church were "empty and longed for a sacred treasure," the cloister acquired the bodies of Saints Julius and Florianus. The cloister subsequently sent the bodies to Augsburg to be even "more beautifully and luxuriously decorated" than the other catacomb saints already at the cloister.[78] Once assembled into holy bodies and adorned with glittering jewels, Julius and Florianus were placed with great ceremony into glass shrines on the formerly empty altars. The decorative nature of the saints was also mentioned during the translation festivals at confraternity and noble church feasts. According to a pamphlet printed to commemorate their translation, Saints Clemens and Constantius were acquired from Rome by the Schmerzhafften göttlichen Mutter unter dem Creutz Bruderschafft in Amberg "for the greater adornment of the Court Chapel, which has just been almost completely renovated from its old state."[79]

The perceived need to provide the new altars with new "sacred treasures" combined with the statistics mentioned above underscore the value older order monasteries and convents—as well as nobles—placed on the fitting decoration of their church spaces. In all of these cases, however, the expressed motivation for obtaining holy bodies is never explicitly anti-Protestant. The cloisters appear most concerned with decorating their new churches as splendidly as possible or competing with their neighboring institutions, not attacking Protestants for their rejection of relics themselves. In this sense, the saints—while they could also function as protectors and intercessors—were also understood in this setting as decorative objects.

The acquisition of a catacomb saint also increased both the prestige of the individual responsible for the achievement as well as the church where it was housed. It indicated that the cloister or noble or layperson had the money as well as the influence and connections to obtain such a luxury object—one that was not easy to procure. The saints and their translation festivals also drew thousands of visitors to the cloisters. In these cases, the abbots' ability to both obtain and decorate Roman catacomb saints for their church was considered a major accomplishment—both in the minds of the abbots themselves and their contemporaries. At the cloister of Aldersbach, Abbot Malachias (r. 1669–81) chose to be buried at the altar where the catacomb saint he brought from Rome—Felicianus—rested. On his gravestone, Malachias kneels before the altar as Felicianus, dressed as a Roman martyr, hovers above the altar surrounded by heavenly clouds as a permanent reminder of the abbot's achievement (fig. 3). At the Augustinian cloister of Gars, Abbot Athanasius also chose to commemorate his acquisition of Saint Felix in 1675 on his gravestone, which notes how much effort and money he spent on the process of bringing the saint to Bavaria.[80] Merchant Johann Evangelist Huber chose a different way to permanently memorialize his donation of Saint Alexander to the parish church in his hometown of Westenhofen bei Schliersee in 1773. After his death in 1778, Huber's skull was placed in the memorial chapel at St. Martin's and painted with a short note about his gift of a holy body to the church.[81] Beyond material monuments, written and visual sources—including cloister histories, funeral, and translation sermons and *Andachtsbilder* (devotional images)—also indicate how notable the acquisition of catacomb saints could be in the record of an abbot, abbess, or nobleman. These individuals

FIGURE 3. Carving of Saint Felicianus on Abbot Malachias's gravestone, Johannesaltar, Aldersbach cloister, 1683. (Photograph by author)

were praised by their contemporaries for their deeds. Benedictine Wolfgang Haeckhl eulogized Abbot Eugenius of Waldsassen and extolled his efforts "to open the graves of the holy martyrs and to transfer five of them, namely Maximinus, Theodosius, Alexander, Valentius and Ursa, a martyred virgin—along with many other assorted relics into the Waldsassen church."[82]

In the decades after the Thirty Years' War, the number of catacomb saints in the duchy increased, and the rising awareness of their availability in Rome spread, encouraging more and more churches and diverse constituencies to pursue a holy body of their own. One of the most important ways early modern Bavarians learned about catacomb saints was through attendance at large translation festivals. In the weeks and months before a translation festival, cloisters especially would send invitations to nearby parishes and monasteries asking them to attend the festivities. Abbot Candidus at Raitenhaslach received at least twenty-eight responses to his invitation for the cloister's translation festivities from other cloisters, parishes, and local governments either confirming their attendance or sending regrets.[83] These invitations were further spread to the populace orally—through announcements at Sunday Mass the week before the translation—and in print. In 1672 in Landshut, the nuns at the Seligenthal convent advertised the upcoming arrival and translation of Saint Cassianus with small flyers they had posted and circulated around the city.[84]

Attendance at such festivals in neighboring towns and villages could inspire individuals who lived in the area to begin their own attempts to obtain a saint. In 1683, parish priest Melchior Thumb had been a guest of honor at the translation of Saint Tigrinus to the Franciscan cloister in Dingolfing.[85] Some twenty-five years later, Thumb was instrumental in helping the parish church of Frontenhausen—less than ten miles from Dingolfing—acquire the body of Saint Amantius in 1709. Just a year later and a few miles away, Adam Lorenz, Freiherr von Alt und Neufraunhofen, obtained Saint Julia for his newly renovated palace chapel. The parish church at Niederaichbach, also in the immediate vicinity, had also managed to import the body of Saint Martialis from Rome in 1700. This small cluster of acquisitions within a ten-mile radius of the Franciscan cloister in Dingolfing indicates that after one institution in a region received a catacomb saint, it could spur others to follow suit.

In some cases, explicit competition between institutions as well as a desire to keep up with the neighbors played a role in bringing saints to the duchy. Abbots, parish priests, nobles, and ordinary Bavarians were certainly aware of the activities of their neighbors—and sometimes even those farther afield—who got catacomb saints. At the translation ceremony for Saint Porphyria in 1694 to the parish church at Arnschwang, the preacher Franz Valentin Fridl mentioned that the city of Kemnath—also in the Upper Palatinate—had welcomed Saint Primianus to their parish church just a year earlier.[86] In Amberg, in 1753, the speaker at the translation of Saints Clemens and Constantius to the confraternity church noted how lucky the church was to have *two* saints, while a similar confraternal church in Munich had only transferred one saint into its church in 1750.[87]

Sometimes the desire to house a catacomb saint in a church even led to protracted and bitter disputes between churches in the same town. In 1678, Father Fortunatus Huber—the Franciscan provincial—traveled to Rome and obtained the body of Saint Theodora. The catacomb saint was earmarked for the Pfarrkirchen Franciscan's new pilgrimage church atop the Gartlberg, which was still under construction at that time. In the meantime, Huber gave the body to the local parish priest in Pfarrkirchen for safekeeping until the pilgrimage church could be finished. However, in May 1680, the parish priest requested permission from the Passau diocese to display Saint Theodora's relics to the public in his parish church and claimed that Huber "had consigned the relics to me with good will."[88] The Franciscans, irritated at the parish priest's impudent claim on their catacomb saint, nonetheless proved unable to wrest Saint Theodora from the parish church when the pilgrimage church opened in 1688. Tensions persisted into the following century. In 1737, the parish church established a rival pilgrimage site to Saint Theodora, in the hope of drawing pilgrims from the wonder-working image of Mary housed up the hill at the Gartlberg church.[89] Clearly, both the parish and pilgrimage church believed possession of Saint Theodora's body was an important issue, which also had the power to increase visitors to their churches.

FIGURE 4. High altar with body of Saint Victor in Taufkirchen palace chapel, Taufkirchen a.d. Vils, 1694. (Photograph by Bodo Gsedl; courtesy of Bodo Gsedl)

As the dispute in Pfarrkirchen demonstrates, commercial ambition and the desire to attract patrons to a church could also be a motivating factor for obtaining a catacomb saint. The arrival of a new patron carried with it the power to draw thousands to a particular church—first for the translation festival and possibly a new pilgrimage site. This is exactly what Adam von Puech hoped would happen when he acquired Saint Victor for the high altar in his palace chapel in Taufkirchen in 1695 (fig. 4). Adam's father, Ferdinand von Puech, had built a new inn and brewery in town when he took over the territory in 1672. His son, eager to increase traffic at both new establishments, believed a catacomb saint would be an ideal way to lure pilgrims—and their money—to Taufkirchen. He commissioned the Capuchin provincial—Father Adrian von Ahaim—to get a martyr for him in Rome, and von Puech's plan came to fruition when Saint Victor was translated with great pomp into his *Wasserschloss*. A small pilgrimage to the saint emerged as dozens of extant *ex votos*—including

FIGURE 5. Silver *ex voto* eyes left by a pilgrim for Saint Victor at Taufkirchen palace chapel, Taufkirchen a.d. Vils. (Photograph by author)

a set of silver eyes—left for the saint attest (fig. 5). These same pilgrims also helped to increase the sale of beer and hotel payments in the town.[90]

The diverse motivations and personal networks used by early modern Bavarians to acquire whole-body catacomb saints from Rome after 1648 highlight the degree to which the process was organized by independent groups and individual actors at the local level. Though the ruling family might have obtained the first catacomb saints to reach the duchy in 1590, it was early modern Bavarians themselves who were responsible for bringing these "holy bodies" to all corners of the territory in the years after the Thirty Years' War and creating the Bavaria sancta once projected on to the pages of a territorial hagiography of the same name commissioned by their rulers. The temporal and geographic distribution patterns of saints also demonstrate that the phenomenon was not part of a Counter-Reformation campaign meant to defend against Protestant attacks on the cult of saints and relics. The ruling family did not flood the re-Catholicized area of the Upper Palatinate with catacomb saint remains as part of a top-down program of confessionalization; rather, churches and communities in the continuously Catholic parts of the duchy led the way in acquiring these saints from Rome. Carried out after European confessional borders had largely been settled, this broad-based movement to bring holy bodies to the duchy was an affirmative expression of Catholic identity and piety as opposed to a defiant act of anti-Protestantism. Bavarians' continued desire to obtain and venerate holy remains led to development of a creative new type of relic presentation, one that matched the label on the authentication certificates sent by the Roman Church: a holy body. Rather than presenting the bones of the ancient martyrs as fragments, as had been customary for centuries, Bavarian nuns, craftspeople, carpenters, doctors, and artists used their expertise to create sparkling full-body skeletons for display to the faithful on altars across the territory. The effort, skill, and financial resources devoted to acquiring and displaying these holy bodies further testifies to the deep significance their acquisition had for the Catholic communities within the duchy of Bavaria during the period from 1648 to 1803.

2

Some Assembly Required

BUILDING WHOLE-BODY CATACOMB SAINTS

In 1753, the Amberg Frauenkirche acquired two catacomb saints, Clemens and Constantius, for its side altars. Jesuit Ernst Geppert, who delivered the sermon on the day of the translation, underlined how incredibly blessed the city was to possess not only relics but the *entire bodies* of these holy martyrs:

> The most distinguished cities and regions consider themselves lucky when they receive only a few bones of a holy martyr from Rome to put on their altars and venerate with privileged devotion. . . . Despite all their solemn delegations, pious deeds, exceptional devotion, and imperial and royal status, Constantia the empress, Justinianus the Emperor, and Pippin the King only received a barely visible chip of St. Peter's chains, a pall from the coffin of St. Paul, some tiny pieces of dust, ash and pieces of the clothing and intestine of St. Zeno. After receiving these relics, they recognized all of them as much greater treasures than all their jewels, riches, scepters, and crowns, and valued them more highly. Learn from this story, Amberg! Learn from this, how highly you must regard this valuable treasure you have received from Rome. You, beloved city, not only received the instrument of martyrdom, but the holy bodies themselves. And from these you received not just a few tiny pieces or motes of dust, but almost the whole thing, and all the bones, and even a large amount of blood from two holy martyrs of Christ. You have received the most precious treasure from Rome.[1]

Geppert's impassioned speech to the gathered crowd focused directly on the importance and prestige associated with having two complete bodies in the Frauenkirche rather than simply having fragments or other secondary saintly relics. His emphasis on this point was not unique and echoed the requests sent to church authorities in Rome which expressed the desire of supplicants for whole bodies rather than particle relics. Once the relics arrived in Bavaria, translation preachers repeatedly used the phrase "whole body" (*gantze Leib*) in translation ceremonies to reiterate the bodily integrity of the catacomb saints' remains. The theater stage also provided a place to dramatically spotlight the special nature of the relics. During the translation festivities for Saint Maximus to Munich in 1750, a local Marian confraternity staged a play about the life of the martyr on the city's main square (Marienplatz). Near the beginning of the performance, an actor playing Saint Maximus gestured to the sparkling skeleton before the audience assuring them that "here you see all my bones, the home of my soul."[2] In this case, the personified martyr himself called attention to the fact that all his mortal remains were present before the onlookers rather than scattered across multiple locations.

Though preachers, actors, and authentication certificates may have declared that the relics of the early Christian martyrs arriving from Rome were "holy bodies," the bones sealed inside the wooden boxes rarely, if ever, constituted an intact skeleton. Before 1648, the recipients of catacomb saints in Bavaria made no effort to forge the fragmented ancient remains into human form or to keep them in a single container. Rather, the bodies were typically housed—as fragments—in opaque or glass-fronted reliquaries. A saint's relics might be kept within a single shrine, but often they were dispersed into multiple reliquaries within a church's collection or displayed alongside the remains of other holy personages. Keeping the bones of the *heilige Leiber* of the catacomb saints together had not yet become a priority.

As the number of "holy bodies" imported to the duchy began to increase sharply after 1648, early modern Bavarians developed a new type of relic presentation that prized bodily integrity and completeness. Instead of splitting the relics into smaller fragments or placing them in reliquaries which highlighted their fragmentary nature, groups of artists, craftsmen, and relic decorators put saintly bodies *back together.* When bones were missing, carpenters created them from wood or other materials. Nuns dressed the saints and carefully crafted facial features for these long-dead heroes using jewels, wire, and sometimes even wax. The sisters then arranged the lavishly decorated bodies into sitting, standing, or lying positions, and finally, communities installed them permanently on altars in glass-walled shrines. Working together, Bavarians developed a relic presentation that matched the label given to the remains by the church on authentication certificates: a *corpus sancti Christi martyris* (body of a holy martyr of Christ).

As with the decision to acquire the saints, the complicated and labor-intensive process of assembling and decorating catacomb saint relics as full bodies occurred at the local level and required time, skill, and financial resources. Instead of relying on Tridentine dictates or guidance from government officials in Munich, nuns, monks, carpenters, painters, relic decorators, and doctors all worked together in a communal effort to create the lifelike skeletons from the jumble of remains brought from the Eternal City. Due to the various states and quantities in which the relics reached Bavaria, the construction of each "body" presented its own unique challenge in terms of physical assembly and decoration. Financing all this work could also be a daunting task. In addition to the money spent in Rome acquiring the saint, the costs for the materials and labor required to present catacomb relics as seemingly intact bodies were high. Communities undertook fundraising drives and sometimes went into debt to make sure the bones of these ancient martyrs were displayed as whole bodies, demonstrating how important it was to them to present the remains in this manner rather than in fragments. All of this effort culminated in the creation of shimmering "holy bodies," an innovative form of relic display that broke with the centuries-long tradition of dividing saintly remains.

Medieval Fragmentation of Relics

To fully appreciate the radical shift the whole-body presentation of catacomb saints in Bavaria in the seventeenth century represented, it is useful to examine how relic display and Catholic theology on the bodily fragmentation of the holy dead evolved in the preceding centuries. The concept of an intact "holy body" had its origins in the miraculously preserved or "incorrupt" bodies of saints discovered in the early period of the Christian church. Theologians, including Ambrose (ca. 339–397 CE), considered an undecayed saintly corpse to be the miraculous result of the glory of Christ's preserved body overflowing onto the bodies of the saints to keep them perfectly preserved.[3] Early Christian writers also used several biblical passages to explain why certain bodies resisted decay: God "shalt not suffer thy Holy One to see corruption" (Acts 13:35),[4] and "a hair of your head shall not perish (Luke 21:18)."[5] Both of these verses—which emphasize God's care for the physical remains of his loyal followers—were interpreted as reasons for the immaculate state of deceased holy people.[6] Upon the discovery of such bodies, often described in hagiographies as miraculously undecayed and smelling of perfume, clerics would remove hair or nail clippings and then rebury the entire body either underneath or behind altars in an enclosed casket reliquary.[7]

As the centuries passed, however, practices surrounding the treatment of saintly remains began to change. By the ninth century, it had become customary across Europe to divide the bodies of the holy dead in order to disperse a saint's intercessory power and protection as widely as possible. This practice rested on the relic theology of *pars pro toto*—that the part could stand in for the whole. First articulated by Christian theologians in the fifth century, these churchmen argued that even the smallest relic particle contained the power and presence of the entire saint.[8] Splitting up holy remains meant that multiple communities could access a single saint's miraculous protection and intercession in churches across the continent. As relic fragmentation became more common and demand for relics increased, the discovery of a saint's preserved body no longer guaranteed it would remain intact. During this era, "the *corpus incorruptum* was less an eternal sign of divine grace, than a means which helped the discoverers of the body recognize a saint's holiness."[9] By 1200, the process of dividing and distributing the remains of a holy figure accelerated further. Rather than waiting to see if the body of someone who died "in the odor of sanctity" resisted putrefaction, it become customary to dismember the bodies immediately to produce relics for quick circulation.[10]

The increasing acceptability and frequency of the fragmentation of saints' bodies led to changes in the reliquaries designed to house and present them to the faithful. Prior to the thirteenth century, relics were typically enclosed in casket (box) reliquaries of varying sizes and materials, with no visual access to the enclosed remains.[11] The earliest surviving reliquaries that alluded to the increasingly fragmented nature of many relics emerged in the ninth century. These so-called "shaped" reliquaries housed saintly remains in containers sculpted to look like a body part and were covered in gold or silver and, often, precious stones.[12] In subsequent centuries, body-part reliquaries—including those shaped like arms, heads, feet, fingers, legs, and toes—became increasingly popular. Though often luxuriously decorated, before 1200 reliquaries in western Europe—shaped or otherwise—never presented the viewer with a direct view of a saint's remains, and physical access to shrines was strictly limited, usually to clergy. For the average layperson during this period, there was no immediate visual or tactile contact with the relics of the holy dead.[13]

In the later Middle Ages, this situation changed as relics that had previously been hidden within reliquaries became increasingly visible to viewers. Several developments spurred this change in presentation. After the 1204 Sack of Constantinople, Crusaders brought back Byzantine reliquaries that featured glass or crystal openings that made holy remains visible. In addition, as veneration of the Eucharistic Host increased, it became more common to display the consecrated Host behind translucent glass or lead crystal. With new models available for the presentation of holy matter, European artists and metalsmiths developed a wide variety of late medieval reliquaries that displayed holy remains directly to viewers.[14] These reliquaries, known as *ostensoria* or monstrances, both allowed direct visual contact with relics and revealed their fragmentary nature. Shaped reliquaries, which experienced a boom in popularity in the thirteenth and fourteenth centuries, also began to incorporate glass and crystal in order to make relic fragments visible within a metallic arm, leg, or foot. Though their use in body-part reliquaries did restore some bodily integrity to otherwise fragmented relics, encasement in a sculpted body part still only represented or referenced a part of a larger holy body.

The larger European trends related to the increasing fragmentation of relics as well as their visibility within reliquaries reached Bavaria during the medieval era. A broadside, printed in 1494, depicts one of southern Germany's largest and most important relic collections, held at the Benedictine cloister at Andechs (fig. 6). The collection features body-part reliquaries—including head busts and arms—as well as many other relic monstrances enclosing the fragmented bodily remains of the church's holy dead. The short descriptions below each reliquary on the broadsheet make clear that the containers hold *fragments* of saints and demonstrate how commonly and frequently their bodies were divided. These display practices meant that when late medieval Bavarians visited church altars or attended feast day processions or annual relic festivals (*Heiltumschauen*), they primarily encountered the remains of the holy dead in reliquaries that emphasized fragmentation rather than bodily integrity.[15]

In the few instances where intact and incorrupt holy bodies had managed to escape fragmentation and dispersal in Bavaria, they were not visually accessible to the faithful. During the fifteenth century, the shrines of Saint Rasso at Grafrath and Saints Richildis and Juliana at the Benedictine cloister of Hohenwart experienced revivals. Each church ceremonially exhumed the saints' bodies and relocated them to aboveground tombs to make them more accessible to pilgrims.[16] Though the tombs may have been newer and grander, they did not offer the faithful a view of the saint's body. The only way pilgrims had

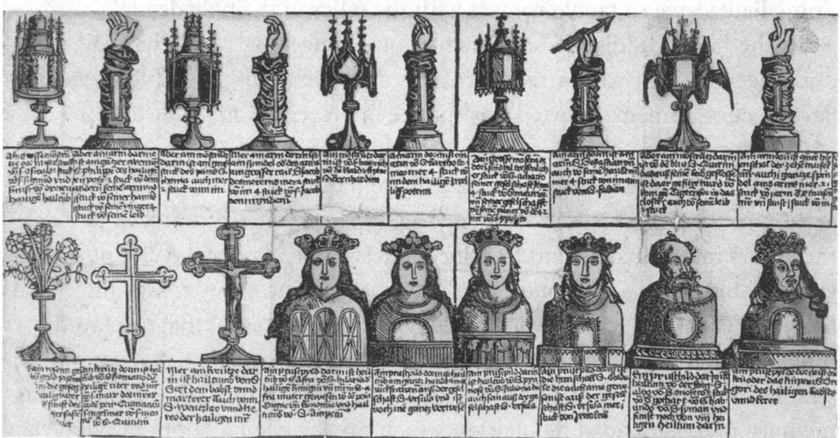

FIGURE 6. Section of woodcut relic-broadside depicting part of the relic collection at Andechs cloister, 1494. (The Trustees of the British Museum)

direct visual and tactile access to the relics of Saint Rasso was through his body's fragmentation. The Augustinian monks at Dießen, who supervised the chapel at Grafrath, removed one of his fingers when he was excavated in the 1460s and placed it a reliquary for periodic display to the faithful on the altar as well as for use during processions.[17]

From Fragments to Whole Bodies: The Evolution of Catacomb Saint Presentation

The outbreak of the Reformation in the early sixteenth century did little to alter the long-established medieval reliquary forms that highlighted bodily fragmentation or the custom of subdividing relics into different reliquaries. The first full-body catacomb saints translated to the duchy in the 1590s, donated to Jesuit foundation in Munich (St. Michael's) by the ducal family, were enclosed in luxurious, and completely opaque, casket reliquaries.[18] Images of these reliquaries appear in the illustrated relic inventory known as the *Schatzbuch von St. Michael* (Treasure book of St. Michael), and each image includes a short Latin description of the content of the reliquary depicted.[19] The label describing Saint Januarius's shrine states that it contains "a large part of the body of the martyr and deacon Januarius,"[20] and the labels for the shrines of Saturninus[21] and Euphebius[22] offer similar descriptions. In this case, the labeling of the saints as fully intact skeletons, and their display as such, was not of paramount importance. The labels openly acknowledge that the relics of these catacomb saints were not, in fact, entire bodies, but parts or particles. Later descriptions of catacomb saints, in sermons, printed relic inventories, and translations sermons, usually describe their saints as "*ganz,*" or complete, even if many bones were missing from the skeleton and artfully filled by wooden or wax replacements.

When more catacomb relics arrived in the duchy in the 1620s, cloisters chose to display them as fragments arranged with other relics behind a large pane of glass. In the wake of the Thirty Years' War, the method of presenting these Roman relics shifted dramatically. Rather than continuing to use more traditional reliquary forms, whole-body catacomb saints began appearing as luxuriously decorated and articulated skeletons housed within glazed shrines. This shift in display coincided with the sharp increase in the number of catacomb saints arriving at parish and cloister churches and quickly became the preferred way for churches in Bavaria—and the larger Alpine region—to exhibit their newfound patrons and protectors.

Several cases illustrate the rapidly changing ideas regarding the ideal way to present catacomb saint relics. Between 1626 and 1689, the Benedictine

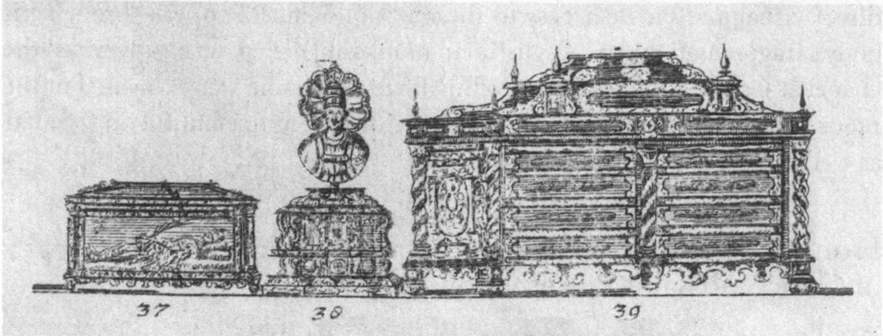

FIGURE 7. Engraving of the reliquaries of Saint Benignus (37) and Saint Antherus (39) at Polling cloister in *Heiliger Schatz* [. . .] *zu Pollingen*, 1729. (Universitätsbibliothek der LMU München, 4 H.eccl. 317)

cloister of Polling in Upper Bavaria received five catacomb saints. The first three saints, Antherus, Perpetua, and Severina arrived in 1626 as gifts from the wealthy Munich merchant Sebastian von Füll. A printed relic inventory published in 1729 includes engravings of the reliquaries designed to hold the relics of these early catacomb saints. The reliquary containing "the majority of the bones of saint Antherus, pope" displays various bone fragments placed in individual niches on the front of a chest-like reliquary (fig. 7).[23] Severina and Perpetua's relics were also arranged on glazed square relic panels, again in a fragmentary manner, with smaller bones placed in niches of various shapes. For the first trio of whole-body catacomb saints to reach Polling, there was no attempt to arrange the bones to form a complete skeleton or to describe the relics as whole. Each label characterizes the relics as "most of the bones" of each saint, and relics from all three saints were dispersed into two or more other reliquaries held at the cloister.[24] The willingness of monks to split relics from the same saint into multiple reliquaries, despite the fact that the cloister possessed the majority of their bones, indicates that the presentation of a *corpus sanctus* was not yet a priority.

When the Benedictines at Polling acquired two more catacomb saints in 1689, more than sixty years after the arrival of the first three, the remains of Saints Constantius and Benignus were staged as complete bodies. Engravings from the relic inventory show each saint lying within a glazed shrine holding the palm leaf of martyrdom (fig. 7). The description of each saint—"the body of St. Constantius" and "the body of St. Benignus"—and the fact that no other relic particles from these two saints are listed in the church's other reliquaries underscore their bodily integrity.[25] In contrast to the martyrs translated in the 1620s, by the 1680s the monastery leaders had clearly prioritized keeping the

FIGURE 8. Engraving of composite relic shrine at the Pütrich cloister in Munich in *Bittrich voll des himmlischen Manna*, 1721. (Bayerische Staatsbibliothek München, 4 H. on. 67)

relics of each of these Roman soldiers together and wanted to visually emphasize the completeness of the remains to visitors of the cloister church.

A similar progression from fragmentation to whole bodies in the display of catacomb saints' relics occurred at the Pütrich convent in Munich, whose inhabitants had surreptitiously acquired Saint Dorothea behind their prior's back in 1662.[26] The nuns continued to pursue more catacomb relics in the years that followed, and between 1664 and 1691, they acquired three more catacomb saints: Saint Hyacinth (1664), Saint Felicitas (1679), and Saint Geminus (1691). An engraving in a chronicle of the cloister's history published in 1721 provides a composite image of the convent's most important relics, including the catacomb saints' reliquaries (fig. 8).[27] The relics of the first two saints to arrive at the convent, Dorothea and Hyacinth, are arranged in vertical shrines. Their skulls are placed on pillows, Hyacinth's wearing a laurel wreath and Dorothea's bearing a crown. Beneath the skulls are larger bones, probably those of the legs and arms, as well as some smaller, rounder bones, all of which are embellished with simple decoration. Beneath the relics of Dorothea and Hyacinth rest the seemingly intact bodies of Saints Felicitas and Geminus. Each of these saints, brought to Munich slightly later than the two above, wear elaborate clothing and hold a vase containing their own blood. The stone gravestones from their burial niches in the Roman catacombs appear at the back of the shrines. Just as in Polling, presentation of catacomb saints in the second half of the seventeenth century evolved in a matter of decades from *pars* to *toto.*

The impulse to arrange catacomb saints into full-body relics did not abate over the course of the eighteenth century. When the Pütrichkloster undertook renovations in 1739, the nuns chose to rearrange Dorothea's and Hyacinth's fragmented relics into whole skeletons.[28] The same occurred with the bones of Saint Serena at the cloister of Andechs. The martyr's remains arrived at the cloister in 1620, and, based on depictions in several cloister chronicles and relic inventories (1657, 1691, 1715, 1745), her disarticulated bones were placed in a heart-shaped reliquary with relics from other female martyrs.[29] Today the saint's full body rests on the Präletenaltar in the Kreuzkapelle at the cloister, indicating that at some point the monks chose to have her fragmented remains assembled into a larger whole. This likely occurred around 1755, when Franz Xaver Schmädl and his workshop created a new altar for the Kreuzkapelle for the three-hundredth anniversary of the Benedictine abbey's foundation.[30] Transformations such as these even occurred in the waning years of the eighteenth century. Abbot Benedikt Lutz of Rott am Inn acquired the bodies of Saints Clemens and Constantius in Rome, and, upon returning to his cloister, he had the saints housed in four copper shrines decorated with silver fruit and flowers. His successor, Gregor Mack, unsatisfied with this state of affairs, sent the saints' relics to Munich for arrangement and decoration as full bodies. The saints returned to the cloister in March 1785 and took their places on two of the church's side altars.[31]

Creating Bodies

Notably, the creation of whole-body catacomb saints was not a presentation promoted or prescribed by the papacy, the Catholic Church in Rome, or the Bavarian ruling family and its clerical elite. In 1577, Charles Borromeo (1538–1584), often described as the model Tridentine bishop, wrote an influential handbook entitled *Instructiones fabricae et supellectilis ecclesiasticae,* which included a section on the proper treatment and display of relics within Catholic churches in the wake of the Council of Trent (1545–63). When it came to whole bodies, Borromeo wrote:

> The bodies of the saints which are to be put in a church having that subterranean part called a *confessio* or a crypt ought to be religiously and properly deposited there, either within stone altars or under them, as is the ancient custom. . . . The bodies of saints may be laid out also in some other conspicuous part of the church other than the altars. Then the chest should be constructed of a more precious marble and be richly decorated on the outside with sculpture that is distinguished for the pious and religious character of its ornamentation. . . . [The chest] should be fittingly placed either within the body of the church in the manner best adapted to its size or in one of the chapels. . . . If it be placed within the body of the church it should stand separate from the wall and on all sides from every other work; but if it is within some chapel it may be placed in the back part of it or at the side of the altar.[32]

These instructions on how to display relics did not include creating a full body from smaller relic fragments or presenting them behind glass to church visitors on or in altars. Within fifteen years, Borromeo's instructions had reached the duchy and begun to influence Bavarian clerics. In 1591, Jakob Müller—vicar of the diocese of Regensburg—published a handbook on proper church decoration and ornament for houses of worship in the diocese.[33] Müller's section on relics hews closely to that in Borromeo's *Instructiones* and likewise does not advise the display of whole bodies on altars nor their construction from fragmentary relics.

Apparently, Borromeo's and Müller's prescriptions for the ideal way to display a whole-body relic did not reach the churches and monasteries across the duchy. Rather than enclosing such relics in marble, individuals and communities across the territory made the decision to begin the long and costly process of assembling the "holy bodies" excavated from the catacombs into lifelike skeletons covered in jewels, pearls, ribbon, and more. Due to the various states and quantities in which these relics reached Bavaria, the construction of each catacomb saint presented unique challenges that required custom solutions and the expertise of a wide variety of individuals. Teams of doctors, sculptors, carpenters, relic decorators, and other artisans all worked together to develop creative techniques for putting together something that resembled a "complete" body out of a jumble of ancient remains.

The process began when the catacomb saints arrived from Rome in a wooden chest tied shut with a red silk ribbon and sealed in three places with the insignia of the vicar general or the papal sacristan. Once approved as authentic by the local bishop, as required by the regulations passed during the Council of Trent, the real task of constructing a holy body from relics received from the Eternal City could begin.[34] Before they were sent away for embellishment—usually to a convent or a laywoman relic decorator—the bones were carefully inventoried to prevent theft.[35] In certain cases, those commissioned to decorate the bones had to swear an oath not to remove particles or insert foreign bones into the skeleton.[36] In preparation for assembly and decoration, the bones were coated with glue in order to strengthen them and placed in the sun to dry.[37] Following this glue coating, the bones were often wrapped with gauze or painted with a white surface layer so they looked cleaner and more intact.[38] The gauze also protected the bones from direct contact with dirt and made the bones recognizable as part of a human skeleton.[39]

Once cleaned and coated with glue and/or paint, the next step was to articulate the available bones into their proper anatomical positions. In many cases, churches or those commissioned to decorate the saints turned to outsiders who were more familiar with human anatomy, namely artists and doctors, to assemble their Roman relics into a skeleton. After the available bones had been inventoried and arranged, care was taken to keep them in the correct order. When examining the remains of Saint Fidelis, brought to the Högerkapelle in 1699, conservator Uta Ludwig discovered that some of the bones were labeled with *Ls* and *Rs* to indicate on which side of the body they belonged and that some of the ribs were numbered, presumably to keep them in order during the construction process.[40]

Despite every effort to arrange the bones that had arrived from Rome into anatomically correct positions, in most cases, a significant number of each saint's bones were either missing or badly damaged. The strong desire, however, to present the imported "holy bodies" as whole skeletons prompted the churches that acquired these saints to come up with a creative solution—they would manufacture the missing bones themselves, most often using wood. This technique of assembling holy bodies using the original relics and manufactured replacement bones can be traced over several years at the parish church of St. Georg in Freising, which welcomed Saints Clara and Timotheus from Rome in the 1740s. In 1742, a carpenter from the town submitted his itemized bill to the parish priest. The list included charges for two wooden reliquary shrines for the saints, repair of a table in the parish rectory, and "three wooden ribs" delivered to the woman responsible for decorating one of the saints.[41] The next year, with the gaps in the saints' anatomy filled by wooden stand-ins, it was time to assemble the bodies into their final recumbent position for display on St. Georg's altars. The church paid one sculptor fifteen Gulden[42] for "putting together the bones of St. Timotheus" and another sculptor the same for "putting together St. Clara."[43] Apparently the sculptor who constructed Saint Clara's skeleton had not done a satisfactory job, because two years later the church had to pay another carpenter, Carl Saifferseid, four Gulden and ten Kreuzer for his work to better assemble Saint Clara's remains.[44]

Material evidence confirms the frequency with which catacomb saints like the pair in Freising had their incomplete skeletons "completed" by the creation of false bones. Over the last twenty years, Ludwig has restored almost fifty catacomb saint bodies, and based on this experience she observed: "Presumably none of the skeletons are made completely of bones. Replacement [bones] are very common, especially in fingers and toes. . . . [I]t is not uncommon to find larger false bones. In most cases, wood was chosen as the material for the replacement bones; more rarely, other materials like wax or fabric soaked in wax was used. Usually the wooden bone replacements were painted a similar color [as the existing bones], so that they stood out as little as possible."[45] Ludwig's observations from her decades of work are consistent with another study that examined the construction of nine catacomb saints from Upper Swabia and discovered frequent use of wooden replacement bones.[46]

Restoration records at the Bavarian State Office for Historic Preservation (Bayerisches Landesamt für Denkmalpflege) also demonstrate the prevalence of this approach to "completing" the bodies of catacomb saints.[47] In the case of Saint Peregrina, transferred to the parish church of Unterdießen in 1700, the use of wood to replace missing bones was quite extensive. According to the restoration report, Peregrina's hands, feet, lower legs, kneecaps, shoulder blades, some ribs, sternum, tailbone, and five vertebrae are made of wood. A missing part of her skull was also filled in with plaster.[48] The care with which these replacement bones were often carved can be seen in the torso of Saint Clemens, a catacomb saint transferred to the cloister church at Rott am Inn in 1760. When Clemens's body is viewed from the side, as it is presented in his shrine, what appear to be his white rib bones are partially visible under a layer of gauze and decorations made of golden wire, pearls, and a variety of stones (fig. 9). When Clemens is turned over, it becomes clear that his spinal column, ribs, and shoulder blades are made of custom-made wooden replica bones (fig. 10). These are not crude approximations of the saint's missing bones—but skillfully carved replacements created by a craftsman with intimate knowledge of the human skeletal system. What is even more striking is that such pains were taken to re-create the missing bones so accurately despite the fact than many of them would largely remain invisible to the viewer. The ribs are painted with a white coating on the surface visible to the viewer, further enhancing the impression that all of Clemens's bones were present in the shrine. This attention to detail indicates that those crafting this body placed a high value on creating as close to an intact skeleton—using real and manufactured parts—as possible.

FIGURE 9. Chest of Saint Clemens decorated with *Klosterarbeit*, Rott cloister, 1760. (Photograph by Uta Ludwig; courtesy of the Archdiocese of Munich and Freising)

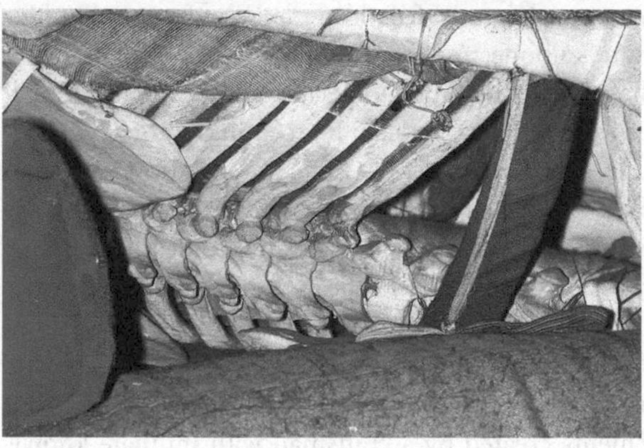

FIGURE 10. Carved wooden ribs, vertebrae, and shoulder blades of Saint Clemens, Rott cloister, 1760. (Photograph by Uta Ludwig; courtesy of the Archdiocese of Munich and Freising)

In certain cases, so few relics were received that replacement bones were not created for all of the missing body parts. Images taken during Ludwig's restoration of Saint Victoria's relics, originally housed at the parish church of St. Nikolaus in Rosenheim, make clear that the church only received some vertebra as well as part of the saint's skull from Rome. In order to craft a whole body from just a few bones, the church enlisted craftspeople to carve almost all of Victoria's leg and arm bones as well as two wooden shells to house her vertebrae and create a torso and lower body, which could be clothed (figs. 11–12). The wooden shells were attached using a flexible joint so the saint's body could be manipulated into a propped position on pillows. At the very top of the torso section of wooden shell, the carpenter or sculptor carved clavicles, which would have been slightly visible to parishioners under a dress that concealed her missing ribs and pelvis. The completion of Victoria's skull required as much creativity as that of the rest of her body (fig. 13). The entire top of Victoria's skull, from just above the eye socket, was missing. In order to round off the top of her head and make the skull fit for decoration, someone used multiple layers of gauze soaked in glue to form the base layer of a rounded

FIGURE 11. Saint Victoria's body before restoration, St. Nikolaus parish church, Rosenheim, 1675. (Photograph by Uta Ludwig; courtesy of the Archdiocese of Munich and Freising)

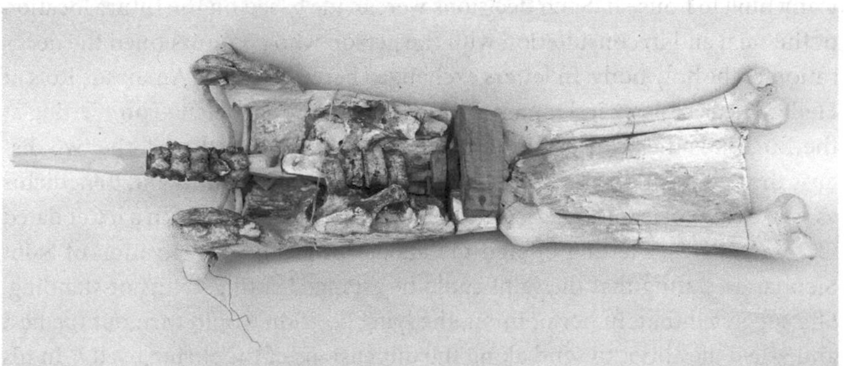

FIGURE 12. Wooden shells constructed to hold Saint Victoria's fragmented relics, St. Nikolaus parish church, Rosenheim, 1675. (Photograph by Uta Ludwig; courtesy of the Archdiocese of Munich and Freising)

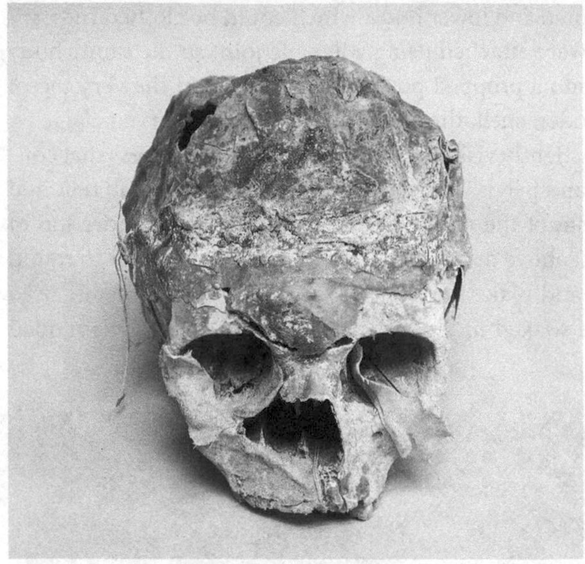

FIGURE 13. Saint Victoria's incomplete skull modified with wax and cloth, St. Nikolaus parish church, Rosenheim, 1675. (Photograph by Uta Ludwig; courtesy of the Archdiocese of Munich and Freising)

skull. A final, molded layer of wax was put on top of the stiffened gauze and finally painted white to resemble bone.

Once the requisite replacement bones or parts had been produced, catacomb saints could be arranged into three different positions—lying or propped up on pillows, sitting, or standing. The lying position was by far the most common in Bavaria, and surviving sitting and standing catacomb saints are relatively rare.[49] The position of the body was partially dependent on whether it would be inserted into an existing altar or integrated into a new altar specifically built to house it. Such decisions were made based on the future location of the saint and in consultation with the person who commissioned the decoration of the holy body. In letters exchanged between Abbot Amandus Röls of Heilig Kreuz cloister in Donauwörth and the nun Magdalena von Fletting at the English Ladies convent in Augsburg between 1725 and 1728, the two discuss the best position for the newly acquired Saints Stephanus and Benedictus as well as the costs for materials needed to decorate the saints. In a letter dated October 4, 1725, Fletting offered the abbot options for the position of Saint Stephanus, stating that the saint could be arranged sitting, lying, or standing. She suggested that, in her opinion, the lying position would turn out the best and asked the abbot to send along the dimensions of the shrine itself.[50] In his reply, Abbot Amandus agreed with Fletting's recommendation to present the saints in a recumbent position, stating that this arrangement would be "most pleasing to the eyes of the pious."[51]

At the cloister church of the Cistercians at Waldsassen, the monastery's chronicler recounts how catacomb saint Maximus miraculously chose a final resting position for himself. After toiling for hours to find a position in which to arrange Maximus's relics, Adalbert Eder, a lay brother who decorated nine of Waldsassen's ten catacomb saints, stood puzzled and desperate before his work.[52] The bells began to ring for a meal, and as the frustrated Eder left the room he told the saint: "St. Maximus, you know that I am losing time with you in vain . . . be so good and see how you, yourself would like to rest, since I cannot put you together." When Brother Adalbert returned to his cell after lunch, he found the relics not as he had left them but arranged facing the opposite direction in a beautiful, pleasing position. Eder broke into tears of joy at the sight and was then able to continue his work in time for the saint to be translated into the cloister church on the night before the Feast of the Assumption in 1766.[53]

Whether through miraculous intervention or earthly exertion, once a position for the saint's skeleton had been determined, decorators went about constructing a substructure, which would hold the real and false bones in the desired position. The example of Saint Victoria in Rosenheim is just one of the many ways in which this task could be accomplished. This process typically involved a wide variety of materials including wire, wooden strips, dowels, cardboard, iron strips and rods, nails, and needles.[54] Gauze and other fabrics soaked in glue or wax were also used to bind bones together or to hold them in place. One of the most common techniques for holding a catacomb saint's skeleton in the desired position was the construction of a supportive three-dimensional frame out of wood, carved specifically to house individual bones. A receipt from Frontenhausen, written by carpenter Franz Stöffauer in 1708, states that in addition to making a shrine for Saint Amantius he had to make a "new body from boards" to hold the saint's body in place.[55]

This type of wooden support system is visible in the skeleton of Saint Albanus, a catacomb saint transferred to the cathedral in Freising in 1758 (fig. 14). Albanus's rib cage, part of his pelvis, and lower vertebrae are stabilized by underlying pieces of custom-carved linden wood that mirrors the shapes of the bones (fig. 15). The same is true for his shoulder blades, tailbone, breastbone, and upper vertebrae, all of which were attached to the wooden substructure with small dowels. Albanus's arms and legs were affixed to carefully carved strips of wood, which had been hollowed out to fit the bones exactly. These frames were attached to the bones using pegs as well cloth bands to keep them in place. Unlike the rather stiff torso of the body, the artists and craftspeople who constructed Albanus chose to make his limbs quite mobile. A closer look at the saint's shoulder reveals a custom metal joint forged by a

FIGURE 14. Saint Albanus, Freising Cathedral, 1758. (Photograph by Uta Ludwig; courtesy of the Archdiocese of Munich and Freising)

FIGURE 15. Saint Albanus's pelvis with underlying wooden support structure, Freising Cathedral, 1758. (Photograph by Uta Ludwig; courtesy of the Archdiocese of Munich and Freising)

metalsmith to connect Albanus's shoulder and upper arm (fig. 16). The joint allowed movement both up and down and backward and forward, providing more flexibility when posing the saint in his shrine. Similar joints were installed at the saint's hips. To complete the skeleton, those constructing the holy body put Albanus's skull on a wooden rod carved to look like vertebra. When the saint was finally placed in his shrine and propped up, his head was held up using a wooden cradle supported by an iron rod.[56]

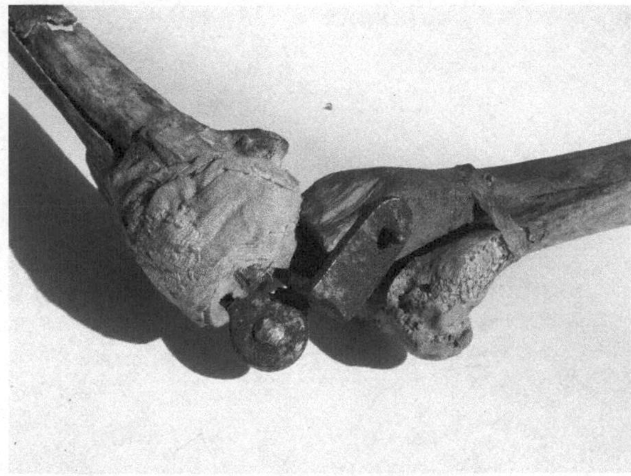

FIGURE 16. Saint Albanus's shoulder with metal joint and wooden supports, Freising Cathedral, 1758. (Photograph by Uta Ludwig; courtesy of the Archdiocese of Munich and Freising)

Decorating the Skeleton

Once the underlying structure of the saints had been completed, the decoration of the bones and the creation of clothing and accessories could finally begin using an art form called *Klosterarbeit* (cloister work). The term is "used to describe objects of devotion which are made out of a wide variety of modest materials, created with simple technical methods, and which, in general, require a great amount of patience and time. Most of this artwork was created in female cloisters, and was frequently produced not by professionals, but by nuns and other female laywomen."[57] Though the technique constantly evolved new forms, its original and primary purpose was the decoration of relics and holy bodies.[58] The earliest *Klosterarbeit* was produced from the fifteenth century onward; however, its peak popularity occurred during the seventeenth and eighteenth centuries in southern Germany, Austria, and Switzerland and was spurred by the importation of thousands of whole-body catacomb saints and particle relics from Rome.[59]

During the early modern period, several convents in Bavaria including the Benedictines in Munich and Frauenchiemsee, the Bridgettines at Altomünster, the Franciscan tertiaries in Ingolstadt and Reutberg, and the Ursulines in Munich and Straubing became quite well known for their skill in cloister work and were frequently commissioned to decorate holy bodies. Several male houses, notably the Jesuits in Munich, the Benedictines in Ettal, and the Cistercians at Waldassen, also specialized in this art form.[60] Each of these communities developed its own style and techniques for decorating holy bodies, with some favoring more visible bones and others preferring to cover the

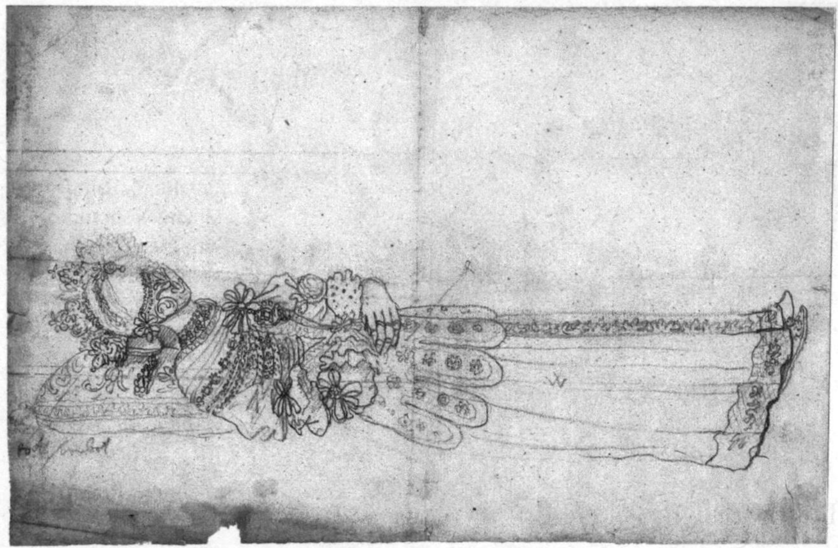

FIGURE 17. Pencil sketch of a design for the decoration of a holy body done at the Pütrich cloister, Munich, 1662–63. (Bayerisches Hauptstaatsarchiv, Plansammlung 20258)

relics (or missing body parts) with cloth or even wax.[61] A pencil sketch of the design for a lying female catacomb saint from the Pütrichkloster in Munich illustrates the careful planning that went into designing the clothing and decoration of a holy body (fig. 17). Though it is likely that one nun supervised and directed the overall project of dressing and ornamenting a saint, the final product was the result of a team effort. Groups of sisters worked together, splitting up the various tasks involved in the saint's adornment, with certain nuns specializing in a particular part of the process.[62]

Despite its sumptuous appearance, *Klosterarbeit* was created by hand and did not require complex technical equipment, particularly expensive materials, or advanced artistic training. In order to create it, practitioners needed to know how to cut, sew, stitch, embroider, and drape cloth. Girls often learned such skills at home as children and could readily apply them when decorating holy bodies.[63] To do so, they used commonly available items including copper wire (gilded or silvered), cloth, paper, wax, glue, colored or clear cut-glass stones, and imitation pearls to cover the relics and give luster to the ancient remains. The clear glass stones were often backed by a layer of colored metal leaf to give them the sparkle and gleam of real gemstones.[64] Though humble materials predominate, wealthier churches or cloisters provided semi-precious stones, real pearls, and jewelry made from silver or gold to embellish the saints.

The most important and common element of all in the creation of *Klosterarbeit* was gilded and silvered copper wire. Relic decorators used the versatile material to create a wide variety of different decorative elements from elaborate flowers and floral patterns to delicate frames for the glass stones. Wire could also be wrapped around a stiff paper core cut into a specific shape to make larger ornaments such as leaves for a martyr's laurel crown. The wire could also be flattened and cut into small metal sequins, which could then be sewn onto a martyr's clothing. To expedite the creation of these intricate decorations, extant artifacts show that nuns sometimes commissioned basic machines for their workshops to speed up the labor-intensive process. They also used other simple tools including hole punchers and awls to bore holes, stamps to create uniform shapes, and patterns and rollers or spindles to furl paper.[65] At the Poor Clares' cloister in Reutberg, several machines designed to craft a variety of different patterns and textures of wire decoration survive. A "spiral machine" was used to wind wire around a needle using a crank to create coils or—if flattened—a curlicue pattern. Another device, likely commissioned from and constructed by a clockmaker, allowed the nuns to flatten and crimp wire into different patterns by feeding it between different grooved gear wheels. The "long wheel" machine, described in a *Klosterarbeit* manual by the Franciscan nuns at Reutberg, was employed to wrap round wire around an already flattened wire to create different decorative patterns.[66]

Many of the ways wire could be used to decorate catacomb saints are visible on the shoulder of Saint Deodatus in St. Nikolas's parish church in Mühldorf am Inn (fig. 18). Directly above Deodatus's shoulder joint, the *Klosterarbeit* artists placed a large flower constructed from gilded and silvered wire surrounding a large red glass stone. The innermost petals of the flower are created from silver loops of wire bordered by golden curlicues. Wide, undulating, petal-like borders created by wrapping golden wire around a cardboard core surround each of these smaller petals. The same technique is used to create the flame-like elements, which extend from the base of this flower. Six additional smaller flowers with green stones at their centers encircle the main blossom. Their intricate petals are made of flattened and looped wire, and the central stones are held in place with small wire brackets. Silver sprigs made of curlicues of silver wire jut out from each of these miniature flowers as a final exuberant flourish.

Saint Prosper in Erding boasts similarly elaborate wire adornment, which incorporates more stones and false pearls all over his body. Atop his skull, Prosper wears a lavishly embellished laurel wreath of golden leaves, a symbol of his martyrdom and victory over death (fig. 19). The paper core of each leaf is wrapped with countless strands of wire that are interwoven with ribbons. Prosper's decorators even chose to fill his eye sockets with small, golden wire

FIGURE 18. Shoulder of Saint Deodatus with *Klosterarbeit,* St. Nikolaus parish church, Mühldorf am Inn, 1745. (Photograph by author)

flowers with striking blue stones at their center surrounded by small pearls. The saint appears to gaze directly out at the viewer, an effect that makes the saint even more lifelike.

Cloth of various kinds (silk, brocade, velvet, etc.) was another important material used in combination with wire decorations and stones to decorate catacomb saints and bring them to life as full bodies. Often convents or churches relied on donations of used clothing from resident nobles or used leftover pieces from the creation of liturgical vestments to create the saint's clothing.[67] In most cases, this cloth was embellished with intricate embroidery, which could include elements of *Klosterarbeit* such as glass stones, wire, or pearls. At Waldsassen, master relic decorator Adalbert Eder—who had once struggled to construct Saint Maximus's remains into a pleasing position—eventually stitched the martyr's name as well as several prayers onto the saint's clothing. Eder did the same for six other catacomb saints at the Waldsassen cloister, painstakingly embroidering each ancient martyr's vestments with gilded and silver thread.[68] Once decorated, cloth elements of a saint's costume were commonly soaked in glue or backed by cardboard to keep the folds and arrangement of the outfit in a particular position.

The meticulous art of *Klosterarbeit* expressed some of the basic values of convent and monastery life: the ideals of poverty, humility, patience, and the

FIGURE 19. Head and shoulders of Saint Prosper with *Klosterarbeit,* St. Johann parish church, Erding, 1645. (Photograph by author)

total giving over of oneself to God. The production of *Klosterarbeit* was extremely labor- and time-intensive, and its creation became a devotional act that produced a "visual prayer."[69] The use of mostly cheap materials (wire, glass or paste jewels, paper, leftover cloth) and the simplest tools reinforced the idea that the poorest things enjoyed the highest value in the eyes of God if they were created in the right frame of mind.

Inspiration for the decoration and costuming of the catacomb saints originated from several sources. First, the clothing of the saints as well as physical attributes such as stone eyes, hair, and crowns all served to create more concrete and realistic patrons for viewers. Rather than a jumble of bones, onlookers gazed at a fully personified skeleton, which in turn gazed back at them with gleaming jewels in place of eyes. Though the complete bodies presented in these glass shrines were certainly identifiable as human, the holy body represented was decidedly not the one the saint had possessed on earth. Rather, according to Bertrandus Leffelleuthner at Raitenhaslach (1698), this was a heavenly body, glorified by God after the martyr's suffering. After their martyrdom, God removed Saints Ausanius, Concordia, and Fortunatus's "old clothing of humanity and, as it were, clothed them in a new one."[70] This new outfit, created from shining golden wire, sparkling jewels, and sumptuous cloth, visually conveyed the martyrs' triumph over death and the heavenly reward that awaited them when they arrived in paradise.[71] In his sermon at the translation of Saint Placidus into the Capuchin cloister in Erding, Jordanus von Wasserburg made a similar point to his audience. He drew a direct parallel between the state of Placidus's body during his torture at the hands of the Romans to the sparkling body resting on the altar before the audience's eyes: "At the time [of his execution] all of the holy martyr's limbs were nothing but flesh and wounds, now these same limbs sink [under the weight] of many jewels. Before [Placidus's] hands and feet were bound with ignominious ropes and chains, now they are decorated with luxurious ribbons and strings of pearls."[72] Though the saint's situation had once been desperate, his loyalty and faith were now rewarded as his bonds were transformed into strands of precious stones and his gloriously resurrected intact body; for his fellow Christians, Pladicus's bejeweled remains provided a concrete preview of the spiritual benefits of a life of faith.

Financing Holy Bodies

Creating magnificently adorned "holy bodies" required not only the skills of a community but also a significant amount of funding. Although the costs for the decorative materials for a catacomb saint were not usually monumental, the acquisition, construction, embellishment, and housing of whole-body catacomb saints represented a significant outlay of funds for both parishes and monasteries. Detailed receipts from the parish church of St. Jakob in Dachau provide insight into the various expenses associated with construction of a whole-body catacomb saint and reveal the number of craftspeople, day laborers, and donors involved in the process of creating a town's new patron. In Dachau, the congregation had planned on acquiring catacomb saints for at least five years before the relics arrived. When new high baroque altars were installed in 1714, a space was left for the installation of holy bodies just above the altar stone.[73] In 1718, a very successful Munich merchant and member of the Electoral Council, Anton Benno Höger, managed to acquire two catacomb saints, Sigismund and Ernestus, on behalf of the church. Höger functioned as an ideal middleman to conduct this business for the church as he had extensive business contacts in Rome and had already procured catacomb saints for his personal palace chapel in Anzing (1699), the parish church of Dingolfing (1701), and the Augustinian cloister at Indersdorf (Julius and Innocentius, 1712). Though Höger managed to acquire the two saints in Rome, this was a costly endeavor. The "expenses and donations" paid in Rome amounted to 300 Gulden, and the transport from Rome to Munich totaled 70

Gulden. An additional 12 Gulden were required to pay for the authentication of the relics and notarial paperwork at the bishop's office in Freising.[74]

Once the administrative tasks had been completed, the church commissioned a young Munich lay "relic decorator" named Josepha Antonia Khroningerin to decorate Saints Sigismund and Ernestus. Khroningerin received 430 Gulden and 2 Kreuzer as payment for her work, though she used an unspecified part of this wage to purchase gold and silver wire, 33.5 cubits of variously colored ribbon, and two wooden shrines with locks used to transport the saints to Dachau. These materials, however, were far from all that was required to complete the decoration of the saints. Höger benefited commercially from his act as middleman as the church paid him 257 Gulden and 35 Kreuzer for other items used to embellish the saints. These included: 53.5 dozen glass imitation gems, nine dozen garnets, 24 loops of pearls, 12 cubits of white gauze, and a mattress and pillows, on which the saints would eventually lie. The final entries into the church account books concerning materials for the decoration of the saints list 2¹³/₁₆ cubits of gold leaf and tin, probably used to make the martyr's laurel wreaths (6 Gulden, 19 Kreuzer); five cubits of unbleached linen and five plaited hanks of horse hair (3 Gulden, 17 Kreuzer); six cubits of silk as well as 14.5 "*loth*"[75] of gilded border to be used on the pillows (60 Gulden, 50 Kreuzer).[76]

While Khroningerin worked in Munich to decorate the two holy bodies, the craftspeople in Dachau stayed busy building the shrines that would permanently house the town's new patron saints. Sculptor Bartolomäus Schuchpaur carved the intricate decorative frames for the shrines, which incorporated foliage and angels. In addition, he made wooden frames for the epitaph stones taken with the relics from the catacombs. For his efforts, Schuchpaur received 27 Gulden, 59 Kreuzer from St. Jakob's. The frame and its decorative elements were then handed over to Dachau painter Johan Georg Hörmann. Hörmann gilded the frames, painted each of the angels with two coats of silver and painted the interior of the shrines silver. Though the fee for the labor was only 40 Gulden, the gold and silver leaf needed to cover the shrine and the varnish to finish it cost twice as much at 80 Gulden. Glazier Georg Älbl enclosed each with large panes of glass (24 Gulden), and then Georg Spizer, a locksmith, finished the project by installing double locks and provided seven "strong rods" to securely fasten the two shrines in place (4 Gulden, 22 Kreuzer) on each altar. By the time the saints' relics had been acquired, transported from Rome to Munich, approved by the diocese in Freising, decorated, transported to Dachau, and transferred into the church in a lavish translation ceremony, the parish church of St. Jakob had spent 1,419 Gulden, 5 Kreuzer, and 5 Heller, quite a large sum.[77]

The sum becomes even more impressive when compared to the yearly average salary of a maid (15–50 Gulden per year) or the amount given *per annum* in alms to a community's poorest residents (1–14 Gulden) in eighteenth-century Bavaria.[78] In Munich, proof of an amassed "fortune" of 100–150 Gulden was required to apply for the privilege of citizenship; in the Dachau region, the same sum of money spent on the acquisition and decoration of Saints Ernestus and Sigismund would have bought a whole farmstead with 120 acres of land.[79] Based on these figures, it is clear what significant financial investment communities—both monastic and parochial—were willing to undertake in order not only to acquire a catacomb saint from Rome but to craft and decorate a holy body from the remains they received.

In the case of Saints Sigismundis and Ernestus, the feat is particularly extraordinary in light of the fact that Dachau had only eight hundred inhabitants. Still, the village managed to pay for the acquisition and lavish decoration of two catacomb saints in the wake of the destructive War of Spanish Succession (1701–14). Finding the resources for this project involved continuous dedication and determination on the part of the entire town. The first attempt to finance the acquisition and decoration of the catacomb saints was a community collection for the cause. Unfortunately, this collection only brought in 120 Gulden, 35 Kreuzer, and 3 Pfennig, far short of the sum the church needed for its effort. The church then turned to the local brotherhoods to help support the relics' decoration and translations, receiving donations from the Saint Sebastian Bildnis-Verwaltung (135 Gulden, 30 Kreuzer) and the Brotherhood of the Rosary (370 Gulden, 59 Kreuzer). The church itself contributed 380 Gulden from its income for the year of 1722 and used donations from the offertory box from 1719 to 1722 (430 Gulden) to underwrite preparation of the whole-body relics and their shrines. Despite all these efforts, the church and the community still did not have enough to cover the full cost of completing their catacomb saint project. Eventually the parish church had to borrow 371 Gulden and 12 Kreuzer from the local hospital endowment, the Jocherschen Spitalstiftung, to be able to pay for the final decorative materials and the translation festival.[80] The willingness of St. Jakob's parish church to pool all available community resources and, in the end, to go into debt to acquire and then outfit its Roman catacomb saints as holy bodies indicates that the community placed a very high value on having these saints in their church and having them presented as whole bodies.

The village of Dingolfing faced a similar challenge. Johann Matthias Weigenthaler, the mason who had fought so hard to bring the body of Saint Faustina back to his home village of Dingolfing in 1770, recorded in his diary that the entire process cost 1,230 Gulden and that "at the beginning of this great work, I had no more than 92 Gulden on hand as capital [for the project]."[81] The potential expense of the endeavor had been one reason the local parish priest resisted providing a letter of support for the acquisition of the saint at the outset of Weigenthaler's campaign. This concern proved justified as a short, final note from February 7, 1784, tucked at the end of the manuscript reveals that Dingolfing, just like Dachau, had had to take out loans to fund the entire project and that it took fourteen years for the loan to be paid off completely. Even in the face of years of continuing costs, the village, led by Weigenthaler, believed it worthwhile to bring a whole-body saint to their home church.

In cases where the parish alone could not afford to acquire and/or decorate a saint, priests often sought the help of local nobles or monasteries. In Frontenhausen, the parish priest approached the noble Egger family and convinced them of the benefits of having a catacomb saint in their burial chapel. The Eggers apparently agreed and helped to finance not only Saint Amantius's decoration but also a new altar and renovations to the chapel itself before the saint arrived in 1708.[82] St. Georg's in Freising, however, faced a different problem. In 1737, Dr. Caspar Andreas Haas, a canon at the nearby collegiate church of St. Andreas, and his sister Rosalia donated the bodies of catacomb saints Timotheus and Clara to St. Georg's. Though delighted with the gift, the parish could not afford to decorate the saints on its own. St. Georg's priest, Joseph Krimmer, wrote to the head of Freising's cathedral chapter and asked for help in finding a benefactor who could pay for the "necessary decoration" of the holy bodies.[83] It seems by "necessary decoration," Krimmer meant that he did not want to display the relics until they had been crafted into whole bodies, a task far more costly than simply presenting the relics as fragments.

Based on the extant account of the donations given to pay for the decoration of the saints, Krimmer never found a single large donor. Rather, he had to rely on a handful of Freising citizens to fund the effort.[84] The need to collect sufficient funds probably also explains the seven-year gap between the relics' arrival in Freising and their construction into whole bodies. In April 1743, Krimmer wrote to the dean of the cathedral to request permission to hold a translation festival because Saint Timotheus's body was "finally far enough along that he could be displayed for public veneration."[85] Krimmer's reluctance to display the saint's relics in the parish church before they had been put together into the form of an intact body underscores the importance Bavarians placed on presenting catacomb in this manner.

While small Bavarian towns had to use all possible sources of income to successfully bring a whole-body catacomb saint to their parish churches, cloisters usually had far greater monetary resources. Still, bringing one or more catacomb saints to a cloister and presenting them appropriately meant a significant outlay of funds. Many cloister translation accounts such as those from Rottenbuch and Sandizell relate the "unbelievable expense"[86] and "very large cost"[87] the decoration of a catacomb saint required. In 1741, the cloister of Indersdorf spent over 10 percent of its income for the year on the transport, decoration, shrine construction, and translation festivities of the catacomb saints Felix and Lucius.[88]

Though some cloisters had plentiful resources, letters between Abbot Amandus at Donauwörth and his decorator, the English Lady Magdalena Fletting of Augsburg, reveal how cost-conscious cloisters could be in relation to the materials used to embellish their saints. In response to Fletting's inquiry concerning the types of stones and gems she should use on the saints, Abbot Amandus replied: "I do not want to dishonor such a precious treasure with fake gold. Using good pearls, on the other hand, would suffice, but would be a mistake and turn out badly because the small ones would barely be visible and the largest ones would be too expensive. Therefore, Your Eminence, try to choose beautiful water pearls and use those for the decoration."[89] Although Abbot Amandus did not want to sacrifice the visual appeal of his catacomb saints Clemens and Constantius, he was aware he could not afford to buy gold or large saltwater pearls in large quantities. Instead, he decided to cut costs by using cheaper freshwater pearls, realizing that it was unlikely that onlookers would recognize the difference and that by doing so, he could get more impressive larger pearls for the holy bodies.

As at parish churches, sometimes private donors helped cloisters—especially convents—afford the decoration of catacomb saints. In a description of the translation of Saint Asterius to the church of Ursulines at Straubing, the writer recounts how the nuns had worked industriously to decorate the relics of the saint themselves according to their ability and that several people had helped them afford both the decoration of the saint as well as his translation ceremony.[90] Similarly, the Franciscan tertiaries at the Angerkloster in Munich relied on the 850 Gulden donated by Joachim von Empacher to complete their adornment of the body of Saint Eleutheria as well as the construction of her shrine.[91] Individual monks and nuns could also donate money and materials to help decorate a newly arrived catacomb saint. At the Pütrich cloister, the nuns donated a variety of items as well as money to help decorate Saints Dorothea and Hyacinth. A small booklet held at the Hauptstaatsarchiv in Munich includes more than fifty entries cataloging the rings, jewels, cloth, and money the sisters presented for the decoration of the newly arrived relics of Saints Dorothea and Hyacinth.[92] Similarly, the sisters at the Benedictine convent at Geisenfeld donated necklaces with rubies, pearls, and diamonds, rings, gold and silver chains as well as money to help adorn Saint Dionysius.[93]

The willingness of early modern Bavarians to fundraise, donate their own jewelry, and even go into debt to present their Roman catacomb saints as sparkling intact skeletons demonstrates the importance placed on staging the relics in this manner. Rather than small pieces, laypeople, parish priests, and abbots across the territory insisted on constructing catacomb saints' relics into holy bodies, reversing a trend toward relic fragmentation that had begun in the fourth century. The decision to present the saints in this manner was a decision made—and funded—at a local level rather than one dictated by Bavarian or Roman authorities. The lengthy process required a community effort involving the expertise of artists and physicians familiar with human anatomy; carpenters and metalsmiths who carved missing bones and built custom support structures for the "bodies"; and nuns skilled in the decorative technique of *Klosterarbeit* who covered the saints' remains in jewels, pearls, and gilded wire. Beyond the striking visual appeal, the reliquary form of the holy body allowed early modern Bavarians to concretely demonstrate their connection to and belief in important movements and doctrines promoted by the universal Catholic Church. At the same time, the concentration of a saint in one place and in human form significantly impacted the saints' ritual arrival (*adventus*), their role as local patrons (*patronus*), and how they were presented within the church (*domus*).

PART II

HOLY BODIES AND THE UNIVERSAL ROMAN CATHOLIC CHURCH

3

Whole-Body Saints and Eucharistic Doctrine

IN 1771, the small parish church in the village of Hahnbach in the Upper Palatinate welcomed the "holy body" of Saint Felix. Constructed into full body and decorated in shimmering *Klosterarbeit,* the saint found a permanent home on the Last Supper Altar holding a vase of the blood he shed in the name of Christ (figs. 20–21). Directly above him, a large panel painting depicts the institution of the liturgy of the Mass when Christ declared the two elements of the Eucharist—the bread and the wine—his sacrificial body and blood. By staging Felix's remains as an intact body and placing them atop the altar in Hahnbach, congregations across Bavaria made certain abstract theological doctrines of the sacred mysteries central to the post-Tridentine Catholic Church—namely the sacrificial nature of the Mass and the transubstantiation of the Eucharist—visually comprehensible and concrete. Here on the altar, where Christ's sacrifice was performed in the liturgy, was a tangible, parallel presentation of a martyr's body holding an ampule of his or her sacrificial blood. Though Christ's "own body and blood" became present in the Eucharistic elements when the priest spoke the words of institution, their external appearance remained the same.[1] By presenting catacomb saints as complete bodies, Bavarian Catholics created an immediate, embodied illustration of "high mysteries hidden in [this sacrifice]," materializing the saint's body to allude to the whole of Christ's body and blood made present during the reading of the liturgy.[2]

To accomplish this task, early modern Bavarians both relied upon and reconfigured the long-standing but *invisible* relationship between Christ's bodily sacrifice in the Eucharist and the sacrificial remains of martyrs. From the early centuries of the church, Christian theologians identified the parallel sacrifices inherent in the body and blood of martyrs and Christ's body and blood in the Eucharist, and brought the two together physically at the site of the altar. In the fourth century, Saint Ambrose explained the logic behind the pairing of these sacrificial bodies: "Let these triumphant victims [martyrs] be brought to the place where Christ is the victim. But He upon the altar, Who suffered for all; they beneath the altar."[3] Ambrose's ideas had practical results as it became

FIGURE 20. Last Supper altar with shrine of Saint Felix, St. Jakob parish church, Hahnbach, 1771. (Photograph by author)

common for early Christians to build churches atop martyrs' graves or to move sacred remains from their original burial site and place them under altars.[4]

As time passed, the connection between martyrs' bodies and church altars became a recognized part of church practice. The Second Council of Nicaea (787 CE) codified the practice, stating that in order to be properly consecrated, altars had to contain relics of martyrs.[5] If no martyrs' relics were available, particles of consecrated Eucharistic wafers began to be used in place of a martyr's remains to consecrate altars because the Host was considered by medieval clerics as "a physical relic of Christ."[6] Though the practice of depositing

FIGURE 21. Blood vase of Saint Felix, St. Jakob parish church, Hahnbach, 1771. (Photograph by author)

Eucharistic wafers in altars for consecration waned after the thirteenth century, the interchangeability of the relics of martyrs and the sacramental bread suggests both were understood to be the sacred *bodies* of those who made the ultimate sacrifice for their faith.[7]

Before the seventeenth century, however, the physical and theological connection between the altar and the bones of the martyrs remained a largely *invisible* relationship, particularly for laypeople. During the consecration liturgy, clerics placed relic fragments in an altar *sepulchrum,* a small cavity in the altar table, which was then covered up to make a flat surface. The creation and placement of catacomb saint bodies upon and within altars behind large sheets of glass in baroque Bavaria visualized and materialized this connection in a radically new manner. No longer were the sacrificial bones of martyrs simply buried in the "tomb" of the altar table. Their bodies, as well as the blood they had spilled while sacrificing themselves in the name of Christ, were permanently visible in the same place where His sacrifice occurred daily in the liturgy of the Mass.[8]

Defining and defending the nature of the Eucharist was a particularly urgent task in the early modern period as Protestants challenged the doctrines on both transubstantiation and the nature of the Mass.[9] Over the course of the Council of Trent (1545–63), the participants issued several decrees on these two related issues. The Council specifically addressed the subject of transubstantiation in 1551, declaring: "by the consecration of the bread and wine, there takes place the change of the whole substance of the bread into the substance of the body of Christ our Lord, and of the whole substance of the wine into the whole substance of his blood. And the holy catholic church has suitably and properly called this change transubstantiation."[10] By defending the concept of transubstantiation, the Catholic Church separated itself clearly from both the Lutheran and Reformed understandings of the Eucharistic sacrament, which rejected the notion that Christ's flesh and blood replaced the substance of the bread and wine during the liturgy.

The Council returned to the issue of the Eucharist once again in September 1562, this time addressing the sacrificial nature of the Mass. It asserted that according to Catholic doctrine, the Mass was a "true and unique sacrifice" instituted by Christ at the Last Supper.[11] The decree explained that in the "divine sacrifice which is performed in the mass, the very same Christ is contained and offered in bloodless manner who made a bloody sacrifice of himself once for all on the cross."[12] In this statement, the Council reiterated its belief that Christ offered himself bodily—not symbolically—each time the sacrament was performed. Thus, by 1562 the Roman Catholic Church had staked out its position on both the Mass and the transformation of the Eucharist, declaring any other interpretations heretical.

Although the Roman Church had defined doctrinal orthodoxy on these issues, the sacred mystery of the Eucharistic wafer and wine's transubstantiation into the *actual* sacrificed body and blood of Christ during the Mass was not visually apparent to the observer. Because these concepts had become such critical confessional markers, early modern Catholics worked to make the reality of this miraculous transformation *visible* and comprehensible to worshippers who were not steeped in the intricacies of sacramental theology. In Bavaria, the ruling Wittelsbach family wholeheartedly embraced this task, stoutly defending the traditional understanding of the real presence of Christ in the Eucharist and the sacrifice of Mass promulgated at the Council of Trent. The dukes and their agents strove to cultivate an increased reverence and veneration for the Eucharist in their domains.[13] Beginning in the 1560s and 1570s, court preachers defended veneration of the Eucharist in sermons, and by 1616, the Bavarian legal code made the theft of a monstrance displaying the Host punishable by death.[14] Besides defending the Eucharist in word and law, the ducal family also promoted devotion to the Holy Sacrament through their own actions. Most notably, the family directed and bankrolled the increasingly elaborate Corpus Christi processions in Munich, Landshut, and Wasserburg and undertook public pilgrimages to bleeding Host shrines at Andechs, Bettbrunn, Deggendorf, and Neukirchen beim Heiligen Blut.[15]

The Wittelsbachs also promoted other paraliturgical devotions to the Eucharist. In 1600, Duke Maximilian I invited the Capuchin order to establish a branch in Munich, and the order helped revive at least sixty Corpus Christi confraternities between 1600 and 1700.[16] Through these confraternities, the Capuchins, as well as the Jesuits, popularized the Forty-Hour prayer vigil, which had begun in late sixteenth-century Italy and entailed constant prayer before a Host displayed within a monstrance.[17] By the mid-seventeenth century, early modern Bavaria offered many opportunities to encounter the body and blood of Christ, whether at yearly Corpus Christi events, Forty-Hour prayer vigils, or at pilgrimage sites dedicated to miraculous Hosts or cult images of Christ. These rituals often relied heavily on visual media to communicate the importance of the Host. Receptacles for reserving and displaying the consecrated host, such as monstrances and tabernacles, became ever more elaborate, and cult images were modified or enhanced to reinforce Eucharistic doctrines. All of these paraliturgical rituals and images, along with weekly attendance at Mass, served to familiarize the duchy's inhabitants with the doctrines of transubstantiation and of the sacrificial nature of the Mass.

Though certainly critical in spreading Tridentine orthodoxy on this most important sacrament, the state did not have a monopoly on how local communities chose to express and materialize their beliefs about the nature of the Eucharist.[18] In the 1660s, early modern Bavarians began forging catacomb saint relics into complete holy bodies that embodied and illustrated the core tenets of Tridentine doctrine on the Eucharist in a creative, material manner. Local festival organizers and clerical preachers along with artists worked together to convey the Eucharistic significance of the whole-body saints during processions and translation sermons. After the welcoming events were over, viewers were permanently reminded of the similarities through the adaptation of altar forms and liturgical vessels typically used to house images of Christ or the consecrated elements of the Eucharist. By presenting catacomb saint relics in this way, early modern Bavarians expressed and materialized their belief in the corporeality of the Eucharistic sacrifice and, thereby, their allegiance to universal Catholic Church doctrine.

Mirror Images: The Sacrificial Bodies of Christ and Catacomb Saint Martyrs

In order to convey the Eucharistic significance of whole-body catacomb saints, it was first necessary to make the connection between the sacrificial bodies of the martyrs and Christ explicit. Even before installation on altars, clerics who designed the iconography for translation festivities and preachers delivering the transfer sermons worked to establish the similarities between both the sacrificial bodies and the attributes of Christ and his martyrs. The ability to make these comparisons was predicated on the visibility and full-body presentation of Roman catacomb saints. The presence of an intact skeleton allowed preachers to bring the physical relics to the audience's attention during sermons and to note the similarities between Christ and the martyrs' bodily sacrifices, especially as they related to the sacrament of the Eucharist.

When delivering a sermon at Arnstorf for the translation of Saint Victorinus to the Schloßkapelle in 1691, Ferdinand Orban told his audience that "this skeleton of a most steadfast hero—presented according to the advice of an anatomist—reminds everyone of the model of Jesus Christ."[19] The presentation and presence of Victor's body on the altar enabled Orban to draw a direct connection between the body of the martyr and the body of Christ for his listeners in a way that would have been very difficult with a small fragmentary relic, especially one buried in the altar *sepulchrum.* The comparisons preachers made between the sacrificial deaths of Jesus and his early followers sometimes went beyond rhetorical juxtaposition and referenced specific forensic details on the bodies of the martyrs themselves. In a printed miracle book cataloging the wonders performed by catacomb saint Dionysius at Geisenfeld, Stephan Malgaritta noted for his reader that, the "stroke of the sword" could still be seen on Saint Dionysius's "vertebrae" where he was beheaded, tangible and incontrovertible proof of his bodily sacrifice.[20] At Inderdsorf, Jordanus von Wasserburg pointed out how Saint Julius's "especially broken skull" was crushed with "a club and cudgel."[21] Julius's sacrifice and wounds, like those of his fellow ancient Christian martyrs, became readily apparent due to their staging as full bodies. These skeletons provided concrete and immediate material evidence, which differed fundamentally from an artistic depiction of a saint's torments or a preacher's sermon on the saint's life and suffering. Their *bodies* and the blows they had borne for love of Christ gave physical testimony to the death they had suffered for their beliefs.

The direct relationship between Christ and the martyrs was further reinforced by the practice of including glass ampules of the catacomb saints' blood within their shrines. These vessels, retrieved from the catacombs and sent with the remains from Rome or produced for the saints in Bavaria, purportedly held blood the saints had shed during their passions.[22] Frequently, the holy bodies held the vases of blood in their hands, proffering them to onlookers as a testament to their violent deaths (fig. 21). The containers could also be affixed inside the shrine with the skeleton in a variety of places: hung from the top on a chain, mounted on the back wall, or on the floor in front of the skeleton. A final option incorporated the vial of blood into the shrine's carved and gilded framing using a small niche. Visible to all, these ampules were sometimes labeled as "*sanguis M.*" for literate onlookers, leaving no doubt as to the substance contained within.

As with their bodies, the prominent placement of the blood vials within the catacomb saints' shrines meant that preachers could draw the attention of translation festival audiences to the presence of the martyrs' blood and highlight its similarity to Christ's sacrificial blood, present though not readily perceptible in the consecrated Eucharistic elements. At Steingaden, Carmelite preacher Andreas von Sancta Theresia went so far as to tell his listeners that when they faced the common travails of life—crop failure, drought, hunger—they should take the "hard morsel and dunk it in the blood-dripping wounds of your savior Jesus Christ and in the blood of the martyr Beninus displayed here and spilled in the name of Christ."[23] In this succinct statement, Sancta Theresia implies that the blood of Christ and his martyrs functioned similarly as a source of comfort and grace, nearly equating the two. Preachers at other translation ceremonies echoed the Carmelite's thoughts on the miraculous potential of the martyrs' sacrificial blood. Hyacinth Frants described the blood at Raitenhaslach's three catacomb saints as a "most powerful balsam," while at Blutenberg, Amadeus Hamilton informed the crowd that the substance had the power to heal wounded souls, turn unbelievers into believers, and strengthen the weak.[24] In each of these cases, the clerics were not speaking metaphorically but making concrete references to the *actual* blood spilled by these ancient Christians during their passions and held aloft by those very saints for parishioners to see. This blood was physically present and perceptible in a way that it was not in the Eucharistic wine and served to remind onlookers of the parallels between the self-sacrifice of Christ and the martyr before their eyes.

Beyond the Body and Blood: Linking Christ and the Martyrs

In addition to the visible physical signs of sacrifice written on the very bodies of the Roman martyrs, preachers and festival organizers used a myriad of creative ways to connect and even blur the distinctions between the lives and deaths of Christ and the catacomb saints. Clerics used parallel hagiographical stories, biblical typology, epithets, and iconographical symbols to reinforce the many similarities between the bodies of ancient martyrs lying before them and Christ himself. The more the martyrs took on Christ-like qualities, the more their bodies and the blood they carried could effectively remind viewers of the real presence of Christ's sacrificed body contained in the two elements of the Eucharist.

The most important resemblance between these ancient martyrs and Christ was their decision to sacrifice their lives for their faith. Wasserburg made this clear for his audience in Frontenhausen during the translation of Saint Amantius in 1708. He noted that among the various types of saints, Amantius and his fellow catacomb saints were "more like Christ since they were martyred."[25] Preachers continuously emphasized this similarity, directly comparing the lives of martyrs to that of Christ, particularly highlighting their desire to sacrifice themselves for their beliefs. At Raitenhaslach, Hyacinth Frants described how during their last moments of torture Saints Ausanius, Fortunata, and Concordia "observed the blood-dripping Jesus on the Cross and desired nothing more than to follow in his holy footsteps."[26] Similarly, at Erding, the preacher wrote dialogue for Saint Placidus that allowed the saint to express his motivations for self-sacrifice. The martyr lamented: "Oh! That I only have one life and not a thousand! Oh, that I have so little blood in my veins and not an entire ocean? Oh, that I can only suffer one death and not a thousand before Christ!"[27]

Placidus's plea to spill an entire ocean of blood for Christ demonstrates how Bavarian preachers understood a martyr's sacrifice to be inspired by and also connected to the Eucharistic sacrifice of Christ. In 1700, Hamilton explained to the assembled crowd at Schloß Blutenberg that during their lives, the five martyrs before them received "the precious blood of Christ in the blessed holy sacrament of the altar; they bore witness and never hesitated to offer their blood for that [His] blood which they enjoyed." By choosing to die in this manner, Hamilton said, the martyrs united the "unbloody sacrifice" of Christ's body and blood they had enjoyed in the Eucharist with the "bloody" sacrifice of their own flesh and blood.[28] Using the very words of the Council of Trent's decree on the nature of the Eucharistic sacrifice on altars, Hamilton explained how the martyred holy bodies before their eyes were a physical embodiment of the substances contained in the communion bread and wine. Though Christ had ascended bodily into heaven, there, on the altar, was a human example of martyrs so like Christ that their sacrifice had been united with that of Christ's daily offering of himself in the Mass. The saints' presence in the form of a full body holding their blood made visibly manifest the mystery of the Eucharist—which did, according to Catholic doctrine—transform into the body and blood of Christ yet still had the "accidental" form of the bread of the Host.[29]

The stories of the bodily sacrifice of Christ and the early Christian martyrs who followed him shared in translation events often centered around their gruesome deaths and the pain and torment they suffered in the process. Yet, contained within the Eucharist—and the bejeweled bodies of catacomb saints—was a message of great hope: the promise of salvation and bodily resurrection. Like Christ, each catacomb saint body had risen to glory. At Pfettrach, Wasserburg described how, according to the will of God, "the body of St. Felicissimus arose out of his grave and was elevated from the Calixtus cemetery."[30] Just a few years later, Wasserburg once again used this comparison at the translation of Saint Amantius in Frontenhausen, telling the audience that, like Christ, this martyr had gloriously risen from his grave. Wasserburg extended the juxtaposition further, comparing the joyous translation celebration held for the newly resurrected martyr to the day Christ's disciples discovered his bodily ascension into heaven.[31]

At Ranshofen, Benedictine Felice Reber extended the parallel between Christ's life and the life of Saint Coelestinus a step further. Reber explained how the martyr had not only risen from the grave like Christ but had taken on His dual nature—both human and divine—as a result of his execution by fire: "In the fire, Coelestinus left behind all that was earthly and human about him; instead, he took on what was divine and is even in a certain way like the Son of God, who was represented and seemed to be a human man. Saint Coelestinus, was the son of a man who became a son of God. From the ashes, in which his skin, his muscles, his body, his bones were burned, shines the radiance of divinity."[32] Though he had been a mortal man in life, Coelestinus's decision to sacrifice himself for his faith had led to his transfiguration into a Son of God, a title used frequently in the New Testament to refer to Christ. Reber's decision to describe Coelestinus in this manner—and to attribute both human and divine nature to the saint—once again demonstrates clerical efforts to draw parallels between the lives and afterlives of Christ and the catacomb saints.

Preachers also used important figures from the Old Testament as an alternative way to connect the lives of catacomb saints to Christ's sacrifice and resurrection. In translation ceremonies, clerics compared catacomb saints to Isaac and Job, who had long been interpreted by Christian theologians as prefigurations for Christ. During the arrival of Saint Hilarius to Maria Thalheim in 1712, Wasserburg noted how both Isaac and the catacomb saint had been led to a place of execution in chains. At the execution site they were stripped, then told to stretch out their innocent necks. Each did so willingly, ready to give up their lives for the love of God. Though Isaac's bodily sacrifice was interrupted by a voice from the heavens, Hilarius did not escape death. Yet, Wasserburg told the crowd, this was not the end of the story: "Before the eyes of these foolish tyrants this martyr seemed to die, but nothing of the sort happened. This Isaac's generous soul, after an ordeal, is now resting in peace. But how is that possible? People only saw a dead body on the battlefield, the spilled blood, the white body; but this was in no way his pure soul. . . . Rather his soul remains undamaged and enjoys the sweetest rest and peace in heaven. . . .

This body, and most valuable relic, has been left behind as a comfort for us to see."[33] Because of his willingness to sacrifice himself for Christ, Saint Hilarius became "an Isaac." Although the parallel was not completely congruent, Hilarius's willingness to sacrifice his body for his faith earned him the title of an Old Testament figure most commonly understood as a precursor to Christ.

Wasserburg was not the only Bavarian preacher to draw a parallel between the risen Christ and the whole-body catacomb saints displayed in the duchy. At Ranshofen and St. Veit, preachers referenced the story of Jonah and the whale, long interpreted by Christian theologians as a typological foreshadowing of Christ's resurrection. At Ranshofen, Reber, the subprior at the Benedictine monastery of Michaelbeuren, noted that even though the martyr Marius seemed dead to the "raging, blinded tyrant" in Rome, he had only been swallowed like Jonah had been by the whale. Though his physical body had died, the martyr's persecutors did not understand that Marius's soul was "on the most blessed shore. He had been transported and translated to the land of the living."[34] The resurrection of Marius's soul, and later his body from the catacombs, paralleled the miraculous restoration of Jonah after his apparent death. Comparing catacomb saint martyrs to Old Testament figures whose stories were most closely associated with the foretelling of Christ's sacrifice and resurrection demonstrates the degree to which key characteristics of Christ's life were made to coincide with the life of the Roman martyrs transferred to Bavaria in the baroque period.

Preachers and festival planners further amplified and reinforced the similarity between the sacrificed bodies of Christ and catacomb martyrs by using epithets typically reserved for Jesus to describe the newly arrived Roman saints. The martyrs were repeatedly described as "innocent lambs" being led to slaughter or "sacrifices" (*Opfer, Schlacht-Opfer*). Originating from the Gospel of John, the epithet "lamb of God" usually referred to Christ and the sacrificial death he endured for the salvation of mankind. As early as the fourth century, the image of a lamb became a common iconographical motif in Christian artwork to represent Christ and his sacrifice.[35] At translation ceremonies in Bavaria, catacomb saints like Munditia, too, became lambs of God, taking on the characteristics of their Savior. Before her transfer to St. Peter's parish church in Munich in 1675, church officials prepared for Munditia's arrival by decorating the nave of the church with sixteen emblems, all of which alluded to certain aspects of her character and martyrdom. One emblem bore an image of a lamb being led to slaughter. The explanation appended beneath the lamb explained its significance: "God blesses you more, Lady martyr, because you were led [to die], like a lamb, completely willing and tame."[36] Munditia's willingness to sacrifice herself like a patient and gentle lamb is a direct allusion to Christ's sacrifice on the cross as well as his continued sacrifice in the Eucharist.

At Raitenhaslach, Cistercian Bertrandus Leffelleuthner took the comparison of the saints to innocent lambs a step further in his translation sermon, explicitly connecting the catacombs saints' sacrifice to Christ's on the altar in the Eucharist. He told the audience it made perfect sense to label Ausanius, Concordia, and Fortunata "innocent lambs" because "[Christ] was led to the slaughtering block, like a lamb . . . and in the same way, your most holy martyrs were first led to a true slaughterhouse in Rome and now are led . . . into a spiritual slaughterhouse [in the cloister church Raitenhaslach]." He continued, explaining that the church was a "spiritual slaughterhouse" because "the Lamb of God [Christ] is daily and so frequently slaughtered in the Eucharist." In the same way, "so many saints offer themselves and are sent to the slaughtering block (altar) and are solemnly buried there where they, and at the same time Christ," are both sacrificed in the same location.[37] For Leffelleuthner, the altars of Raitenhaslach cloister that housed the martyred bodies of Ausanius, Concordia, and Fortunata became the site where the bodily sacrifice of Jesus and the martyrs' converged and became visibly manifest. The martyrs—innocent lambs whose remains lay on, rather than being hidden in, the altar "tomb"—were so like Christ that they embodied and materialized the sacrifice made the by first innocent lamb in the daily Mass.

In addition to lambs of God, catacomb saints were sometimes compared to another animal commonly used to allude to Christ's Eucharistic sacrifice: the pelican. According to legends popularized during the medieval period, in times of scarcity a mother pelican would nourish her chicks by wounding her own body and feeding them with her own flesh and blood.[38] At Raitenhaslach, Adam Plaichshirn compared the three recently arrived martyrs to pelicans, "because they had spilled their blood for love of God and true belief like the pelican that feeds its young from its own breast."[39] Applying rhetorical titles like pelican or lamb of God to saints, rather than their traditional referent, underlined the close resemblance between Christ and the Roman catacomb saints arriving in Bavaria.

Large translation processions provided another opportunity to highlight and reinforce the similarities between the sacrificial bodies and lives of catacomb saints and Christ. Like verbal epithets, iconographical motifs generally associated with Christ could be transferred to catacomb martyrs. The monks at Aldersbach designed a *tableau vivant* for a portable stage carried during the translation procession for Saint Valerius in 1746. In the scene, the allegorical character of the Church offers the catacomb saint a golden crown of thorns rather than the traditional martyrs' crown made of laurels.[40] Similar imagery was used on a flag carried at the translation of Saint Beninus at Steingaden. The martyr was shown wearing a crown of thorns and carrying a chalice in his hand, tying him iconographically to Christ's Passion and sacrifice as well as to the consecrated wine of the Eucharist.[41] At both Aldersbach and Steingaden, catacomb saints were given iconographic motifs typically used only for depictions of Christ himself. The transfer of such exclusive symbols and titles from Christ to catacomb saints demonstrates the degree to which these Roman martyrs had assumed Christ-like qualities and become associated with his sacrifice.

Triumphal arches erected for translation festivities also incorporated the iconography of sacrifice and resurrection. The town of Kemnath built several triumphal arches for the arrival of Saint Primianus to Kemnath in 1693. The largest arch featured two large painted panels. The first painting depicted the saint rising from a tomb, a direct illusion to Christ's resurrection. Angels accompanied the saint, carrying bones and banderoles with quotations from Psalm 33 ("the lord keepeth all their bones")[42] and Psalm 138 ("my bones are not hidden from thee").[43] The citation of Psalm 138 is particularly significant. Saint Priminus's bones, long buried underneath Rome, were now visible—put together in human form—for all the residents and visitors of Kemnath to see during the translation procession and then permanently in the parish church. This visibility hinged on the conscious choice to present the body within a glass shrine. The second painting depicted Primianus, now ascended into heaven, holding two censers with burning incense. Below the saint was an altar labeled with the motto: "blood and bones are my sacrifice."[44] The choice of motto and its placement directly above the altar reinforces the dual sacrifice of Primianus—body and blood—and links it to an altar where the liturgy of the Mass and Christ's sacrifice was routinely performed. Primianus's resurrection and rebirth into heaven, above the image of the altar, illustrated the glorious reward for laying down his life for his faith in God.

In addition to the associated iconography, the placement of the catacomb saint bodies at the center of translation processions also had particular significance. The format for these processions mirrored the annual Corpus Christi processions in which the Eucharist, the most holy object of the event, was placed at the center of the processional order and carried by a priest in a monstrance underneath a lavish portable canopy. The most sought-after positions in these processions—which closely reflected the established social hierarchy—were directly in front of or behind the Eucharist.[45] During catacomb saint translation processions, the consecrated host was replaced by the body of a catacomb saint carried under a baldachin.[46] The saint's sacrificed body, treated with the same respect and physical trappings of the consecrated Host, had replaced the body of Christ as the center of attention and veneration in these festivities. This transposition once again highlights the ways in which martyred catacomb saint bodies were visually presented in rituals in ways that alluded to—and sometimes even replaced—the Eucharist.

Permanent Framing after Translation

After the translation festivities ended and the large crowds dispersed, the physical framing of catacomb saints and their blood by Bavarian artists, sculptors, and architects continued to reinforce the Eucharistic significance of the holy bodies. Craftsmen and craftswomen used altar design and other decorative elements to reinforce the close relationship between Christ's sacrificial body and blood, present but invisible in the Host, and the martyred body and blood present before the eyes of supplicants. Making the parallels between the sacrifice of Christ and the whole-body saints visually apparent began with a small item contained within the shrines themselves that preachers repeatedly referenced in their sermons: a blood ampule. These vessels' shapes and framing show marked similarities to monstrances and chalices used to hold the consecrated Host and wine respectively. Modeling the containers for catacomb saints' blood on those used to hold the Eucharistic wafer or wine framed the substance in a way that underscored the connection between the blood of Christ and that of the Roman martyrs.

A surviving *Andachtsbild* (devotional image) depicts the shrine of Saint Maximus, housed at the confraternity church (Bürgersaal) in Munich until its destruction in World War II (fig. 22).[47] Above the holy body, a winged putto presents onlookers with a monstrance topped with a crown and cross. Instead of the Eucharistic wafer, the glass disc in the center of the container reveals the "blood of Saint Maximus, Martyr" (*Sanguis S. Max. M*). The container for Saint Maximus's blood appears rather modest when compared to that designed for Saint Honoratius's in the parish church of Vilsbiburg (fig. 23). Surrounded by sunbursts, the container of blood takes pride of place at the center of the shrine, directly behind the holy body. The gilded sunbeams draw attention to the contents of the container and its form, which would likely have been familiar to early modern Bavarians from frequent displays of the Host. During the baroque period, sunburst or solar monstrances—in which the Host was exhibited for veneration within a glass disc surrounded by gilded or silvered rays of light—became increasingly popular.[48] In both cases, artists adapted the familiar forms of the Eucharistic monstrance and used it to hold another sacred substance associated with sacrifice, the blood of catacomb saints.

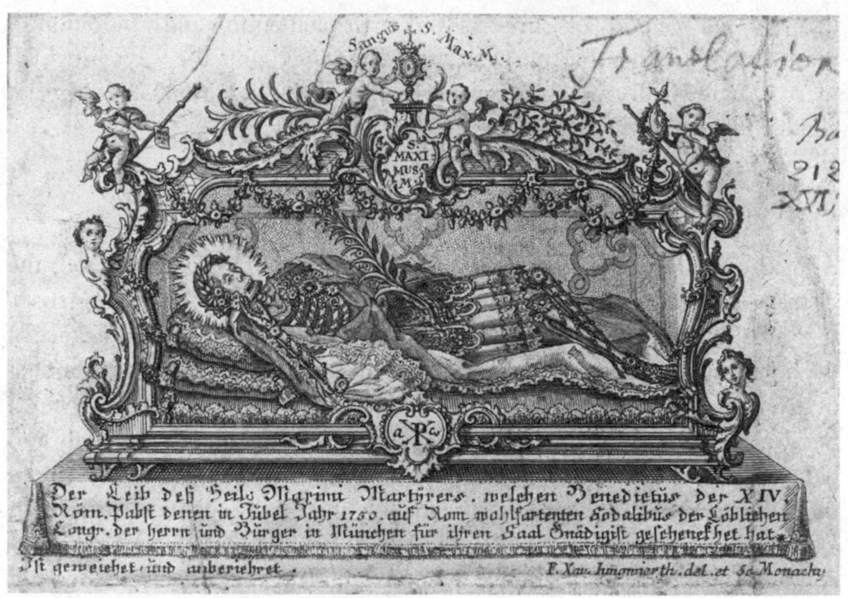

FIGURE 22. Devotional image of Saint Maximus's shrine in *Translation* [. . .] *des hl. Leibs S. Maximi,* Francis Xavier Jungwierth, 1750. (Bayerische Staatsbibliothek München, Res/4 Bavar. 2120,XVI,33)

FIGURE 23. Devotional image of Saint Honoratius, Mariä Himmelfahrt parish church, Vilsbiburg, Johann Michael Söckler, 1769. (Museum Dingolfing, Inv. Nr. 2566)

FIGURE 24. Altar with shrine of Saint Victor and *Ecce Homo* sculpture, Kalvarienberg pilgrimage church, Bad Tölz, 1754. (Photograph by author)

At the pilgrimage church of Heilig Kreuz in Bad Tölz, the blood of Saint Victor, who was transferred to the church in 1754, is affixed to the back wall of the shrine in a similar glass cylinder (fig. 24). The container is surrounded by golden sunbeams and sits on a small pedestal base. A small, gilded putto hangs nearby holding a scroll that announces that the shrine contains the "*corpus et sanguis Sti. Victoris, Martÿris*" (the body and blood of Saint Victor, martyr). As in Vilsbiburg, the transubstantiated bread often housed in such a container has been replaced with another element of the Eucharist: sacrificed blood. Though the blood belongs to a martyr and not to Christ, the connection between the two is further underscored by the "*Ecce homo*" statue directly behind Saint Victor's shrine. Bound and wearing a crown of thorns, Christ's body is surrounded by gilded sunbeams explicitly echoing those that encircle Victor's spilled blood below and visually linking the two.

FIGURE 25. Model designs for Eucharistic chalices in Müller, *Kirchen-Geschmuck*, 1591. (From the collections of the Hanna Holborn Gray Special Collections Research Center, University of Chicago Library)

Though artists and relic decorators sometimes borrowed the design of sunburst monstrance, it was more common for them to use a container modeled on a Eucharistic chalice to hold the blood of the ancient Roman martyrs. By using this form, the blood of the martyrs was more explicitly visually linked with the sacrificial blood of Christ, just as it often had been in translation sermons. In 1591, Jakob Müller, vicar of the diocese of Regensburg, published a book entitled *Kirchen-Geschmuck*. The book provided a guide for proper church furnishings and included a description and illustration of what model Eucharistic chalices should look like in his Bavarian diocese (fig. 25).[49] Müller's book hewed closely to the influential post-Tridentine handbook on church furnishings written by Bishop Charles Borromeo after the Council of Trent. Many containers created to hold the blood of catacomb saints resembled the prototypes in Müller's guide, with a cup on top and a small knob in the stem and pedestal base. In Munich, Saint Munditia holds a blood vase that, though made of glass for maximum visibility, looks very much like Müller's model. Several others from Kollbach and Oberviechtach are quite similar in form (fig. 26). Saint Desiderius's chalice has also helpfully been painted red on the inside to reinforce the fact that it contains the martyr's blood.

The form of the sunburst monstrance and the chalice could also be combined to hold a catacomb saint's blood. An engraving from a chronicle of the Pütrich cloister in Munich shows such hybrid vessels held by Saint Geminus (fig. 8). At first glance, the saint holds a chalice with what appears to be a

FIGURE 26. Blood vase of Saint Desiderius, St. Martin parish church, Kollbach, 1770. (Photograph by Uta Ludwig; courtesy of Pfarrverband Gangkofen)

Eucharistic wafer encircled by a sunburst floating above it, a common early modern motif for depicting the two elements of the Eucharist.[50] Upon closer inspection, however, the word "*sanguis*" (blood) becomes legible on the disc above, identifying the chalice's contents as the blood of the saint. The close resemblance between Geminus's reliquary vase and the well-known iconography of the Eucharistic chalice and wafer indicates the degree to which artists and their patrons associated the blood of Roman martyrs with that of Christ. It also demonstrates the degree of interchangeability and slippage that had emerged between the holy body of Christ and the intact and visible sacrificial bodies of his earliest followers.

Beyond the housing and artistic framing of the blood of catacomb saints in their individual shrines, artists incorporated the holy bodies into contemporary altar types that were frequently used to present a static host or to highlight Christ's suffering. In these altarpieces, the space normally dedicated to the display of the consecrated host or holy image/statue of Christ was used to present a whole-body saint instead. The similarity of these altar formats is evident in the language preachers used to describe the resting places built for the newly imported saints. At Raitenhaslach in 1698, Leffelleuthner stated that the cloister would become "a more comfortable Mount Tabor for those three holy martyrs, where . . . the three most beautiful tabernacles and luxurious altars were built and raised for them."[51] The use of the word "tabernacle"—an "ornamented receptacle for liturgical vessels containing consecrated bread reserved for the Communion of the sick, for communion services, and for adoration"—to describe the shrines designed to house catacomb saints was especially significant in the post-Tridentine context.[52]

Before the sixteenth century, tabernacles were separate from the main altar. This changed after Trent as the defense of the Eucharist and transubstantiation took center stage in Catholic regions. Local ordinances began to require the reservation of the consecrated host on the main altar in tabernacles visible from all parts of the church, which made the Host constantly available for veneration. By 1614, the Roman Ritual codified this prescription further, stating that the Host must be reserved in a tabernacle on the main altar. As a result, tabernacles became essential to Bavarian baroque high altars and often provided places to both reserve and display the Host in a monstrance.[53] In the section of Müller's handbook on proper church decoration, he notes that such tabernacles should be decorated with "beautiful etched or painted holy images that place the bitter pain and death of our Lord Jesus Christ or the most holy sacramental mystery before the eyes."[54]

In some cases, the bodies of catacomb saints were used to materialize this "most holy sacramental mystery" for parishioners, as sculptors began to appropriate the form of the altar tabernacle to house the bodies of catacomb saints. In doing so, they made the connections among the saint's body, the Eucharist, and the altar even more concrete than Leffelleuthner had in his sermon at Raitenhaslach. At Gars am Inn, sculptor Christian Jorhan created one such altar-tabernacle for the holy body of Saint Felix in 1752 (fig. 27). The gilded shrine is carved in the shape of an elaborate facade. At the bottom of the shrine is a small door incised with an image of the Eucharist above a chalice used for the reservation of the Host. Directly above the door, behind a large pane of glass, sits the decorated body of Saint Felix, who gazes out at the viewer while holding a martyr's palm in one hand. Here, Felix has replaced the monstrance or an image of Christ that would have usually appeared in the same space, something that becomes clear when this tabernacle altar is compared to similar contemporary tabernacles like the one designed and sculpted by Johann Georg Lindt for the high altar at the pilgrimage church in Marienberg in 1765 (fig. 28). In the case of Felix's tabernacle-altar, the sacred mystery of the Eucharist and its miraculous

FIGURE 27. Altar-tabernacle with shrine of Saint Felix at Gars cloister, Christian Jorhan, 1752. (Photograph by author)

transubstantiation are "placed before the eyes" and made manifest in the body of a martyred catacomb saint. The body itself has become the visual embodiment of and proxy for Christ's sacrificial body contained under the species of the bread and wine.

The link between the sacrifice of the Eucharist and the sacrifice of the martyr is further emphasized visually by the combination of attributes held by the putti who surround the altar. On the bottom left, a putto holds an image of the Sacred Heart, representing the side wound of Christ and His sacrifice for mankind, while above, another angel holds a single flame representing religious ardor.[55] On the other side of the altar-tabernacle, one angel holds an anchor, a symbol of hope and salvation that was extremely common on catacomb epitaphs from the second and third centuries.[56] Above, the angel on the right holds a cudgel, the instrument used—according to the hagiography constructed for the saint—in Felix's martyrdom.[57] The altar presents a combination of symbols that represent Felix and Christ's sacrifice (sacred heart, cudgel) and reinforces the larger Eucharistic message embodied by Felix's housing within a tabernacle-altar.

A similar placement of a catacomb saint's body in the position often occupied by a Eucharistic Host occurred on another type of altar: those dedicated

FIGURE 28. Altar-tabernacle at Marienberg pilgrimage church, Johann Georg Lindt, 1765. (Photograph by Uta Ludwig; courtesy of Pfarrverband Burghausen)

to the Holy Cross. At the summit of these altars, a crucified Christ hangs on a large cross, crowned with thorns and bleeding from his wounds. At the base of the cross stands Mary as Our Lady of Sorrows (Schmerzensmutter, Mater Dolorosa), with a sword protruding from her chest, a reference to her co-suffering with Christ at his crucifixion.[58] Underneath the sculptures of Mary, these altars typically feature a niche in which the Host or a cult image of Christ was displayed. One such altar takes pride of place at the pilgrimage church of Heiligenstatt in Tußling outside Altötting (fig. 29), the site of a late medieval Host miracle.[59] Like the altar in Heiligenstatt, the Holy Cross altar designed by Ignaz Günther for the Weyarn cloister around 1755 presents a vertical axis of sacrifice (fig. 30). This altarpiece—with large sculptures of Christ on the cross above a suffering Mary—is almost identical to the one at Heiligenstatt except for one major difference: the tabernacle for the consecrated Host has been replaced by the body of the catacomb saint Valerius. Similar Holy Cross altars survive at Oberalteich cloister and the parish churches of Saint Laurentius in Königsdorf and Mariä Himmelfahrt in Bad Aibling.

FIGURE 29. Devotional image of the Holy Cross of Heiligenstatt, eighteenth century. (Stadtarchiv München, HV-BS-A-10-04)

The cross on these altars physically connects the crucified body of Christ and that of the martyrs. It visually emphasizes the connection between their sacrificial deaths, materializing a link Plaichshirn made verbally at the Raitenhaslach translation ceremony for the martyrs Ausanius, Fortunata, and Concordia. He told the assembled crowd that the martyrs died "at the base of the Cross, suffering and finally ending their lives in martyrdom with the spilling of their precious blood."[60] At Sandizell, Kurz also highlighted the connection of Saints Maximus and Clemens to the Cross: "Maximus and Clemens, through heavenly advice, recognized that eternal life grew from none other

FIGURE 30. Holy Cross altar design with shrine of Saint Valerius, commissioned by Weyarn cloister, Ignaz Günther, ca. 1755. (Münchener Stadtmuseum, Signatur G-MI-1206)

than the tree of the cross, and Jesus hangs on this cross. Therefore, they must also hang as branches from this tree."[61] The design of the Holy Cross altar brought these connections into material existence as the sacrificed bodies of catacomb saints rested directly below their Savior.

The seeming interchangeability of the two "bodies" in these Holy Cross altars as well as their housing in tabernacle-altars indicate that early modern Bavarians also connected the sacrificial body of a martyr with the body and blood of Christ contained in the Host. When visitors entered the church, they could sit and contemplate the body of a martyr just as they would if they had come to observe a Forty-Hour devotion. The whole-body presentation of a catacomb saint within tabernacle-like altars concretely evoked the body and blood contained in the Host. Rather than a small piece of bread or a single small bone, Christ's sacrifice was embodied in the lifelike skeleton of a Roman martyr. By framing the saints in this fashion—and due to their presentation as intact bodies—viewers were reminded of their Eucharistic significance in a more enduring way than could be accomplished at a translation festival lasting for a single day or celebratory octave.

It is important to note that catacomb saint relics, along with the blood ampules sent with them, did not arrive in Bavaria with instructions from Rome to be used as a teaching tool for Eucharistic doctrine. This didactic function was made possible due to the decision of local communities to carefully construct holy bodies from the fragmented bones that could proffer their sacrificial blood to onlookers during translation ceremonies and later atop altars in churches across the territory. As the whole-body presentation of the relics became dominant after 1648, clerics, festival organizers, and artists began to associate the characteristics of these saints more closely and directly with those of Christ, who Catholics believed sacrificed himself in a bloodless manner each time the liturgy of the Mass was read. Though consecrated altars had held the remains of martyrs since the Middle Ages, their saints' visibility in bodily form encouraged and enabled preachers to associate the relics of the early Christian martyrs with the Eucharistic sacrifice in a concrete and material manner. Clerics expounded on the many ways the physical bodies of the martyrs as well as their life stories paralleled Christ's, employing a variety of rhetorical techniques that conflated or closely aligned the common elements of bodily sacrifice and resurrection. Adopting artistic forms like the chalice and the monstrance to hold the martyrs' blood as well as the placement of the saints' shrines on altars in spaces typically used to house a reserved Host or cult image of Christ perpetuated the parallels between the sacrificed body of Christ and the martyrs long after the initial translation sermons and festivities. By using a locally developed form of relic presentation, early modern Bavarians were able to materialize and affirm their allegiance to universal Catholic doctrine on transubstantiation and the sacrifice of the Mass and to directly participate in the church's defense of incarnation and the immanence of God in the physical world.

4

Semper eadem

CATACOMB SAINTS AND CATHOLIC SACRED HISTORY

While holy bodies materialized important facets of Roman Catholic Eucharistic doctrine, Bavarians also used this creative relic form to participate in a larger, church-wide intellectual movement known as the paleo-Christian revival.[1] The major goal of the scholars who initiated this erudite campaign was to use historical and archaeological evidence to prove a central thesis: the Roman Catholic Church had been "ever the same" (*semper eadem*), unchanging across the centuries.[2] This had become an urgent task in the sixteenth century because the history and rituals of the early Christian church had become an important battlefield between Protestants and Catholics during the Reformation.[3] Both sides vigorously contested the history of the early church by "professing complete identity between their own beliefs and practice and those of their earliest ancestors."[4] Protestants of all denominations alleged that many contemporary Catholic doctrines, institutions, and practices—the papacy, the veneration of images and relics, and so on—lacked a basis in Scripture and instead reflected accumulated human error and invention over the centuries.

In the eyes of Catholic archaeologists and theologians, catacomb saint remains provided material evidence that countered such claims. The relics came from a period of church history that was celebrated by Protestants themselves as untainted by corruption, and thus, venerating them could not be considered unorthodox. The significant number of holy bodies in the catacombs also bolstered the case for Rome as the true "cradle of Christianity,"[5] a concept consistently reflected in these scholars' attempts to equate the terms *Romanus* and *Catholicus* in the period after the Council of Trent.[6] The additional assertion, made by important paleo-Christian scholars like Cesare Baronio (1538–1607) and Antonio Bosio (1575–1629), that all those buried in the labyrinthine passages were martyrs was especially resonant in an era of renewed religious violence and martyrdom. Catholic writers connected the persecution of early Christians with the deaths of early modern martyrs as a way to illustrate the movement's key argument of continuity over time. From the earliest years of the church to the present day, they argued, martyrs had been willing to sacrifice their lives to defend their Catholic beliefs against tyrants and heretics.[7] The conviction that the bodies of catacomb saints "incorporated the [paleo-Christian revival's] key themes of antiquity, martyrdom and Roman provenance" underpinned the decision of the church in Rome to send the remains across Europe and the wider world.[8]

Although the significance of these "holy bodies" in the arc of Catholic sacred history was clear to church officials and scholars in Rome steeped in paleo-Christian scholarship, when the catacomb saints' remains arrived in Bavaria, local communities were faced with the task of crafting an identity for their new patron using a box of jumbled bones and scarcely any information beyond the fact that the saint had been an ancient, Roman martyr. Once these skeletal remains arrived, the clergy and laypeople collaboratively undertook an innovative, multistep process of identity creation that began with the costuming of a holy body and the composition of a written vita and was then reinforced through a variety of visual media.

To begin, the saints' identities as antique, Roman martyrs were rendered legible through costume and symbolic attributes (laurel wreaths, palm leaves) as well grave goods placed within their shrines. By looking at the body and the material objects that surrounded it, a viewer could quickly draw conclusions about the saint's suffering, place of burial, and period of origin. In addition to carefully curating the physical presentation of whole-body catacomb saints, clergy and laypeople in church communities researched the lives of these martyrs to create hagiographies for their saints. This research was based on church-sponsored scholarly works produced as part of the paleo-Christian revival and more popular works, such as Roman pilgrimage guides, that provided background information on the saints' origins and significance in Catholic sacred history. Though these texts provided a general context for the importance of catacomb saints in the paleo-Christian revival, they did not contain any concrete information about the specific saints arriving in Bavarian towns and villages. Undeterred by the seeming dearth of information about the saints' individual lives and deaths, local clergymen used these texts to develop a life history for each saint consistent with the generalized ecclesiastical texts, which emphasized the historical context of early Christian persecutions as well as the physical environment and sacred meaning of the catacombs themselves. Just as they were willing to craft missing bones and long-decayed clothing, when the sources offered scant information, the clergy supplied the missing elements in the history of their saint.

By building bodies and crafting backstories for unknown ancient Roman martyrs, Bavarians used the relics of catacomb saints to participate in larger conversations occurring at the highest levels of the Roman church hierarchy about sacred history, the suffering of early Christian martyrs, and the primacy of Rome. Using a combination of local artistic invention and knowledge gained from scholarly paleo-Christian sources, communities across Bavaria demonstrated how relics, iconographies, and texts that came from the heart of the universal church could be reinterpreted and re-formed to express confessional adherence to Roman Catholicism in an environment far from the Eternal City.

Costuming Ancient Roman Martyrs

The first step in creating an identity for these unknown martyrs began after the herculean task of creating a saint's "body" from fragmented remains was complete. At this point, relic decorators began the process of clothing the saint in a manner that made them legible to early modern eyes as ancient Roman martyrs. The attire chosen to convey two of these identifying characteristics—antiquity and Roman provenance—was the uniform of a Roman legionary soldier. The outfit usually consisted of a knee-length tunic over which waist-length body armor (*lorica*) was worn. The bottom of the tunic as well as the sleeves were often decorated with strips of cloth that hung over the tunic (*pteruges*). To complete the look, the soldiers wore sandals (*caligae*) and, in some cases, a cape or helmet. This outfit had become stylized in Western iconography in Roman sculpture and funerary monuments and was adopted into Christian art as both the typical garb of Roman soldiers was well as Roman soldier saints. Saint Hyacinth, translated to the Cistercian cloister at Fürstenfeld in 1674, provides a typical example of a male catacomb saint dressed as a Roman soldier (fig. 1). Lying on his side, the saint's chest is covered by sparkling "body armor" made of *Klosterarbeit*. Beneath his armor, Hyacinth wears a skirt covered with *pteruges* and knee-high sandals, also made of cloister work. The *pteruges* are echoed once again on his sleeve caps.

Dressing female martyrs as soldiers was a more difficult task. No costume for women was as recognizably "Roman" as the legionary garb. As a result, relic decorators borrowed several elements of the legionnaires' costumes and integrated them into female catacomb saints' attire to make the clothing distinctly "Roman." At Niederaltaich, Saint Julia wears *Klosterarbeit* "body armor" on her chest and a full-length pink skirt, from which her sandaled feet peek out (fig. 31). On top of the long skirt lies another shorter skirt that is almost identical to those worn by male catacomb saints. It is knee-length and has *pteruges* covered in *Klosterarbeit* embellishments. The epaulets on her sleeves appear identical to those worn by Saint Hyacinth in Fürstenfeld.

In the rare case that a church or cloister had evidence that a male catacomb saint might *not* have been a literal Roman legionnaire, this information tended

FIGURE 31. Saint Julia with skirt, Niederaltaich cloister, 1731. (Photograph by author)

to be ignored. Capuchin preacher Josephus Münchner in St. Veit noted that, "when [Lucius's] holy body was taken out of the grave, a piece of a Mass chasuble was found, which was probably a sign of his episcopal majesty."[9] Instead of presenting the saint in clerical robes, however, the cloister chose to have his body dressed as a Roman warrior. A large sculpture atop his shrine, depicted in a devotional image of the saint's chapel, reinforced Lucius's identity as a youthful Roman soldier by dressing him in an outfit of a legionnaire (fig. 32). The label below the shrine clearly identifies him as "S. Lucius Martyr." Rather than dressing or describing him as a bishop—who could have hailed from any time or place in Catholic history—the monks at St. Veit chose to have the saint represented in a familiar iconography that communicated to onlookers his antique origin as well as his Roman provenance. In this case, the need to convey his antique Roman identity as well as his status as a Christian fighter took precedence over his clerical rank.

Costuming catacomb saints—especially male catacomb saints—so they were readily identifiable as Roman soldiers also functioned on a more symbolic level. In sermons, they were consistently labeled as soldiers of Christ, brave knights and military heroes who prevailed over their pagan foes. In some cases, this related directly to the vitae written for the saints by Bavarian clergy, in which the saints were depicted as members of the Roman legion.

FIGURE 32. Devotional image of Saint Lucius's holy body and altar in *Neues Liecht oder Neuschein,* Johann Ulrich Biberger, 1696. (Universitätsbibliothek der LMU München, W 4 Homil. 1764#16)

More frequently, their representation in this manner suggested their implied combat with and triumph over heretical beliefs—a narrative that could be directly tied to the Roman church's dispute with Protestant doctrines.

Though churches across the Electorate uniformly chose to costume whole-body catacomb saints as Roman warriors, this was not an unambiguous iconographical motif. After all, in many stories of early Christian martyrdom, Roman soldiers acted as the Christians' persecutors. Such legionary soldiers—wearing outfits almost identical to those adapted for catacomb saints—can even be seen torturing and killing early Christians in paleo-Christian texts, such as Antonio Gallonio's *Trattato degli instrumenti di martirio e delle varie maniere di martirizzare* (1591) (fig. 33).[10] Similarly attired legionnaires also appear as villains in the images of early Christian martyr-saints in Maximilian I's great territorial hagiography, *Bavaria Sancta.*[11]

Despite these less than favorable iconographical associations, in most cases the imperative of making saints' temporal and geographical origins visually

FIGURE 33. Roman soldiers defleshing Christian martyrs in Gallonio's *Trattato de gli instrumenti di martirio,* Antonio Tempesta, 1591. (Henry Charles Lea Rare Book Collection, Kislak Center for Special Collections, Rare Books and Manuscripts, University of Pennsylvania)

clear was more important than the link between Roman soldiers and Christian persecution. The degree to which the outfit of the legionnaire was identified with the Eternal City is evident in documents that recount the translation festivities held for the saints' arrival in Bavaria. When planning these events, local parishes and churches eagerly sought out or created "Roman" clothing for participants who would accompany the remains of these ancient Roman martyrs into their towns and villages. Johann Chrysostomos Hager, a monk at the Benedictine cloister Gars am Inn appointed to organize the translation festivities for Saint Felix, eagerly tried to borrow "Roman" clothing from the court in Munich. According to his *Tagebuch* (diary), Hager wrote to the Elector and asked that the custodian of the royal *Kleiderkammer* (wardrobe) allow the cloister to borrow "Roman" clothing for the event. Receiving no response, Hager traveled to Munich himself, where he was eventually able to obtain the desired costumes to use in the cloister's translation events for Saint Felix.[12] Hager's determination to find "Roman clothing" for these celebrations

FIGURE 34. Young boys wearing "Roman clothing" in the translation procession for Saints Marius and Coelestinus to Ranshofen cloister in *Saeculum octavum*, 1702. (Staatliche Museen zu Berlin—Preußischer Kulturbesitz, Kunstbibliothek; photograph by Dietmar Katz)

was not unique. Similar "Roman" outfits were used in other Bavarian catacomb saint transfer processions. At the translation for Saint Leo in 1685 to the Benedictine cloister at Kühbach, the mounted lead rider in the procession was "dressed in the Roman fashion,"[13] as were participants in the procession for four catacomb saints to the Angerkloster in Munich in 1738.[14]

Surviving visual evidence confirms that "Roman clothing" or dressing "in the Roman fashion" in baroque Bavaria meant wearing the outfit of a legionary soldier. In an engraving of a transfer procession in Ranshofen in 1699, the numerical key identifies several pairs of young boys in "Roman costume" (fig. 34).[15] Each of the boys wears a short skirt with *pteruges*, tight body armor, sleeves with epaulets, and sandals. At Raitenhaslach, those dressed up in "Roman clothing" were none other than actors playing the catacomb saints themselves, whose outfits matched those of their skeletal counterparts. The actor-saints rode in the ceremony in a triumphal wagon, wearing laurel crowns on their heads and holding palm leaves (fig. 35). Riding alongside them in the wagon was another actor dressed in a papal tiara representing "the triumphant church." By including the figure of the pope, the designers of the procession further underscored the catacomb saints' close connection to the institutional church in Rome as well as their origin in the Eternal City itself.

The saints' "Roman costumes" even made their way onto the temporary architecture built for the often-lavish translation ceremonies that welcomed catacomb saints to their new homes. Triumphal arches, themselves a nod to

FIGURE 35. Saints Ausanius, Concordia, and Fortunata riding in a "triumph wagon" with a figure of the pope during their translation procession to Raitenhaslach cloister in *Glorwürdiges Sechstes Jubel-Jahr,* 1699. (Staatliche Museen zu Berlin—Preußischer Kulturbesitz, Kunstbibliothek; photograph by Dietmar Katz)

the antique origins of the saints, built along the procession routes typically featured images of the martyrs wearing the outfit of a Roman legionary, just like their holy bodies. An engraving of one such arch built for translation of Saints Marius and Coelestinus to the Augustinian cloister in Ranshofen (1699) illustrates how the iconography of a Roman soldier was transferred directly to festival architecture (fig. 36). Marius and Coelestinus stand atop the arch wearing their "Roman costumes"—one gesturing to the onlookers below, the other pointing toward the heavens.

The fact that "Roman clothing"—worn in processions and used to depict the catacomb saints in other media—was largely identical to the costumes worn by catacomb saints demonstrates why this clothing was chosen for the saints' bodies: to communicate their ancient Roman origins. With little information to go on, using the iconography of a Roman soldier was an effective means of making clear that the newly arrived saints hailed from the purest period of the early Christian church; the outfit also underscored for onlookers the city's status as the center of the Roman Catholic Church and the source of numerous holy relics.

Though legionary dress could establish ancient Roman provenance, it was insufficient by itself to communicate a saint's identity as a martyr. This required additional iconographical attributes and objects that could indicate to viewers that the ancient Roman before them had sacrificed his or her life in the name of Christ. Once again, the form of the complete body as well as the large transparent shrines in which they were housed proved critical in conveying this additional piece of a saint's background story. In addition to the legionnaires' costume, relic decorators also created laurel crowns and palm

FIGURE 36. Triumphal arch built for translation festival of Saints Marius and Coelestinus to Ranshofen cloister in *Saeculum octavum*, 1702. (Oberösterreichisches Landesmuseum, Ha III 675, fol. 42)

leaves—the traditional iconographical symbols of Christian martyrdom—with *Klosterarbeit* for the saints. At Fürstenfeld, Saint Hyacinth wears a laurel crown made of gilded wire, colored gemstones, and pearls. In his left hand, he holds a large golden palm leaf, a symbol of his victory over death (fig. 1).[16] Each of these attributes is readily visible to the onlooker and drew on a visual vocabulary familiar to contemporary Bavarians to inform the viewer that the person before them died a martyr. The large hammer Hyacinth cradles in his right arm provides another concrete clue as to his violent manner of death. Though the inclusion of an instrument of martyrdom in Bavarian catacomb saints' shrines was fairly rare, the laurel wreath and palm leaf became standard parts of catacomb saint decoration.

The attributes worn and held by Bavarian catacomb saints were not the only physical reminders to viewers that they had sacrificed their lives in the name of Christ. In some cases, grave goods found at the saints' excavation sites in Rome were sent along with the relics to churches and cloisters in the Electorate. These items included carved gravestones as well as small containers made of either glass or terracotta. These vessels purportedly contained the blood of the martyrs, collected after their executions and buried alongside them in the catacombs by fellow Christians. In order to understand the meaning of these objects—both for themselves as well as their parishioners—monks and parish priests turned to sources produced by scholars associated with "institutional" paleo-Christian scholarship in Rome. In *Roma sotterranea* (1635), the most influential and comprehensive book written on the catacombs until the nineteenth century, Antonio Bosio asserted that the glass and terracotta vases found in the catacombs had once contained the blood of martyrs.[17] This interpretation of these objects received official church sanction in 1668, when the newly founded Congregation for Indulgences and Relics determined that these "blood ampules" were one of the most certain signs of a martyr's death.[18] This position was further reiterated in the eighteenth century by representatives of the Roman church such as Marc' Antonio Boldetti, who served for several decades as the custodian of sacred relics. In 1720, he published *Osservazioni sopra i cimiteri de' santi martiri ed antichi christiani di Roma* as a handbook for the identification of relics. He dedicated close to one hundred pages of the tome to proving that the ampules found in the catacombs held nothing but martyrs' blood.[19] Thus, the discovery of a blood vial alongside a body in the Roman catacombs became incontrovertible material proof that the remains belonged to an early Christian martyr.

In Bavaria, Jesuit preacher Ernst Geppert turned to sources like Boldetti's book and other texts produced as part of the paleo-Christian revival to interpret the grave goods accompanying the holy bodies of Saints Constantius and Clement to Amberg in 1753. In his translation sermon, Geppert told the assembled worshippers that he did not know a single word about their holy lives, virtues, and heroic Christian deeds.[20] However, all was not lost. He assured the audience that the presence of the saints' remains and the blood vials alone served as an "infallible sign" that the holy bodies in front of them belonged to martyrs.[21] Across the territory, preachers repeatedly emphasized the probative properties of these grave goods—visible within saints' shrines—as a way to verify that these new holy bodies were ancient Roman martyrs. At the Raitenhaslach cloister in 1698, Adam Plaichshirn, a Cistercian monk, drew the festivalgoers' attention to the shrines of Saints Ausanius, Concordia, and Fortunata. He explained that their lives had ended "with the spilling of their precious blood, which they show to you now in beautiful vessels as testimony and proof."[22] The saints' presentation as complete bodies allowed them to proffer their own blood—evidence of their violent deaths—directly to viewers in a single relic ensemble that conveyed a larger hagiographical narrative in material terms.

The gravestones that arrived from the catacombs along with the saints' relics functioned in a similar manner to the blood ampule: material proof of martyrdom at the hands of ancient Roman persecutors. These slabs of stone were usually engraved with a saint's name, date of death, and symbols such palm leaves, crosses, and Chi-Rhos (☧). Catholic archaeologists, most prominently Bosio, asserted that these symbols were signs of a martyr's grave.[23] In *Roma sotterranea*, Bosio wrote that the Chi-Rho symbol was one way a martyr's grave could be identified and provided illustrations of several versions of the symbol.[24] When describing the verification process for identifying martyrs' graves in the catacombs, Geppert told his audience at the translation of two saints to Amberg that early Christians used the Chi-Rho as a "marker and martyr's sign." These two letters, he continued, were an "infallible sign that desire[d] to say so much: that this or that person, whose bones rested in that grave, spilled his blood *pro Christi* or for Christ."[25] The combination of these signs and the apparent antiquity of the stone itself gave further credence to the idea that Clemens and Constantius were early Christian martyrs who hailed from Rome. Geppert's insistence that the Chi-Rho symbol was proof of a martyr's death demonstrates that knowledge produced and propagated by scholars in service of the paleo-Christian in Rome was known and used beyond Italy and was being marshaled by Bavarian clergy to inform the creation of hagiographies for the new and unknown saints.

In some cases, the inclination of local clerics to read such signs as proof of martyrdom relied more on textual sources from Rome than on the written text on the gravestones themselves. At St. Peter's parish church in Munich, Saint Munditia's shrine contains a large gravestone with a Latin engraving that reads: "To the pious memory of Munditia, a one-of-a-kind, well-deserving woman. She lived sixty years and died peacefully on November 17."[26] Although Munditia's epitaph does not mention martyrdom, emphasizing her long life and quiet death, she was still dressed and described as a martyr in her translation ceremonies and vita. Though "no one [knew] in what year or in which persecution she was killed," she was accepted as a martyr for two key reasons: her gravestone featured engraved Chi-Rho symbols, and she had been identified as one on the authentication certificate sent by church authorities in Rome.[27] As was the case for Saint Lucius at St. Veit, when material evidence pointed to the possibility that a catacomb saint might *not* have died for their faith, this information was sometimes discarded or put to the side in favor of a more straightforward narrative of martyrdom.

Though Munditia, Clemens, and Constantius were sent to their respective locations with grave goods, not all catacomb saints arrived in Bavaria with a gravestone and/or a blood ampule. Today, however, the vast majority of the 259 in situ catacomb saint shrines in the former Electorate feature one or both of these items. As with the holy bodies' missing bones, when a blood ampule or gravestone did not arrive from Rome with the relics, local Bavarian artisans simply created them.[28] In 1724, the Premonstratensian cloister at Neustift-Freising received the bodies of Ascanius and Ascania. Ascania's gravestone, decorated with a Chi-Rho and palm leaves, lists her death date as "CXXXXI" (fig. 37). This is not a valid date in Roman numerals and indicates the gravestone's engraver was not familiar with this numerical system. The last letter of Ascania's name has also been changed from an *O* to an *A*, another sign that the gravestone probably was not commissioned at the time of the saint's death by someone who knew her well.[29] The gravestone of Ascania's fellow saint, Ascanius, also features an invalid Roman date, listing his year of death as IXXI. The willingness to commission and install what appeared to be ancient gravestones in catacomb saint shrines indicates that these physical markers—and the symbols they bore—had become essential in the process of creating an identifiable antique Roman martyr. A similar phenomenon developed in relation to blood ampules. In one of the most obvious examples of this practice, Saint Desiderius at the parish church in Kollbach holds a glass in his hand—likely not antique—that has been painted bright red on the inside, presumably in an effort to make its contents unmistakable to viewers (fig. 26).

FIGURE 37. Gravestone of Saint Ascania, Neustift cloister, Freising, 1724. (Photograph by author)

By using or creating missing archaeological objects like gravestones and blood vases, early modern Bavarians were able to make visible their new catacombs saints' status as ancient Christian martyrs. Their understanding of these objects rested on assertions of archaeologists who had never set foot in Raitenhaslach, Kollbach, or Amberg but whose ideas were consulted and deployed in a local context to help communities understand the significance of these ancient Christian grave goods.

Writing Hagiographies for Roman Catacomb Saints

Once the saints' bodies were fully decorated in Roman garb and ready to transfer into their new homes, early modern Bavarians turned their attention to constructing vitae for their new patrons. The printed authentication certificates that arrived from Rome along with the box of catacomb saint relics only revealed their name, the catacomb where the remains had been located, and a date of excavation. Left with few details and the desire to glean every possible piece of information about the saint, monks and clergymen in communities across the Electorate turned to textual sources to find background information about ancient Roman history and the catacombs themselves. Using this raw material, they crafted hagiographies for these ancient Roman martyrs—of varying levels of specificity—to share at translation sermons, in printed vitae, and in devotional texts.

To begin the process, clergymen consulted a range of textual sources. These included texts commissioned by the Catholic Church for the paleo-Christian revival as well more popular works such as Roman pilgrimage guides and medieval martyrologies. Much of the information conveyed in these sources relied on "catacomb clichés," hagiographical tropes established in the passion accounts of the early martyrs and repeated for more than a millennium.[30] These clichés included the idea that the Roman catacombs only contained the graves of Christians and that there were innumerable martyrs buried in the ancient underground passages. These beliefs about the catacombs and Rome as a hub of martyrdom were amplified and repeated by the likes of Baronio and Bosio in major works of the paleo-Christian revival, such as the *Roman Martyrology* with historical notes (1586) and *Roma sotterranea* (1632). Common catacomb clichés and established models of passion narratives provided the building blocks amateur Bavarian hagiographers needed to start writing the lives of their new saints. Despite knowing next to nothing about these martyrs, local monks and priests creatively used genre and content to reinforce Baronio's claim that the church had been "ever the same."

A booklet produced for the arrival of catacomb saint Antoninus to the Cistercian convent of Seligenthal in Landshut in 1668 provides a prime example of how textual sources that relied upon catacomb clichés and the structure of ancient passion narratives could be deployed to provide a compelling identity for an unfamiliar saint. Although they knew little about the history of their new set of Roman remains, the convent managed to produce a sixty-three-page devotional booklet that included the saint's vita. The account states that Antoninus was a noble young Roman who lived during the reign of Emperor Gallienus (r. 253–68 CE) in the third century. Gallienus was a tyrant who, with his predecessors, was responsible for killing thirty thousand Christians.[31] After personally witnessing the execution of several of these victims, Antoninus was so moved that he decided to convert to Christianity. Despite being offered many inducements by the emperor to return to the pagan faith, Antoninus refused and was then beheaded. On the night following his execution, Antoninus's fellow believers "buried his body in the tombs of the graveyard of Saint Callisti by the church of Saint Sebastian, which is on the Appian Way outside the city of Rome. These tombs are made of carved vaults and small passages and were built by the Christians. They go on for two German miles. At night, the Christians gathered there because they were afraid of the [Roman] tyrants. Popes also said Mass and preached there to help strengthen the faith of the people. According to the *Roman Guide,* 174,000 martyrs are buried in these vaulted tombs."[32] In the space of a few sentences, this text demonstrates how one amateur Bavarian hagiographer stitched together a variety of different sources to give the reader information about the saint's death and his burial as well as pertinent details about the catacombs and the role they played in the early Christian history.

In the vita, the author cites a mixture of scholarly sources produced as part of the academic paleo-Christian revival as well as more popular texts. The writer mined both Baronio's *Annales ecclesiastici* and *Roman Martyrology* as well as Tommaso Bozio's *Annales Antiquitatem* (1637) for information about the first centuries of the church and the severity of persecutions under pagan emperors. Antoninus's hagiographer also consulted German guidebooks produced for Roman pilgrims—referred to as the "Roman Guide"—for raw material.[33] Between 1620 and 1803, publishers printed nine different German-language guides for pilgrims to the city of Rome that contained information on the city's most famous sites.[34] The Basilica of Saint Sebastian Outside the Walls, one of seven main pilgrimage churches in Rome and home to one of its most famous catacombs, was featured prominently in many of these works. The books frequently described the underground cemetery beneath the basilica, providing Bavarian writers with key information about the history and construction of the catacombs as well as the holy bodies buried there. Importantly, the guides propagated the idea that the ancient passages contained thousands upon thousands of martyrs. Catacomb saint hagiographers often included the "fact" that 174,000 martyrs were buried in the catacombs of Saint Sebastian in the vitae of catacomb saints. This was not a random number. During the sixteenth century, a plaque was posted over the stairwell used to descend underground that stated there were 174,000 martyrs and forty-six popes buried in the catacombs below. Although not accurate, these figures—and often the entire Latin text of the plaque itself—were reproduced in most of the German-language guides to Rome printed in the seventeenth and eighteenth centuries and then included in the biographies of catacomb saints.

As the years passed, the number of martyrs allegedly buried in the catacombs continued to rise in translation sermons and devotional literature dedicated to the imported saints, reinforcing the importance of Rome as the center of the church and the home to countless precious relics. Priests like Cistercian Hyacinth Frants at Raitenhaslach cited passages from paleo-Christian texts to back up his claims about the number of holy bodies available in the Eternal City during his sermon for the translation of Saints Concordia, Ausanius, and Fortunata in 1698. Frants informed the thousands in attendance that, according to Bozio's *Annales Antiquitatem,* "the Catholic Church has eleven million martyrs . . . and the city of Rome alone has 300,000 martyrs."[35] By 1708, at a translation sermon for Saint Amantius, Jordanus von Wasserburg did not even bother sharing numbers with the crowd in the parish church of Frontenhausen; rather, he asserted that there were "no evildoers" buried in the catacombs and that "only the holy bones of martyrs" could be found there.[36] By the early eighteenth century, priests, preachers, and their audiences had become familiar with the idea that all those buried in the Roman catacombs—including the bodies recently translated to their churches—belonged to martyrs.

In addition to impressive numbers, preachers used information from recently produced histories of the early church to bring the Christian persecutions in ancient Rome dramatically to life. With background information in hand, they placed the martyred catacomb saints center stage in an ancient theater of cruelty. At Sandizell, on the occasion of the translation festivities for Saints Clemens and Maximus, the preacher, Maximilian Emanuel Kurz, set the scene for his audience, telling them that "the ancient, world-conquering city of Rome will be the arena where [we] will pitch a blood-frothing stage."[37] Shortly thereafter, he rhetorically "led" the congregation to the ancient city's gates and asked them to enter it with him. Together they knocked on the door of the city, and when it finally opened, he cried: "Oh horrible sights! O blood-frothing theater! Oh Rome! Alas! Close your blood-boiling theater! Stop these horrible scenes! It is not wild animals, but rather Christians among the wild animals who are bleeding and must fight to the death."[38] With this dramatic rhetoric, Kurz placed the audience directly into the brutal persecution of Roman Christians, explaining how Sandizell's martyrs Maximus and Clemens—whose bodies sat right before their eyes—had undergone such torture. They were, Kurz assured his listeners, not the only ones to endure such torture in Rome for their Christian faith. After witnessing these awful scenes, Kurz's listeners continued their "tour" through Roman history, where they "saw" other persecutions that he had learned about through his consultation of Bozio's *Annales Antiquitatum.* These attacks included Diocletian's murder of 17,000 Christians in one day, the martyrdoms of Peter and Paul, and the killing of 260 Christians at the Hippodrome by Claudius.[39] Kurz's extremely vivid presentation of the execution of early Christians in Rome—and his inclusion of the catacomb saints Maximus and Clemens in this sacred drama—highlighted the role of martyrs in the larger arc of Catholic sacred history and—using references from an important text of paleo-Christian history—made clear that the main stage for this history was the city of Rome.

Outside of translation sermons and printed devotional booklets, word of mouth could also spread paleo-Christian ideas about the importance of the Eternal City as the true home of the church and the innumerable martyrs buried there. In 1757, a wandering hermit—who had been on many pilgrimages, including one to Rome—donated the body of Saint Innocentius to the parish church in the small village of Oberaudorf in Upper Bavaria. Inspired by this hermit's actions, shoemaker Sebastian Pichler decided he would go to Rome in the next Jubilee year, 1775, and attempt to obtain another holy body for the town church. When the year finally arrived, Pichler, along with a friend and the local priest, set out for Rome. Pichler kept an extensive diary of the group's journey, which survives in manuscript form. In the diary, he described the group's descent into the catacombs beneath Saint Sebastian's basilica. He reported that the "catacombs have narrow passageways that only one person could pass through at a time, though sometimes they are a bit wider. The tunnels are not walled with brick but carved out of hard earth. The holy bodies that still remain are in carved openings; this is where our holy body will be taken from."[40]

In addition to the physical description of the catacombs, Pichler recounted in his journal how popes and clergy held Mass in the subterranean spaces during persecutions, administering the sacraments as well as holding councils. Furthermore, he wrote that during these persecutions Christians lived in the underground chambers, surviving on food and drink sympathizers squeezed through holes in the ground. He also quoted the plaque above the entrance to the catacomb, noting the large number of martyrs buried below.[41] Once again, the familiar tropes about the catacombs and the relics available therein, were repeated, demonstrating that they had penetrated beyond the level of educated priests to devout lay pilgrims from a small rural town.

That a shoemaker living in Oberaudorf in the eighteenth century knew about the persecution of early Christians also illustrates the power of martyrs' bodies to connect the church's ancient past with the present in a concrete manner. Augustinian preacher Joseph Angerer emphasized the enduring importance of martyrs in church history during the celebration of the arrival of Saint Coelestinus in Ranshofen in 1698. In a sermon, he observed that Coelestinus suffered death by fire and noted: "Similar saints—some of the most noble and pleasing to God—were also burnt to death. These include Saint Lawrence, Saint Tiburtius, Saint Eustachius, Saint Polycarp, Saint Afra with her companions, the glorious Carolus Spinola from the Society of Jesus and many others who—just a few years ago—were also killed with fire in Japan."[42] In one sentence, Angerer made an explicit connection between well-known ancient Christian martyr-saints, the newly arrived catacomb saints, and contemporary early modern martyrs. This kind of rhetoric placed catacomb saints alongside much more prominent martyrs, equating their importance within church tradition, and drew a direct line between church practice from the remote past to the early modern period. From the very beginning of the church, he argued, martyrs had been willing to sacrifice their lives to defend their Christian/Catholic beliefs against tyrants and heretics. At Raitenhaslach in 1698, Frants stated the connection more explicitly. Echoing Baronio's main thesis, the Cistercian preacher attributed the quality of "semper idem" to all martyrs because they were "always united, always strong and always united."[43] Now that Raitenhaslach had the bodies of such martyrs in its midst, the village was part of and witness to the unbroken history of the Catholic Church.

Sermons were not the only way to bridge the temporal and physical distance between ancient Rome and early modern Bavarian villages. A three-act play written by Father Maurus Pfendtner and performed during the weeklong celebration of Saint Lucius's arrival in St. Veit connected these disparate periods and locales in a powerful and compelling performance. The first act of the play features Roman emperor Hemiarchus arresting, jailing, and then torturing Lucius for his refusal to sacrifice to the Roman gods, a typical story arc familiar from the passion stories of older martyrs. The play's action is then briefly interrupted by a ballet scene with dancing gladiators after which Lucius is beheaded and welcomed to heaven by a choir of angels. The scene then shifts back to earth, as the audience then observes Lucius's burial in the

Roman catacombs and subsequent transfer to the cloister. The last scenes depict the translation festival in Neumarkt, including a procession and supplications to the new patron, which had occurred just a few days prior to the play's debut.[44] Using a short, linear timeline, onlookers were transported from ancient Rome to present-day St. Veit by the story of the same martyr whose very body now lay in their church.

Rather than rely solely on catacomb or passion tropes, some church communities consulted additional sources published at the behest of the Catholic Church during the paleo-Christian revival in search of more specific information about the "holy bodies" that had arrived in their midst. For example, when the bones of Saint Julius arrived in Indersdorf in 1712, examination of the remains revealed that the saint's skull had been badly damaged. The monks at the cloister surmised it was possible that a head wound could have been his manner of martyrdom. They then consulted Baronio's *Annales,* combing it for references to a Saint Julius who had died in the same violent manner. Wasserburg, who gave the translation sermon, concluded that the saint who had come to the cloister was a particular Saint Julius who, "as one can see in the *Annales* of Baronio and in the very damaged skull of this holy martyr, was eventually crushed with clubs and cudgels."[45] In this case, the monks used the remains of the saint as forensic evidence to push their research on his life beyond the more generic passion narrative to a specific time and place in church history.

Similarly, the monks at Gars—eager to learn more information about their new patron, Felix, than his authentication certificate could provide—turned to both material and written sources. According to the cloister's chronicle, Felix's tomb had included a blood ampule, and two small glass images lay near the grave when it was unearthed by excavators. One glass image showed a person in Roman clothing with a laurel wreath and palm frond in his hand. This was supposedly labeled with the name "Saint Felix." The second image showed a man in priest's clothing and was labeled "Saint Calixtus." A piece of Calixtus's bones supposedly also lay nearby. Based on this information, the chronicler made an interpretive leap: "By leaving the glass images, the Holy Father wanted to leave a clue, that Felix and Calixtus both suffered a martyr's death in Rome and were buried in the same place."[46] With this information in hand—and a desire to learn more—the monks next consulted Baronio's revised *Roman Martyrology* to find a feast date that included both a Saint Calixtus and a Saint Felix. After some searching, they found a date that fit their criteria: "in the *Roman Martyrology,* this saint is commemorated on December 29; therefore, the feast day for St. Felix in Gars is also observed on this date."[47] Although this particular bit of information was useful, the traits of another Saint Felix were pressed into service to create a more well-rounded hagiography for the martyr. Over the years, the saint came to be identified as one of the "Seven Brothers." These brothers, supposedly the sons of Saint Felizitas, were also buried in the Calixtus catacombs and had been martyred at a young age using a cudgel. These seeming similarities led the Augustinians at Gars to adopt certain aspects of the "Seven Brothers" Felix for their own saint, effectively merging the lives of two separate saints with the same name into one.[48] In this particular case, the brothers at the cloister in Gars started with the objects and information given to them about Saint Felix by the church in Rome and then proceeded to use a mash-up of paleo-Christian written sources to form a more detailed hagiography for the saint.

This use of the sacred histories and martyrologies produced by Baronio, Bosio, and others demonstrates the degree to which paleo-Christian sources had made it over the Alps and were being used at the local level as Bavarians sought to learn as much as possible about the lives and deaths of their new saints. This likely did not occur in exactly the way the church historians and archaeologists might have expected when they were exploring the catacombs or plumbing the depths of the Vatican archives. Instead, early modern Bavarians, eager to learn about their new saints and their origins, creatively fused scholarly sources with older hagiographical traditions and popular tour guides to make these martyrs' lives vivid and memorable to a population unfamiliar with their deeds.

A Persistent Identity: Catacomb Saint Iconography in Visual Media

The immense work early modern Bavarian laypeople and clergymen did to build holy bodies, as well as research and write the vitae of Roman catacomb saints was only the beginning of the process of creating long-lasting and memorable identities for these martyrs. After the catacomb saints were safely ensconced in glass-walled shrines in churches across the Electorate, the effort to perpetuate and solidify their status as ancient Roman martyrs continued both inside and outside the church walls in a variety of media including engraved book illustrations, devotional images (*Andachtsbilder*), sculptures, paintings, shrine covers, votive images, and public monuments. The Roman costumes and martyrs' attributes present on the constructed bodies of the catacomb saints provided the basis for the iconography used for the saints in other media and continued to reinforce the major themes of the Rome-driven paleo-Christian revival in a Bavarian setting.

Inside churches, altar paintings highlighted pivotal points in catacomb saints' lives—often their execution—and echoed the spoken rendition of their

FIGURE 38. Altar painting of Saint Claudius's martyrdom and ascent into heaven, Altenhohenau cloister, Griesstätt, Andreas Wolf, 1703. (Photograph by Georg Arnold; courtesy of Georg Arnold)

constructed hagiographies delivered in translation sermons. The Claudius altar at Altenhohenau features a large painting of its titular saint, whose body sits directly beneath the panel (fig. 38). At the bottom of the image, Saint Claudius burns on a pyre as a man stokes it with more wood. To the martyr's left, several Romans gesture to a statue of the emperor on a pedestal, seemingly imploring the saint to sacrifice to it. In the background the viewer can see several other Roman soldiers with helmets and shields, and in the deep background the artist has outlined several classically inspired Roman buildings. In contrast to the torment below, the top two-thirds of the image depict angels lifting Saint Claudius into heaven and crowning him with the laurel wreath of victory. Like his holy body below, Claudius is dressed in a Roman soldier's uniform and holding a palm leaf. Statues of Saint Sebastian and Saint Florian—wearing similar outfits to Claudius—flank the altar painting and present the viewer with an ensemble of ancient Roman martyr-soldiers. Placing the statues of these well-known figures alongside the more recently arrived Claudius reinforced his origins and antiquity and—as Angerer had in his translation sermon at Ranshofen—his status within the company of the church's unbroken history of martyr saints.

In contrast to the altar painting at Altenhohenau, a 1677 painting by Franz Josef Geiger at the cloister of Landshut-Seligenthal focuses largely on the

FIGURE 39. Altar painting of the martyrdom of Saint Victor at Landshut-Seligenthal cloister, Franz Josef Geiger, 1677. (Photograph by Toni Ott; courtesy of Toni Ott)

moments just before catacomb saint Victor's martyrdom (fig. 39). The image shows the saint dressed in a Roman soldier's costume looking heavenward as the emperor condemns him. Though the saint appears calm, one soldier takes off his leg guards while another ties him up. Earthly temptations—a crown and money—lie on the ground. At that very moment, a terrifying reddish bolt of lightning descends from heaven, breaking a statue of Jupiter in two and apparently scaring the nearby onlookers and the emperor. Saint Victor, undisturbed by the commotion, gazes calmly toward heaven while an angel hovers overhead bearing a palm leaf and crown of laurels foreshadowing Victor's impending martyrdom. Details such as the Roman statues, architecture, and costumes reveal the geographical and temporal setting of the scene, while the palm leaf and laurel crown reinforce that Victor—whose remains rest upon the altar directly below and bear their own versions of these symbols—was an early Roman martyr. Large altar paintings like those at Altenhohenau and Landshut-Seligenthal also more permanently evoked and reinforced—through their consistent presence within the church space—many of the events and common passion tropes found in the vitae written for the saints and relayed in translation sermons.

Small devotional images (*Andachtsbilder*) produced for distribution to those who attended translation events or visited the saints' shrines as pilgrims also helped to propagate the cult and the iconography of the saint beyond the walls of a church and could even be made into secondary relics through contact with the holy body itself. In Landshut, the nuns decided to produce small images of Saint Victor in addition to the large altar painting of the saint they had already commissioned for their convent church as a way to increase devotion to the martyr (fig. 40). The saint's outfit in the *Andachtsbild* mirrors the costume used to clothe his holy body as well as the one he wears in the altar painting above his shrine: that of a Roman soldier. He sports body armor, a

FIGURE 40. Devotional Image of Saint Victor as Roman soldier, Landshut-Seligenthal cloister, C. Schmitt, 1700. (Museum Dingolfing, Inv. Nr. 2565)

FIGURE 41. Devotional image of Saint Lucius as Roman soldier and patron of St. Veit cloister in *Neues Liecht oder Neuschein,* Johann Ulrich Biberger, 1696. (Universitätsbibliothek der LMU München, W 4 Homil. 1764#16)

skirt, and sleeves with *pteruges* while holding a martyr's palm. At the top of the engraving, one angel removes his armored helmet as another replaces it with a crown of laurels.

A surviving devotional image of Saint Lucius engraved by Johann Ulrich Biberger uses similar iconography (fig. 41). Dressed in legionnaire's clothing, with body armor and sandals, Lucius hovers over the St. Veit cloister buildings as a protector and patron. He holds the martyrs' palm as well as a sword, reminding the image's owner of his manner of death. At the bottom of the engraving is a short line of text noting that the devotional image had been "touched to the holy body" itself, imbuing it with the sacred aura of the saint. Production and distribution of small devotional items like this meant that,

FIGURE 42. Statue of Saint Primianus on Primianusplatz, Kemnath, 1695. (Photograph by author)

rather than remaining confined within the interior of a particular church, the image, identity, *and* the power of ancient Roman catacomb saints could be taken home and used in a domestic setting.

In addition to private devotion using *Andachtsbilder,* Bavarian Catholics encountered images or reminders of catacomb saints in outdoor monuments or place-names. The town of Kemnath, which received the body of Saint Primianus in 1693, erected a column with a statue of the saint atop it two years after his arrival near the main square (fig. 42). The statue, which still stands at the center of Primianusplatz today, shows the saint—who became a town patron—dressed as a Roman soldier in body armor, a skirt with *pteruges,* high sandals, and a plumed helmet. In his left hand he holds what appears to be the ampule of

FIGURE 43. *Ex voto* painting with Saint Felix as a Roman soldier, Gars cloister, 1790. (Photograph by author)

his own blood, and his right hand touches an axe. Without entering the nearby church, passersby were reminded of the antique Roman martyr in their midst.

Surviving evidence demonstrates that the immense work early modern Bavarian laypeople and clergymen did to build bodies, research and write the vitae of Roman catacomb saints, and reinforce their origins in a variety of media successfully produced long-lasting and memorable identities for these imported ancient martyrs. In Gars, Saint Felix still sits in a gilded altar in his eponymous chapel at the former cloister. One of the walls is covered in *ex voto* paintings left to express gratitude to the catacomb saint for his intercession. In these, Felix consistently appears in the garb of a Roman legionnaire wearing a crown of laurels, indicating that his identity—and the iconography used to convey it—had been absorbed by local supplicants and artists and replicated for centuries after his arrival (fig. 43).

By following the remains of catacomb saints over the Alps, it becomes clear that it was not just scholars or rulers who attempted to bring the early Christian church back to life. While the Roman church had assigned a particular meaning to the relics within the paleo-Christian movement—as material evidence in the debate with the Protestants over early church history—it was up to early modern Bavarians to figure out how to make their identities both legible *and* significant in an environment far removed from the scholarly milieu of Baronio and Bosio. Choosing to present the relics as intact bodies provided the platform on which to construct an identity for the saints, first through costume and then through the composition of vitae that creatively deployed the texts of paleo-Christian scholars in Rome for their own hagiographical project. In doing so, Bavarian clergy and the local community used holy bodies to communicate the larger themes of the paleo-Christian revival—antiquity, the centrality of Rome as the home of the Catholic Church, and martyrdom—and to incorporate their small villages and towns in the unbroken history of the universal Catholic Church.

meaning to their lives within the paleo-Christian movement—as much a tendency in the debates within the Protestants over early church history—it was up to early modern Bavarians to figure out how to make these identities both legible and significant in an environment far removed from the scholarly milieu of Rome and Bosio. Choosing to present the relics as intact bodies provided the platform on which to construct an identity for the saints, first through names and then through the composition of vitae that creatively deployed the tenets of paleo-Christian scholarship in Rome for their own hagiographical project. In doing so, Bavarian clergy and the local community used holy bodies to communicate the larger theses of the paleo-Christian revival—emphasizing the centrality of Rome as the home of the Catholic Church and martyrdom—and to incorporate their small villages and towns in the unbroken history of the universal Catholic Church.

PART III

ROMAN CATACOMB SAINTS BECOME BAVARIAN

5

Welcoming the Saints Home

TRANSLATION PROCESSIONS AND FESTIVITIES

EARLY IN the morning on September 26, 1694, parish congregations in the region around the small village of Vornbach set out in procession toward its Benedictine cloister. Carrying crosses and flags, the eight groups eventually converged on the town to join in the "triumphal introduction" of the Roman catacomb saint Clarus to his new home in Bavaria.[1] After arriving, the local parishioners joined a larger procession organized by the cloister's monks that carried the bejeweled body of the saint through town and into the courtyard of the monastery. Along the way, participants passed through three triumphal arches built and decorated for the occasion. As they marched, thirty-eight cannons announced the martyr's arrival to the surrounding countryside. After reaching the doors of the cloister church, seven Benedictines brought Saint Clarus into the church for a Mass and sermon. So many people were in attendance—from all ranks of society—that not everyone could fit inside to hear Capuchin Romanus Austriacus's homily in praise of the ancient martyr's heroism in the face of Roman persecution.[2] As the sermon drew to a close, Austriacus shifted his focus from Clarus's origins to his new role in Vornbach: a patron and miracle worker for the community.[3] He succinctly described how Saint Clarus, over the course of the translation ceremonies, had completed a critical rite of passage: "[he] had his triumphant entrance as a foreign guest, but he is no longer a guest; he is a most welcome resident, who will stay here."[4] Over the course of the day, the Roman Saint Clarus had gone from unknown outsider to permanent resident.

As with Clarus, when Roman catacomb saints showed up Bavarian communities, they were strangers with unfamiliar stories and no proven record when it came to intercession and protection. A relationship between these outsiders and their new hometowns—both in the heavenly and earthly realms—had to be formed. Translation festivals were critical moments in the saint's transition from foreign outsiders to local patrons and citizens.[5] Examining this process of adoption, integration, and subsequent veneration reveals that whole-body catacomb saints—in addition to communicating Bavarian Catholics' allegiance to Rome and the universal church—simultaneously functioned as intensely local patrons who became quickly embedded in the daily praxis of religion in towns and villages across the territory. Sitting at the nexus between the universal and local Catholic Church, these holy bodies—built by Bavarians—materialized the negotiated nature of sanctity in the early modern period.

The saints' first introduction to a community typically occurred in a meticulously planned procession with clerical and lay participants from the surrounding area. While communities had long celebrated the arrival of relics with *adventus* (arrival) ceremonies, sources created for translation events, including festival pamphlets, procession engravings, translation sermons, plays, and songs, demonstrate how Bavarians made significant modifications to these traditional ceremonies of welcome and adoption after 1648; these changes coincided directly with the shift in the presentation of catacomb relics from fragments to intact bodies. After the Thirty Years' War, festival organizers added elements from secular entry ceremonies including triumphal arches and military escorts to the processions held to welcome holy bodies to their towns and villages. Parading into town, the new saints were greeted with all the trappings of an illustrious out-of-town visitor or dignitary. The elaboration of the transfer festivities indicates the importance communities placed on greeting the new saints with great fanfare and highlights the degree to which they were perceived as fully present, human individuals worthy of a royal welcome.

These often-lavish festivities also frequently featured actors—drawn from the town or village—who took on the role of the catacomb saints in plays or *tableaux vivant* created specifically for the occasion. In other cases, these living body-doubles marched alongside the skeletons of the catacomb saint they represented in the transfer procession. The addition of actors to these celebrations—like the triumphal arches and military escorts—represented a departure from pre-1648 rituals for relic translations. Previously, actors did not typically appear as living embodiments of saints whose remains were being transferred to new locations. The unprecedented use of personification hastened the introduction and adoption of foreign saints into localized spiritual and earthly communities. Local clerics wrote and produced plays starring the catacomb saints, bringing them to life and allowing them to personally introduce themselves to their new communities and to seek approval from the existing patron saints of the area. In addition, preachers and playwrights used the language of kinship to forge bonds of mutual duty and affection between the Roman catacomb saints and their new earthly and heavenly communities. The dramatized introductions and adoptions staged to integrate the holy interlopers into towns and cities across the Electorate made these connections concrete and relatable to the gathered faithful and relied heavily on the fact that the saints were entirely present before their eyes. Rather than small bone fragments, catacomb saints were perceived as people with whom a city, town, or village could form a relationship. As a result, by the end of the translation festivities, Roman catacomb saints had become firmly ensconced in their local Bavarian communities as fellow citizens and heavenly protectors.

Translation Festival Logistics and Attendance

Catacomb saint translations, like the one held for Saint Clarus at Vornbach, were singular cultural events in the life of a community and its hinterlands. They lasted from a single day to an entire week in a celebratory octave.[6] Printed festival accounts and manuscript sources recount how local citizens and clerics devoted months to planning every detail of the celebrations including designing and building ephemeral architecture, devising the procession order, writing songs and plays, and acquiring costumes for actors and procession participants. Preparations could last from six weeks to several years and predated the arrival of the relics themselves, particularly when the holy bodies were acquired in conjunction with anniversary celebrations.[7] The most elaborate translation festivities occurred at male cloisters, especially those with considerable financial resources. Several surviving engravings from festival books printed to commemorate the translations of catacomb saints to the Cistercian cloister at Raitenhaslach (1698) and the Augustinian cloister at Ranshofen (1699) illustrate the scope of the festivities. The procession at Raitenhaslach featured forty different groups including trumpeters and timpanists, seventy riders in "Roman costume," confraternities from nearby villages, and, of course, the holy bodies of catacomb saints Ausanius, Concordia, and Fortunata (fig. 44). Just a year later—and not far down the road from Raitenhalsach—the Augustinian Canons welcomed Saints Marius and Coelestinus to town with a massive procession that included 101 separate groups of participants. Convents and parishes often held quite impressive processions and festivals, though they were usually smaller in scale due to financial constraints.[8] Strict convent enclosure implemented by the Council of Trent also meant that nuns were also not allowed to participate in translation activities outside of their church, though they played active roles in planning the public events and decorative programs for the transfer ceremonies for holy bodies. At the parish level, various groups including guilds, mayors, city councils, as well as ordinary citizens organized the translations.[9]

No matter how modest or ornate, the coordination and execution of catacomb saint translations required significant time, labor, and financial investment. Vornbach's acquisition of Saint Clarus began two years prior to the

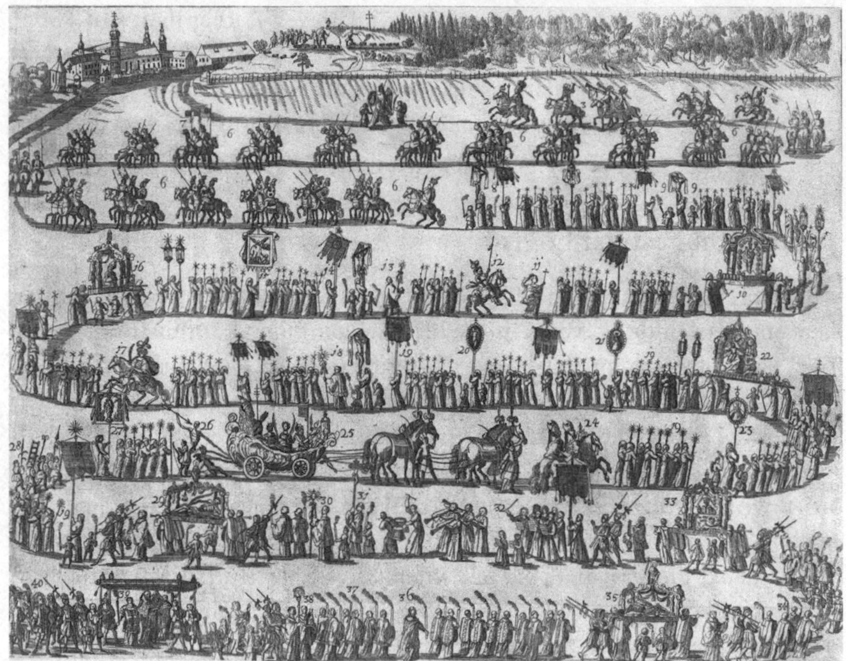

FIGURE 44. Engraving of translation procession for Saints Ausanius, Concordia, and Fortunata to Raitenhaslach cloister in *Glorwürdiges Sechstes Jubel-Jahr,* 1699. (Staatliche Museen zu Berlin—Preußischer Kulturbesitz, Kunstbibliothek; photograph by Dietmar Katz)

cloister's six-hundredth anniversary in 1694, when the cloister's prelates approached Father Willibald and urged him to request a catacomb saint from the pope for the occasion. Soon thereafter, in April 1692, a box tied with red silk ribbon containing the bones of Saint Clarus arrived. After authentication by diocesan authorities, the abbot sent the relics to the Benedictine nuns of the Niedernburg cloister in Passau for construction into a "complete, lying male figure" and decoration with *Klosterarbeit.*[10] As the nuns proceeded with their work, the brothers at the cloister commissioned a custom altar—described as a "royal mausoleum or resting place"—for the saint. The monks even managed to procure indulgences for Masses read at Saint Clarus's new altar as well as a plenary indulgence for attendance at the saint's translation festival.[11]

Having spent months planning for the transfer events, churches and cloisters paid special attention to making sure the ceremonies were well attended as they were eager to promote the cult of the new saints and to introduce them to a wide audience. It also seems likely that parish and cloister communities wanted to make sure their neighbors were aware they had acquired such a valuable set of relics. As a result, they worked diligently to draw large crowds to the events, sending out invitations to nearby churches as well as to local officials and nobles. To promote the translation of Saint Cassian to the cloister of Landshut-Seligenthal, the nuns had flyers posted throughout the entire city; at Fürstenfeld, Abbot Martin sent letters to ten neighboring parishes asking priests to bring their congregations to Saint Hyacinth's translation in 1672.[12] As at Vornbach, procuring indulgences was another strategy used to increase the attractiveness of the festivities. The cloister at Ranshofen managed to obtain an indulgence from Pope Innocent XII (r. 1691–1700) for the translation of Saints Marius and Coelestinus, and the indulgence was announced publicly prior to the translation from area pulpits "to remind the Christian people to take advantage of such a great spiritual treasure."[13]

As a result of these efforts, as well as the Bavarian Catholics' devotion to saints and relics, these events drew massive and, in some cases, unprecedented crowds. At Hohenpeißenberg, Augustinian Anselm Mannhardt wrote that the translation events for Saint Clara attracted an "indescribable and truly unbelievable number of people, the likes of which, up to then, had never been seen in Peißenberg."[14] Some of the participants, he noted, had come all the way from the parish of Ammeragau, which was six or seven hours away.[15] Many other printed festival books and manuscript sources describe the large number of attendees at these translation events. They recount "astonishing" and "unbelievable" crowds, often numbering in the thousands.[16] Several even include more concrete information on the number of participants at the festivities. The cloisters of Kühbach and Gotteszell drew 12,000 and 16,000 visitors respectively to welcome Roman holy bodies from the catacombs. The translation of Saint Victor to the Bürgersaal confraternity church in Munich drew 30,000 onlookers, just 2,000 people short of the city's entire population.[17]

Though the reports may be subject to exaggeration due to the desire of the writer to enhance the reputation of a particular church and its new saint(s), the numbers remain impressive, particularly in light of the fact that 80 percent of Bavarians still lived in small villages or on farms in the eighteenth century. Munich, Landshut, and Straubing were the only cities in the duchy with populations larger than 4,000 people, meaning that the crowds attending these festivities often far exceeded the number of inhabitants living in a typical village or town.[18] The popularity of these religious festivals demonstrates the enthusiasm of Bavarian Catholics for the holy Roman bodies arriving in their midst. The large crowds at these events also meant that thousands of locals witnessed the introduction of the saint and became familiar with them and their stories. This began the process of embedding the saint within the particular local religious landscape, one that was not duchy-wide but often restricted to a town or monastery and the surrounding countryside.

Development of Translation Festivities and Rituals

The crowds that gathered to witness the *adventus* (arrival) of whole-body catacomb saints experienced—in many cases—an elaborate and magnificent baroque spectacle that could last from several hours to multiple days. Festival organizers freely borrowed elements from other contemporary secular and religious rituals, particularly royal entries, and Corpus Christi processions to welcome and introduce the Roman martyrs to their new Bavarian hometowns.[19] The most elaborate festivities, chronicled in printed festival books and handwritten eyewitness accounts, included large processions, temporary architecture, music, sermons, plays, cannon fire, and even fireworks. Actors playing catacomb saints marched in the processions, appeared in *tableaux vivant,* and introduced themselves to the faithful on stages built for the occasion. Such extravagant translation festivals, however, only became the norm after 1648, when catacomb saints began to be staged as whole bodies.

Prior to the Thirty Years' War, translations of catacomb saint relics, while celebratory, were more subdued affairs that closely followed transfer rituals established for holy remains in the Middle Ages. Typically, on the night before the transfer, the relics would be held at a second nearby church. The following morning, the head cleric would lead a procession of religious officials and laypeople to go pick up the relics and bring them back into town to their destination. People in the processions would carry candles, crosses, and flags, and the event would often be accompanied by singing and the tolling of bells. As time passed, the entry ceremonies grew more complex. Wagons transported the arriving relics while a church's existing relics were carried in the procession by members of the clergy. Once the group reached its destination, clerics sang a litany outside the front doors of the church receiving the relics and then went inside to prepare the altar. When they were finished, the clergy reemerged from the church to carry the relics inside, where they deposited them on an altar and held a Mass for the guests.[20]

When the Wittelsbach family welcomed the first whole-body catacomb saints to Munich in 1593, the translation largely followed medieval precedents. Before the transfer, the saints' relics—enclosed in opaque reliquaries—were held in the St. Salvator Chapel outside the city's Sendling Gate. On August 13, the city's clergy, accompanied by members of the local Marian Congregation, craftsmen, and a large crowd of laypeople set out in a solemn procession to pick them up as church bells rang across the city. On the way back into the city, the ducal family, members of the court, and the bishop of Cremona met the relics at the gate and joined the larger procession as it accompanied the relics through the city to St. Michael's Jesuit church.[21]

A similarly solemn and traditional relic translation occurred at Benediktbeuren for the catacomb saint Primenius in 1626. According to the cloister's chronicle, on the morning of the event, several of the brothers processed out of the church, picked up Saint Primenius at the nearby parish church in Bad Heilbrunn, and brought his remains back to the monastery. Upon arriving at the cloister walls, the monks placed Saint Primianus's relics on an outdoor altar and waited for the abbot and the rest of Benediktbeuren's monks to come meet the saint. This group emerged from their church carrying white candles and singing songs of praise to the martyr. Four monks then went up to the altar and picked up the saint's relics, which they then marched back into the cloister under a baldachin.[22] Though certainly celebrated, the arrival of holy bodies from the catacombs in the period before 1648 did not spark major innovations or changes to existing ritual forms of relic transfer.

Other relic translations in the duchy prior to 1648 also lack many of the more dramatic features later added to catacomb saint translations, notably the personification of saints as well as some elements of royal entries. The Wittelsbach family organized two other high-profile translation of saints' relics during this period. After rescuing Saint Benno's relics from Protestants in Saxony, Duke Albrecht V brought the holy bishop's relics into his capital city in 1576. Though a temporary triumphal arch was built for event, the saint himself was not personified onstage or in the procession.[23] In 1604, Duke Wilhelm V personally oversaw the translation of Saint Castulus's body from Moosburg to Landshut. Though the event included a procession, there were no actors representing Saint Castulus or any other saints, an element that would become a staple of catacomb saint translations after 1648.

After the Thirty Years' War, the ceremonies held for the holy bodies of Roman martyrs that flooded over the Alps and into the Electorate became much more elaborate. This was largely driven by the staging of catacomb saints as full bodies. This shift materialized the saint's personhood and allowed early modern Bavarians to greet them in the same way they would a living ruler or dignitary. Saints, much like rulers, passed through triumphal arches and by columns of honor and obelisks as they made their way along parade routes festooned with garlands and emblems. The use of temporary architecture was borrowed from customs that had begun to be used by territorial rulers in the Holy Roman Empire after 1500.[24] As was customary for high-ranking visitors, honor guards of soldiers recruited from local garrisons often also accompanied new catacomb saints into town, where dignitaries and local government officials waited to welcome them to the community.[25] As a procession began to enter the town, church bells, trumpets, drums, singing, and cannon fire added to the multisensory experience.

The translation held for Saint Leo at Kühbach in 1685 was typical and incorporated all the same pomp displayed when rulers and high dignitaries entered cities and towns during this period. The day before the translation of Saint Leo, nuns and craftsmen worked to decorate the courtyard, setting up two triumphal arches, a large altar, trellises, paintings, and tapestries. The arches were decorated with an emblematic program that depicted Leo as a patron and protector.[26] In the early morning on the day of the translation, trumpets and drums began to play, and the first salvo from the cannons and other weapons placed on nearby hillsides were fired.[27] The neighborhood was on notice—a royal guest would be arriving that day.

As the sun rose, processions left from nearby villages and converged at the Schloßkapelle at Haslangreit, where the saint had been kept overnight. After a Mass, the procession set out for the first triumphal arch, which had been set up in a field just outside the cloister. The procession included the local cavalry from nearby Schrobenhausen, multiple "triumph wagons," *tableaux vivant*, and musicians of all kinds.[28] At the first arch, the bishop of Augsburg and his assistants, the high nobles, as well as the clergy met the body of Saint Leo with "a great welcome." Once they entered the cloister courtyard, the holy body was placed on the decorated altar. The day closed with fireworks—including rockets and spinning fire wheels.[29] A heavenly prince had graced the town and cloister with his presence, and in many ways, his grand welcome mirrored the reception given contemporary rulers.

Though saints were routinely dramatized onstage and in religious processions in the centuries prior to 1648, it was uncommon to see a costumed person acting out the role of saint—catacomb or otherwise—in conjunction with their bodily relics. The Jesuits, in particular, staged many Latin plays about martyrs at their colleges in the region that included actors playing saints. Actors playing saints and other holy figures also appeared regularly in Corpus Christi processions; and Passion plays like the one held yearly in Oberammergau dramatized Christ's last moments.[30] Only after catacomb saints began appearing as sparkling intact bodies did actors playing the Roman martyrs begin to appear in translation festivities. They walked in processions alongside their bejeweled bodies and stood atop litters or wagons in *tableaux vivant* that depicted hagiographical scenes from their lives. Visible and present, the saints were embodied not only in their full-body relics but by actors drawn from the local population who became the living, breathing body-doubles of these ancient heroes. The holy was present in flesh *and* bone, right before the eyes of the spectators.

One of the biggest advantages of including actors in catacomb saint translation processions was that it allowed organizers to introduce the saint's heroic martyrdom story to observers. Since the saints were imported from Rome and had no history in the region, the procession provided the first opportunity to publicly communicate the hagiographical identity carefully crafted for the martyrs by local clerics. Actors embodying these ancient Roman martyrs, whose relics would follow later in the procession, proved a favored way to accomplish this task. When the parish church of St. Martin welcomed Saint Porphyrius to Arnschwang in 1694, the procession included two "living images"—one of the saint before the Roman court and another that showed his execution.[31] Seventy-six years later in Dingolfing, the village put on an *adventus* procession for Saint Faustina that included four *tableaux vivant* acted out by citizens' daughters as well as residents of the nearby town of Schwaiger. These depicted Faustina's capture and incarceration by Roman soldiers, her appearance at the court of the Roman emperor, the delivery of her death sentence, and finally her beheading. Shortly behind the decapitation scene, sixteen more daughters of Dingolfing bore the shrine containing the body of the martyr herself.[32] Those attending the procession would have first witnessed the major events of Saint Faustina's life followed by her dramatic death. Instead of that being the end of the story, the saint's body itself came marching by, reinforcing the saint's physical presence in their midst and the connection between the acted scenes and the gleaming body before them.

Another elaborate dramatization of a Roman catacomb saint's triumph over paganism and persecution occurred in the Angerkloster's translation procession for Saints Victor, Aurelius, and Felix in 1738. Armored Bavarian soldiers marched through Munich's streets, escorting a group of actors playing captured Roman prisoners. The captives included Roman priests carrying images of Jupiter, Saturn, and Mars—a nod to their heretical beliefs—as well as Roman judges and emperors in chains. Interspersed between these groups of defeated Romans were "triumph wagons" carrying actors playing Saints. Victor, Aurelius, and Felix as well as angels in Roman costume carrying their instruments of martyrdom.[33] This dramatization illustrated the victory of the martyrs over pagan superstition and their Roman persecutors. The arriving saints—through actors—participated actively in their defeat, looking down on their former persecutors, who were now vanquished. The use of actors in direct proximity to the saints' bodily relics helped introduce them to their new communities as living people with a dramatic and vivid story of martyrdom.

Roman Saints Become Bavarian

At the same time that the personification of catacomb saints highlighted their Roman heritage, it also facilitated and hastened the integration of the newcomers into local Bavarian communities. One of the key steps in the process of adoption was to incorporate the new catacomb saint into the local pantheon—another ritual concept early modern Bavarians inherited from their forebears but modified due to the presence of whole bodies. In the medieval period and beyond, a church's relics or statues of its patrons would often be brought to consecration ceremonies for neighboring communities or brought out for relic translations.[34] These were static displays that did not include any dialogue or dramatic personification of the saints whose remains were present for the ceremony. Relic arrivals in Bavaria, whether for the remains of catacomb saints or "rescued" relics from Protestant regions, largely conformed to this formula. When Saint Primenius arrived at Benediktbeuren in 1626, no actors participated in the translation procession. Instead, Abbot Joannes placed the saint's relics "on the altar of saint Anastasia, doubtless believing that no one would receive this new Roman guest more worthily than another holy Roman."[35] Though the abbot believed there was a relationship between these two saints—both Roman martyrs translated to the cloister centuries apart—this relationship was not further explicated or dramatized as would be the case after 1648, when catacomb relics were forged into complete bodies.

After the Thirty Years' War, the dramatic moment of greeting between old and new saints became more pronounced as saints were embodied and present in their holy bodies and/or personified by actors.[36] The meeting of older patron saints and the new catacomb saints dramatized the integration of the newly arrived martyrs into a very particular community of local patron saints. Since catacomb saints' bodies were intact and present in one location and nowhere else, the melding of these new and old saints resulted in a unique heavenly community that could only occur in a single locale. Unlike more famous saints, whose cults often spread independently of their bodily remains, catacomb saints and their hagiographies were unknown upon arrival in new hometowns. Their veneration was instead solely dependent on the presence of their relics. Since all of their relics were ostensibly in one location, a catacomb saint's addition to a group of patrons made a church or town's group of protectors distinct from those in all other locations and helped to further particularize the sacred landscape of Bavaria sancta.

The integration of a saint into a local pantheon occurred in several ways. Often, previously translated catacomb saints were processed out to meet new catacomb saints. Actors representing older local patrons also interacted with their new compatriots. At Dingolfing, the body of Saint Martialis, translated in 1701 to the town's Franciscan cloister, was taken in procession to greet his new "fellow patron" Saint Faustina when she made her festive entrance in 1770.[37] Once she had been picked up, the procession wended its way back to the parish church. In Munich, two Franciscan convents—the Pütrichkloster and the Angerkloster—regularly brought out their previously transferred catacomb saints for inclusion in subsequent translation festivities. Hyacinth, Dorothea, and Felicitas were carried in Saint Geminus's arrival procession in 1691, and Saint Eleutheria greeted Victor, Aurelius, and Felix in 1738.[38] Given the saints' origin in the Roman catacombs, festival organizers believed it fitting that those ancient martyrs who had preceded them across the Alps should be part of the delegation that brought a new fellow patron into the community or church.

Often, it was not left up to catacomb saints alone to greet their Roman brethren and welcome them to their new towns. Munich's religious houses brought out many of their most famous relics alongside more recently arrived catacomb saints to welcome Saint Felicissimus to the city in 1698. Before his final installation in the chapel of the English Ladies, priests bore the body through the streets and into the Our Lady Cathedral, where they placed him on the high altar for public veneration. Arrayed around the altar, a company of saints from religious houses across the city awaited their new compatriot. The display included the relics of Saint Benno (Unser Liebe Frauenkirche) and Cosmas and Damian (St. Michael's) as well as a host of Roman catacomb saints: Honoratus (St. Peter's), Benignus (St. Michael's), Alexander (Augustinian Eremites), Constantius (Josefspital Chapel), and Felicitatis (Pütrichkloster).[39] After Balduin, a prelate from the Cistercian cloister at Fürstenfeld conducted the Vespers service, a procession with all the relics set out through the streets of the capital accompanied by trumpets, drums, and music.[40] Attended by prelates from Fürstenfeld, members of the ducal court, nobles, government officials, members of the clergy and an "innumerable crowd of all sorts of highly honorable men and women," the procession eventually made its way to the courtyard of the English Ladies, where five large altars with baldachins awaited the holy bodies.[41] On the following day, Balduin held a high mass, and then Saint Felicissimus took up his permanent residence inside the convent chapel. The impressive festival to usher Saint Felicissimus into Munich and the presence of heavenly and earthly residents of the city embedded him firmly into a local religious community unique to the city itself.

Actors playing older patrons—rather than their relics—also traveled to pick up the relics of the new catacomb saint or appeared alongside them in processions, effectively greeting the Roman outsider. At Arnschwang, a *tableau vivant* in the arrival procession featured the parish church patron, Saint

Martin, welcoming Saint Porphyrius to his new hometown. This *tableau* followed two others in the procession that depicted his Roman origin story. Over the course of the parade, the focus of the narrative shifted from the saint's early years in Rome to his integration into his new Bavarian home in Arnschwang.[42] Similarly, an actor playing catacomb saint Lucius rode at the head of his own entry procession into the town of St. Veit, escorted by none other than an actor playing Saint Veit himself, the cloister's medieval patron and town namesake.[43] Though the actors had no dialogue in these cases, the sight of a long-standing community protector side by side with their new Roman counterparts indicated to onlookers that the new saint was a trustworthy addition to their town's company of heavenly guardians.

The most explicit adoption and integration of new catacomb saints into a community's preexisting pantheon of patron saints occurred in theatrical performances, sometimes called salutation plays.[44] These could be interspersed in processions with scenes staged at stops along the translation route. In Bavaria, they most commonly occurred at the end of processions on purpose-built stages at the end of the parade route.[45] In these dramas, the catacomb saints were brought to life before the eyes of large crowds attending the translation ceremonies—in some cases introducing themselves directly to the community and taking up their place among the older patrons. Unlike most Jesuit drama performed in the duchy during this period, the plays written for catacomb saints were performed in German in order to reach the widest possible audience, regardless of education level.

The plays varied in complexity from a simple greeting to those that included several acts and extensive dialogue. The dramatic reception for Saint Beninus at Steingaden in 1664 was fairly straightforward. After the translation procession ended, the priests carrying the saint's body placed it on an altar in front of a triumphal arch in the cloister's main courtyard. Three "heavenly emissaries" then greeted the new saint's relics in a "living musical play." After welcoming Beninus, the emissaries called on the older patrons of the cloister to do the same. Actors playing these holy patrons emerged from the church, surrounded the saint's holy body, and "took him into their company with great joy." To end the "action," the patrons picked up the "newly adopted" martyr and took his body into the church as the bells rang, salutes were fired, and trumpets and drums played.[46] In this particular case, not only did the older patrons greet the new saint as a person, they physically bore him into the church, reinforcing their welcome and acceptance of him into their domain.

A more elaborate greeting with both processional and stage drama elements occurred on October 8, 1724, for the translation of the catacomb saints Wenceslaus and Gaudentius to the pilgrimage church of Hohenpeißenberg.

Supervised by the Augustinian cloister of Rottenbuch, the church, set on the peak of a mountain, housed a wonder-working statue of the Virgin Mary. Inspired by his acquisition of five catacomb saints for the Rottenbuch cloister, Abbot Patritius Oswald decided to outfit the pilgrimage church with several holy bodies.[47] Saint Clara arrived first in 1719, followed by Wenceslaus and Gaudentius in 1724. Early in the morning on the day of the translation, amid cannon fire, all three catacomb saints were carried down to the base of the mountain and guarded by soldiers. Several hours later, a procession set out from the pilgrimage church and wended its way down the mountain path to meet the relics. When the procession arrived, the participants along with the gathered crowd saw not only the saints' shrines containing their bodies but also actors embodying the saints standing in front of them. An actress playing Saint Clara, who had preceded her fellow catacomb saints to the site by five years, was the first to welcome them to their new home. Described in the chronicle text as an emissary from Christ and Maria von Peißenberg, Saint Clara began her greeting by singing a song of invitation to the new saints to join them in their church. Wenceslaus and Gaudentius, also played by actors, replied favorably and then joined the procession as it headed back up the mountain to the pilgrimage church.[48] The saints' welcome, however, was just beginning.

Once atop the hill, the procession made its way through an "alley" of forty trees leading to the cloister doors, which were decorated with emblems. One very large emblem depicted not only the saints from Hohenpeißenberg but eight martyrs whose bodies rested at the cloister church in Rottenbuch, about eight miles away.[49] This company of saints came to life shortly thereafter on a stage set up in front of the church's facade. With the bodies of Wenceslaus, Gaudentius, and Clara placed, the eight Rottenbuch martyrs welcomed their new companions in an hourlong "Begrüßungs-Action" (salutation play). As the play drew to a close, the Hohenpeißenberg and Rottenbuch saints made an "eternal alliance and union" between Rottenbuch and Hohenpeißenberg with the approval and power of Mary and Jesus, who also promised their constant protection for both places.[50] Using actors, images, and the holy bodies themselves, the festival planners and playwrights in Hohenpeißenberg created a coterie of heavenly intercessors dedicated to protecting a small patch of the Bavarian countryside.

The transition from guest to permanent resident took its most dramatic form in longer plays written for the arrival of the saints and staged at the end of the procession. Actors playing older medieval patrons, angels, or even the role of local parishioner or pilgrim appeared in the welcome plays. They often voiced a degree of curiosity about how the Roman saint had ended up in Germany. In 1750, pilgrims from the Marian sodality in Munich who had traveled to Rome for the Jubilee year returned, having obtained the body of Saint Maximus for their public chapel. The saint's large and elaborate translation procession ended at the town center on the Marienplatz, where a stage had been erected. The confraternity staged a play to introduce the new "welcome guest" to the city and its church. The cast included the guardian angel of the Marian Congregation; the Archangel Raphael, who had accompanied the Bavarian pilgrims on their journey to Rome and back; Saint Maximus; and two of the pilgrims from the sodality. To begin, the guardian angel asked the saint what his name was, where he was from, and why he had come to Bavaria. Saint Maximus replied that he had been sent to Bavaria from Rome, where he had originally rested, and that he was a martyr who had been killed due to his confession of Christianity. He told the congregation to take his body—which rested near the stage—to its church and display it on the altar, promising that he, along with the Blessed Virgin Mary, would safeguard their flock and dispel any dangers. He also asked the members of the sodality to take him as a patron saint, saying that if they accepted him, he would faithfully serve them. The guardian angel of the congregation, played by another actor, replied that the congregation considered it the greatest of honors that he had traveled to them and then invited him to come and take up "your quarters in my palace."[51] Two congregation members, playing pilgrims, then invited Maximus to come and see his new place of rest, promising to accompany him to the church. They told the saint that the congregation had his new "home" all ready and that his blood and bones would be their treasure, comfort, and wealth forever. In the grand finale, Maximus promised that he would always remain the patron of the congregation.

Though the Marian sodality and its guardian angel welcomed Maximus with open arms, in other dramatic introductions local medieval patrons expressed much more skepticism about the saintly strangers arriving in their midst. In 1688, the Bridgettine cloister at Altomünster received the first two of its nine catacomb saints. For the occasion, Prior Simon Hörmann wrote a play dramatizing the initial encounter between the cloister's eighth-century founder and guardian, Saint Alto, and a pair of new catacomb saints, Maximian and Alexander. To begin, an actor playing Alto took to the outdoor stage and addressed the crowd, reminding them that he had protected the cloister and surrounding area from all dangers for more than one thousand years. He told them that he had come outside on this particular day because he had heard loud shooting—the celebratory gunfire that began the translation festivities—and wanted to know if the cloister was in danger from enemies.[52]

At that moment, actors playing Saints Maximian and Alexander walked onstage. Spotting the Roman martyrs, Alto demanded to know who they were, where they had come from, what they were doing in his "fatherland,"

and if they had come in peace. Both martyrs, in turn, explained that they were once soldiers in Rome, but that they had been killed because of their Christian beliefs.[53] Astonished by both of these answers, and seemingly still a bit suspicious of their motives, Alto continued to pepper the martyrs with questions: "You were both important people and both Roman citizens, why did you not stay there? People there would have given you more honor than we can show here."[54] Unfazed, Maximian replied: "Indeed, Rome is a noble place, but we had to hurry from there because our highest general Christ has given us an order to go to Altomünster and find our rest here." Still unconvinced, Alto replied: "No soldier is sent out without his passport, were you all provided with proof? Let me see it!"[55] At this point in the action, an actor playing the Roman church and wearing the papal tiara brought out the saints' authentication certificates from Rome and the bishop in Freising. After the reading of the authentication certificates, Alto's skepticism began to soften, though he had a few last questions for the saints: "What are you going to do here? Do you want to stay here forever?"[56] The saints responded enthusiastically, with Alexander reiterating that they "came to this place so that we can protect it forever more." They then asked Alto to take them into his "company" and into his church, where their bodies could rest together. Alto consented to their requests, responding: "I will grant you your wishes, you are one-thousand times welcome noble Alexander, pious and beloved Maximian; with this kiss, I adopt you all. Come here, you all shall be my knights."[57] With this traditional gesture of homage between lord and vassal, the two catacomb saints pledged loyalty not only to Alto but to the Altomünster community, adopting the language and gestures used to create the relationship of military fealty.

After formalizing their relationship, Alto invited the martyrs into his domain with a short poem: "Follow me! Come I will show you the resting place that you all, as most beloved friends, will occupy. It is decorated with lots of gold . . . as is fitting for such heroes. Come here, I will lead you there!"[58] Amid the sound of muskets firing and the clanging of the church bells, "a very beautiful procession" carried the two holy bodies along with an image of Saint Alto into the cloister church and where the holy bodies were placed together on the main altar.[59] Though they retained their Roman heritage, over the course of the play the catacomb saints had transitioned from potentially threatening outsiders to members of Alto's honor guard sworn to protect the cloister and surrounding town. The dramatization of this interaction vividly demonstrated the incorporation of the new holy residents into the group of local heavenly patrons for the thousands gathered for the translation festivities.

Six years later, Hörmann composed another play for the arrival of three additional catacomb saints: Victoria and Fortunatus, a pair of twin child martyrs, and the matron Mercuria. Saint Alto reprised his role as the guardian of the cloister.[60] The twins, Victoria and Fortunatus, were introduced by their mother, Fabia, whose body still rested in Rome. Fabia explained she had traveled with the young pair to Altomünster but could not stay, and she pled with Alto to take in her two children.[61] Saint Fortunatus and Saint Victoria themselves then approached Saint Alto to ask if he would be their father and accept them into his home.[62] Alto granted both twins their wish. He told them: "Come my beloved Fortunatus. You have my promise that you and Victoria will stay with me. I will always be your father, and you will be my son and daughter. You are truly accepted and a thousand times welcome."[63]

After this encounter, Hörmann was not finished creating familial ties between the new saints. Once Alto had adopted the twins, Fabia asked one more favor of Saint Alto, saying that since she could not stay in Altomünster, she wanted the third catacomb saint, Mercuria, to serve as the children's mother.[64] The twins happily agreed to this arrangement, and by the end of the play Altomünster had become home to a new family of saints.[65] In this particular play, Hörmann created more than a community of saints; he created a holy family that resided in the cloister church. These relationships helped to immediately enmesh the Roman saints into a heavenly kinship network, whose head was the very familiar Saint Alto. Alto's acceptance of the saints into his family indicated to the assembled crowd that they, too, should welcome these former interlopers into their local set of patrons. This act of welcome was made all the more concrete for onlookers through the use of actors and the presence of catacomb saints' bodies. As in the processions, those in attendance could not only see the bodies of the saints themselves but also witness actors taking on their personas being integrated seamlessly into the local heavenly pantheon by other long-standing patrons.

In addition to becoming members of a group of local patrons, catacomb saints were also embedded in local earthly communities during the translation festivities, as preachers and playwrights established communal, familial, and historical ties between the residents of Bavarian towns and villages and their newest inhabitants. In sermons and songs, the saints were commonly referred to as citizens (*Bürger*),[66] neighbors (*Nachbar*),[67] and friends (*Freund*).[68] When Saint Amantius arrived in Frontenhausen, Jordanus von Wasserburg described the saint as a "local inhabitant" and later as a truly "truly blessed citizen" of the town.[69] By using terms like these, clerics reinforced the notion of the saint's belonging and presence within a very specific community. They also implied—through the use of the word "citizen"—that these new residents had certain obligations within the community as well as to their fellow residents.

While saints in parish and cloister churches became integral parts of their local communities as neighbors and friends, saints in noble chapels took up residence in private, family homes and were understood as new members of the household. Such a living arrangement occurred at *Wasserschloss* at Taufkirchen. In 1694, the von Puech family welcomed Saint Victor into their home chapel, where the lady of the house, Maria Adelheidis, was reported to be happy to have such a "steward and inhabitant in her house" (fig. 4).[70] At translations at the palaces of Pfettrach and Poxau, Wasserburg portrayed the new saints as members of each noble family. At Pfettrach, the Capuchin told Freiherr von Mändl, the "aristocratic housefather," that he could take Saint Felicissimus "as a son into his home."[71] Through this adoption, the Freiherr von Mändl not only gained a son, but Saint Felicissimus became part of "a whole house, and entire aristocratic family."[72] With this declaration, a once-foreign Roman martyr—whose body rested in the private chapel—was placed squarely on the von Mändl family tree to be treated as a son and relative.

Wasserburg's enthusiasm for integrating newly arrived catacomb saints into families was also on display at the 1709 transfer of Saint Julia to the chapel of the von Frauenhofen family at Poxau. Rather than a son, Wasserburg told the audience that "the most generous heavenly father wanted not only to give our baronial lordship St. Julia's relics for veneration, but also to give him the saint as a desired heir and spiritual daughter."[73] Saint Julia's relics were not given to the family as inanimate objects for safekeeping. Instead, the von Frauenhofens received a "spiritual daughter and an heir," a living and longed-for member of their household. The establishment of such a personal relationship between relics and the noble families housing them was facilitated by the presence of the saints' complete bodies. In order to be integrated into a family, a saint had to be perceived as a *person*, a task that was accomplished by the arrangement of his or her relics into a complete skeleton.

Beyond integration into families and local communities, festival planners and playwrights created relationships between newly arrived catacomb saints and important local historical figures. At Beuerberg, the arrival of the catacomb saints was presented as part of a longer play on the history of the cloister. In the sixth act, which covered the years from 1600 to 1725, the catacomb saints Claudius and Bonifacius appear onstage and interact with brothers Otto and Conrad, Counts of Iringsburg—two of the founders of the cloister—as well as the cloister's first provost, Heinrich.[74] In these exchanges, the saints are brought to life and converse with the foundational figures in the cloister's history. Much like the new saints' interactions with older saints in welcoming plays, the acceptance of the saints by such authority figures within the history of the cloister and the area—as well as their embodied interactions on

Ven: BOSO
Clericus, pri
mus Funda.
tor et Præpo
situs Monast
Garsensis.
MONASTERII GARSEN„
SIS Ord: Canonicorum Regular:
S. AVGVSTINI posita sunt Primordia
circa An: Dñi DCCLXVIII.
THASSILO
III. Bojorum
Dux censi-
bus et prae-
diis auxit·

FIGURE 45. Painting of Gars cloister with patron saints and founders, after 1675. (Photograph by Father Anton Dimpflmaier; courtesy of Father Anton Dimpflmaier)

stage—tied the martyrs to the foundation story of the cloister and included the saints in integral local historical events.[75] While the saints had been integrated into the universal history of the Roman Church in their constructed hagiographies, the inverse could also occur as translation plays embedded the saints into the history of particular Bavarian towns and villages.

The historical bonds between catacomb saints and their heavenly and earthly communities were further reinforced and reflected in artwork commissioned by Bavarian churches. One painting that now hangs in the refectory of the cloister at Gars displays these multiple bonds. The cloister founders—the cleric Boso and Bavarian duke Tassilo III (r. 748–96 CE)—hold a small model of the cloister church between them. Directly under the church is an image of the cloister buildings and the town of Gars when the painting was executed in the eighteenth century (fig. 45). Above is a company of the town's protectors, including the Virgin Mary along with Saint Radegundis, to whom the cloister was dedicated. Just below Radegundis sits Saint Felix wearing the outfit of a Roman martyr and carrying both a palm frond and a vase of his sacrificial blood. Within decades, this Roman outsider had not only become wholly integrated into the long-standing group of local patron saints but was also tied historically to the town and cloister's earliest history.

Like many other Bavarian catacomb saints, Felix began the journey to his position as part of the heavenly coterie protecting the cloister of Gars at an elaborate translation into town in 1675. During these festivities, whole-body Roman catacomb saints completed their rite of passage from unknown foreigner to cherished citizen and protector of communities across the Electorate. The perception of catacomb saints as people rather than objects spurred festival organizers to modify long-standing traditions in the rituals associated with the arrival of relics. Personified in their remains as well as by actors, the arriving saints were brought fully to life before the eyes of the faithful, who rushed by the thousands to welcome the ancient martyrs to their towns. Using processions and dramatic performances, preachers and playwrights established familial, communal, and historical relationships between local communities and the foreign saints, quickly converting them from outsiders to beloved neighbors, friends and kin. In the years and decades after their arrival, catacomb saints continued to serve as trusted local patrons whose shrines were visited by pilgrims and supplicants asking for help and protection with many challenges of early modern life.

6

Roman Catacomb Saints as Local Residents and Patrons

As THE translation festivities welcoming Saint Amantius began to wind down in 1708, Capuchin Jordanus von Wasserburg told the assembled faithful that "[the saint] has risen from his grave gloriously and has appeared to give them comfort in Frontenhausen." This noble Roman, brave martyr and heavenly knight, Wasserburg continued, was "now corporeally here and wants to live with you all."[1] Wasserburg's emphasis on Amantius's bodily presence in Frontenhausen and his future role as patron foreshadowed the significant impact the whole-body reliquary form had on how catacomb saints functioned in a local religious environment.

Since the fourth century, saints had been understood to reside in the churches—their *domus* (home)—where their bodily relics lay. Catacomb saints embodied and materialized this concept in a new and concrete manner.[2] Instead of fragments of bones encased in reliquaries that could be easily taken on and off display, catacomb saint shrines were integrated into baroque altars and became permanent fixtures within churches across the Electorate. These were not the "invisible friends" described by early Christian writers like the theologian Theodoret (393–457 CE) when discussing the presence of saints within a church.[3] Rather they were *visible* friends, who could be easily approached and seen within the sacred space of Bavarian churches. The saints' typical placement on side altars made them particularly accessible to lay worshippers, where they could serve as identifiably human role models for Christian behavior as well as sources of comfort and protection for individuals and the community at large.

The presence of their whole bodies at one site also had a significant impact on the traditional role of saints as patrons and protectors, simultaneously concentrating and limiting their power. Catacomb saints inverted the concept of *pars pro toto,* in which a small part of the saint stood in for the whole. Through division, a saint's body could be present at multiple locations at the same time. This was not the case for the holy bodies of catacomb saints, which were not scattered across Europe and beyond in tiny fragments but present in a single locale. As a result, catacomb saints became extremely local patrons who had a special relationship to the one and only place their bodies lay. In sermons, they were conceived of as patrons of a single church, community, or area—not the territory at large. The veneration patterns that developed for catacomb saints in the decades after their translation—evident in pilgrimage accounts, *ex voto* gifts, miracle books, parish baptismal records, and town patronage—reflect how this understanding of the role of catacomb saints played out in practice. Though catacomb saints did tie Bavarian churches to the Roman church and materially embodied core Catholic doctrines, these foreign saints were also quickly adopted and embedded within a localized religious culture that was far from universal. Because their bodily remains were concentrated in one place, the saint formed an exclusive bond of a single heavenly and earthly community. This resulted in the development of extremely local cults, as early modern Bavarians carved out small, particular devotional microclimates within the larger landscape of Bavaria sancta.

Saints Living in the Church

After members of the heavenly and earthly communities of a town or village had greeted and adopted catacomb saints during translation processions, their shimmering skeletons were installed atop or within side altars in cloister, parish, and pilgrimage churches across Bavaria. The belief in the "presence of an invisible person" (*praesentia*) had drawn people to churches to visit saints' relics from the earliest period of Christianity, when relics were buried out of sight.[4] Though relics had become more visually accessible over the course of the medieval period, the arrival and staging of catacomb saints in glass shrines on or within altars represented a major shift in the type of holy remains Bavarians encountered. Smaller reliquaries could be moved on and off view and required viewers to make an imaginative leap from a small bone fragment to a full human body. Conversely, catacomb saints were a constant and corporeal presence within baroque churches who permanently inhabited their *domus.*

For early modern Bavarians, the visibility of whole-body catacomb saints within the sacred space of the church was of utmost import and critical to their ability to function as holy helpers. Again and again, sources relating to catacomb saints—sermons, festival accounts, the text of devotional images—mention the display of the bodies and emphasize how they lay directly before the eyes of worshippers in a specific community. Vision—above all other senses—was of paramount importance when it came to encountering the holy bodies. During a translation sermon in Ranshofen in 1699, Bonfacius Kranz acknowledged the power of objects—like the bodies of catacomb saints—to awaken faith. He said that "of all creatures," humans were the most moved and affected by "the appearance, shape, form and sight of external things."[5]

Kranz's estimation of the spiritual value of *seeing* the holy bodies in their shrines is apparent in sources from the very beginning of their introduction to new communities—even before the saints reached altars inside churches. Festival book authors repeatedly note the visibility of the holy bodies during translation processions. In a list of the procession order for Saint Asterius to the Ursuline cloister in Straubing in 1697, the writer notes that the saint was "lying in a high, beautiful, luxurious and artistic shrine with transparent glass, through which he can be seen by everyone."[6] At Steingaden, Saint Beninus's bones were "very visible through the glass."[7] Indeed, it was the desire to see the saint in person that, according to Maximilian Emanuel Kurz at Sandizell in 1769, was a motivating factor for the "countless crowd of devout souls from the nearby cities, markets, hamlets and villages" who had come to the translation festivities.[8]

Once the saints were translated into a church, they did not disappear from view but, rather, took up permanent and highly visible residence in their new homes. At Poxau, Wasserburg repeatedly reminded the audience throughout his sermon that the holy bodies "lie here before our eyes."[9] At Burgrain, Gelasius Hochenleutner noted that "we have received the body of the holy martyr Albert from God to venerate publicly."[10] The emphasis on public display echoes the text of the authentication certificates, which generally contained a clause requiring the public exhibition of the relics.[11] This accorded with a papal bull issued by Pope Clement X in 1672 concerning the regulation, excavation, and distribution of catacomb saint relics. One of the major points of the bull stated that whole bodies or important relics such as heads, shins, or arm bones should not be kept in private buildings but in churches where they were accessible to the worshippers.[12]

For Kranz and his fellow clerics, the very efficacy of the holy bodies rested on early modern Bavarians' ability to *see* them. In his sermon for the translation of Felicissimus at Pfettrach, Wasserburg asked the crowd: "Of what use were they, when the beloved saints were hidden in Rome in their graves and crypts, and remained invisible? How could the faithful, especially here in Germany, get any use from them?"[13] Buried in the catacombs, the saints were hidden from view and therefore could not be venerated. By excavating the remains from the catacombs and transferring them to Bavaria, the Roman church had brought the "dead bodies of the holy martyrs back to life; now they can begin a new life with the pious people, who will venerate and honor them."[14]

Many catacomb saints in Bavaria began their "new lives" on side altars in baroque churches across the Electorate, a placement that made them accessible, approachable, and, above all, visible to worshippers. According to Tridentine reform measures, church interiors were supposed to be laid out to serve the needs of laypeople rather than solely oriented to the activities of the clergy.[15] Though the high altar and the choir became more visible through the removal of large choir screens, these areas were still set off from the rest of the church by steps and low railings, and entry was reserved for clergy or monks.[16] In contrast, side altars were meant for individual prayer and contemplation and were spaces that were much more accessible to the general public.[17] The placement of most catacomb saints in or on such side altars made them easier to approach at close range than many of the relics in the medieval period, which had often been stored in sacristies or placed on or near the high altar.[18] These large shrines could not simply be moved on and off display periodically for feast days or particular liturgical seasons; they were permanent parts of the altars themselves.[19] As a result, whole-body catacomb saints physically inhabited their *domus* in a prominent manner where they were no longer "hidden treasures in the graveyard" but, like Saint Lucius at St. Veit, became a "light on the altar," where he could "shine his graceful radiance on all those who will pleadingly ask [for help]."[20]

The intention to permanently showcase the bodies and shrines of catacomb saints inside Bavarian churches is evident in surviving blueprints for new altars and altarpieces, often created for the renovation of monasteries and convents. Extant designs for altars at the Angerkloster in Munich and for the cloister at Weyarn demonstrate how artists and builders made catacomb saint shrines integral—and immoveable—components in their schematics. A pen-and-ink drawing of a design for a new side altar at the Angerkloster (1738) depicts how catacomb saint shrines were placed front and center at the eye level of a supplicant (fig. 46). The saint's shrine is physically and stylistically integrated into the overall design of the altar ensemble with the intricate carved framing around the holy body echoed by the filigree décor around the frame of the future altar painting. The design is a small *Gesamtkunstwerk*, and its focal point is the future home of a Roman holy body. Ignaz Günther's sketch for a new altarpiece, commissioned by the cloister church of Weyarn in 1755, provides another example of how catacomb saint bodies were included in altar plans. Saint Valerius's glazed shrine is fully integrated into the overall design scheme as an essential part of the altarpiece (fig. 30). Statues of angels sit atop it and gesture upward to larger statues of the Maria Dolorosa and the crucified Christ. Valerius's shrine provides the base on which the rest of the altar was built; it was not meant to be portable or stored out of sight but on constant display.

The permanent and visible presence of these saints upon altars helped perpetuate their influence beyond initial translation celebrations and the yearly

FIGURE 46. Pen-and-ink drawing of a design for a new altar with a catacomb saint shrine at the St. Jakob am Anger cloister, Munich, 1738. (Bayerisches Hauptstaatsarchiv, Plansammlung 19366)

events held on their feast days. At a sermon to celebrate the renovation of the Augsburg Kollegiatstiftskirche St. Mauritius in 1760, Jesuit Ignatius Bonschab discussed the significance of having relics present on altars:

> On the altars . . . [there are relics and images] so that everyone can see what cannot always be heard: that which a person must do and suffer in order to reach heaven as a friend of God. Living preachers, even if they are the best at their art, do not preach to every person, at all times or always in a divine manner. But the saints on their altars, and in their images, preach to everyone at the same time without hindrance and without respect to their station. They preach without stopping to every person without a single flaw.[21]

According to Bonschab, the bodies of the saints spoke for themselves and did not need to be interpreted or framed by the words of a mortal preacher. By placing them on side altars, early modern Bavarians gave catacomb saints a stage from which they could "speak" throughout the year and where a person in need of help could find an intercessor, exemplar, and patron without clerical mediation.

Though typically visible year-round, in some churches, customs varied with regard to how long and how often catacomb saint bodies were displayed or covered. The periodic display of relics was not a new phenomenon in the early modern era. Despite the ever-increasing pressure from the public to see relics during the medieval period, relics were often only exhibited on feast days, during Mass, or at relic shows (*Heiltumschauen*). Likewise, in certain churches, catacomb saint shrines were only open on certain feast days or during specific seasons of the year. At the Altomünster cloister church, the traditions concerning the display of holy bodies varied even within the church itself. Five saints of the cloister's nine saints are hidden behind altar paintings on the main altar and the choir area. To this day, these saints are traditionally visible only on All Saints' Day, when the paintings that cover them are lowered into recesses built into the altar frames. In the nave of the same church, however, Saints Maximilian and Sebastian are on constant display on side altars. Additionally, the amount of time a holy body was visible throughout the year was sometimes contingent on the demands of the donor who had procured the relics. At St. Peter's parish church in Munich, the Höck family requested that Saint Honoratus's remains be displayed only on feast days.[22]

Although some churches only displayed the holy bodies periodically during the year, the relics did not disappear fully from the church space. Frequently, custom-fitting, painted wooden or linen covers for the front of the shrines revealed almost as much as they hid.[23] Two types of images appear on surviving shrine covers (*Verschlußtafel*) from the Electorate.[24] The first type is a "skeleton portrait," which depicts the relics hidden just behind it in exact detail.[25] The painted wooden *Verschlußtafel* made for Saint Theodor at the pilgrimage church of Maria Brünnlein, today mounted next to the shrine, portrays the holy body in meticulous detail. Theodor's skeleton sits upright holding a martyr's palm, blood ampule, and instrument of martyrdom (cudgel). The artist has very carefully painted the saint's pink cuirass and white-and-green skirt, as well as his sandals. The saint's skull, ribs, arms, and leg bones peek through the decoration, and the *Klosterarbeit* is correct down to the wire flowers on the saint's neck, shoulders, elbows, wrists, and knees. Had worshippers visited on a day when the shrine was not open, they would have seen a faithful representation of the contents of the shrine itself, reminding

FIGURE 47. Shrine cover for Saint Justus, Marienberg pilgrimage church, 1762. (Photograph by Uta Ludwig; courtesy of Pfarrverband Burghausen)

them of the constant presence of the saint's whole body in the church. The four shrine covers for Felix, Justus, Prosper, and Vinzentius at the Marienberg pilgrimage church present similar skeletal portraits (fig. 47). In this case, the images of the saints' remains were painted on canvas panels that hung on a dowel affixed to the top of the shrine; when turned, the dowel rolled up the skeletal portraits to reveal the bodies behind the paintings.[26]

A second type of *Verschlußtafel* image showed a portrait of the saint within the shrine as a human, typically dressed as Roman martyr. At Waldsassen, four shrine covers survive for standing catacomb saints Gratianus, Maximinus, Vitalianus, and Viktorius, who still stand on altars in the church's crossing (fig. 48). All four panels show the saints as protectors hovering over the cloister and the small surrounding village as they rise toward heaven. They, like their skeletal counterparts, are dressed as Roman legionary soldiers. At Niederalteich, each of the cloister's five catacomb saints were provided with shrine covers that presented portraits of the catacomb saints as living people. In this case, each painting depicts the saints in positions that mirror those of the relics behind—lying, with hands propping up their heads—staring out at the visitors. No matter the style—all of these paintings indicated to the viewer what was directly behind the images in the shrines—a complete saintly body. Even in cases where a holy body might not be visible at all times, these images constantly reminded—rather than obfuscated—the saint's constant presence within their church *domus*.

Whether the catacomb saints were covered by painted shrine covers or visible behind large panes of glass, worshippers across Bavaria were able to visit the ones living in their churches in times of need. Sermons instructed

FIGURE 48. Shrine cover for standing catacomb saint at Waldsassen cloister, Stiftlandmuseum Waldsassen, eighteenth century. (Photograph by author)

visitors on how to approach the catacomb saints. In all cases, the visibility of the saint's body as well as access—visual and physical—to their altar is emphasized. At Sandizell in 1768, Kurz described the catacomb saints Maximus and Clemens as fountains and told the audience to "pour out your sorrowful heart with all trust at the altar of our two saints."[27] Kurz's statement implies that the saints were placed on altars that would be accessible to laypeople. Furthermore, several devotional images of catacomb saints include prayers that explicitly mention and assume the worshipper's presence before the saint's body. The prayer printed on the *Andachtsbild* produced for Saint Amantius at Frontenhausen includes the phrase, "I worship you before your holy body, in which you suffered pain and martyrdom."[28] Another devotional image of Saint Victor at Taufkirchen includes identical wording, which indicates the understanding—at least on the part of these prayers' authors—that the venerator would be able to stand directly in front of the saint, viewing the holy body without impediment.[29] Access to the saints was an essential component in the process of asking for intercession and could be easily accomplished by a person who sought to visit the saint in their residence.

A miracle report from the Angerkloster in Munich records just such an incident. In October 1736, Johann Anthony Ignatius Barbier—a member of the Bavarian Privy Council and a mayor of Munich—testified that fifteen years previously he had suffered from bad headaches, exhaustion, and weakness. The pain was so bad he could not perform or even understand his duties and several times wished to die. One night, he fell asleep and dreamed that he was in the Angerkloster's church before an altar with a holy body and that the saint helped relieve his suffering. The next morning, he got up and asked his servant if there was a holy body in the Angerkloster. His servant did not know of any and said that in the eight years he had worked for Barbier, they had never visited the church. Barbier dressed quickly and hurried to the Angerkloster in search of the mysterious saint. As soon as he entered, he saw the holy body on an altar in the same form and shape that it had appeared in his dream. Barbier fell to his knees before his saint, read the name plate on the reliquary, and discovered his intercessor's name was Eleutheria. He directed his prayers to her and vowed to visit her monthly for devotion and to give a small donation of alms in her honor. From that moment, he was freed from his pain.[30] Barbier's dream of the altar and his recognition of Eleutheria's altar as soon as he entered the cloister church indicate that the saint's relics were visible on the altar.

Barbier's experience as well as the text on prayer cards suggest that in the seventeenth and eighteenth centuries, a majority of the holy bodies were visually and physically accessible to visitors and not hidden by external covers. Itemized receipts from Dingolfing, Freising (St. Georg), Frontenhausen, Habach, Indersdorf, and Munich (Pütrichkloster) that list all items associated with the construction of the catacomb saints and their shrines also support this conclusion. None of the receipts include costs associated with the commission of a shrine cover or the materials needed to create one. Descriptions of the altars built for catacomb saints at Donauwörth, Munich-Bürgersaal, Raitenhaslach, and Vornbach also make no mention of shrine covers. The visibility and access to the bodies of catacomb saints within the sacred space of Bavarian churches represented the culmination of the *Schaufrömmigkeit* (visual piety) that began to affect relic display beginning in the Middle Ages.

Once only visible through small openings, the embodied remains of saints now rested on altars in transparent shrines waiting for petitioners in need of aid to visit them.[31]

Catacomb Saints as Human Role Models

When supplicants like Barbier approached the side altars where *heilige Leiber* rested, what they saw was qualitatively different than the particle relics. Whole-body catacomb saints were *recognizably* human. They were not pieces of a human—a small bit of vertebrae or a lone finger separate from a larger whole. Nor were they like the universally venerated and familiar saints like those listed in the *Golden Legend* or commonly depicted in panel paintings and sculptures in Catholic iconography. A church might or might not have a small relic of one of these saints, like Lawrence, Sebastian, or Catherine of Alexandria, but none of these saints were physically present or staged in the same manner as catacomb saints were. They were aspirational, almost mythical examples. Catacomb saints were concrete and present, their humanity unmistakable due to their presentation as intact skeletons. *Klosterarbeit* provided them with eyes, mouths, and noses. They had arms, legs, and wore clothes. They stared through the glass at their equally human counterparts.

This immediate and perceptible humanity made the catacomb saints easier to emulate, for they had once been simple believers just like those who stood before their shrines in baroque Bavaria. Preachers urged their flocks to look at these bodies not as exalted, distant paragons of ideal Christian behavior but as humans like themselves, who had endured bodily and emotional hardship with patience and steadfast belief. Wasserburg underscored this point during his sermon for the translation of Saint Julia to Poxau in 1709: "It is amazing for us men, how much power the good example of another pious and virtuous man before our eyes can have. A preacher can speak as brilliantly as he could wish, but [Julia] will teach far more with silence. Because, according to the old saying: *Verba movent, exempla trahunt,* words move people, examples compel them."[32] Later in the sermon, Wasserburg once again emphasized the close connection between the physical presence of a martyr's body and its exemplary power for the faithful. He told the assembled crowd: "It is necessary to place the holy martyrs before the eyes of men in order to remind them how strong and noble the martyrs were in the face of extreme persecution. These martyrs, like us, were also made from flesh and bone."[33] Rather than lofty images of the calendar saints, the bodies of catacomb saints were tangible, concrete role models available for ordinary visitors in local parish, cloister, and pilgrimage churches. By viewing a body much like their own, early modern

Bavarians were "especially reminded what and how much the holy martyrs suffered and withstood for the love of their God."[34]

Though they frequently praised the sacrifices of the early martyrs, the preachers at the catacomb saint translation sermons did not expect those in attendance to die for their faith. After the Peace of Westphalia stabilized confessional borders in Europe in 1648, the prospect of execution for religious reasons became a more distant prospect for Catholics across the continent, including those in Bavaria. Instead, catacomb saint martyrs became "models for Christian living, if not necessarily patterns for dying."[35] Clerics encouraged their congregants to pursue a "white martyrdom"—patiently enduring hardship, difficulties, and illnesses—and to use these visible martyrs as an "edifying high example" on the path to a virtuous Christian life.[36] At the translation of Saint Albert to Burgrain in 1723, Gelasius Hochenleutner explained to his listeners that there were "two kinds of martyrs—public ones who are killed for beliefs and private ones who persist in belief despite all hardships." He assured his audience that "God rewards private martyrs as well." Hochenleutner then urged his flock to look to Saint Albert as a model during their everyday trials: "Oh beloved Christians! The body of the holy martyr Albert lies before our eyes. And we also see so many arenas and events in this miserable life, which we can face by following him in his bravery."[37] Later in the sermon, he once again returned to this point: "I should be delighted that the relics of saint Albert lead us, like a burning light, on the path to wisdom. They clearly and brightly instruct us that—even if we cannot succeed in becoming bloody martyrs for God—at least we can follow him bravely in patient tolerance of our hardships."[38] Hochenleutner's message of fortitude in the face of misfortune was echoed by other preachers who listed illness, crop failure, drought, hunger, and even unhappy marriages as trials their listeners should endure patiently, using catacomb saints as their example. For as Andreas von Sancta Theresia noted in his translation sermon for Saint Beninus in 1695, such persistence would be richly rewarded—as the audience could see by looking at the body of the lavishly decorated martyr.[39]

The martyrs' names, in addition to the prospect of rich heavenly rewards, could even be pressed into service to encourage a positive disposition in the face of crisis. At the transfer of Saint Hilarius to the pilgrimage church at Maria Thalheim, the festival preacher—playing on the Latin meaning of *hilarius*—urged those in attendance to be "cheerful and happy in the service of God," just as their new patron had been. He elaborated, saying that "at all times, even in times of pain and martyrdom, the martyr's face is cheerful and light-hearted. Our faces should also be that way, and we should learn this point from our St. Hilarius . . . when we see his martyred body, we should happily follow him."[40] The saints' function as human role models, reinforced during translation sermons, lasted far beyond their initial arrival. Permanent fixtures, they remained on altars serving as examples of patience, fortitude, and steadfastness to their fellow human believers.

Catacomb Saints as Local Patrons and Intercessors

In addition to serving as embodied role models for Bavarian Catholics, catacomb saints' bodily concentration in a single location also had an important impact on their function as patrons and shaped the veneration patterns that developed around them in local communities in the decades and centuries after translations. Since the early period of Christianity, church theologians asserted that the souls of saints in heaven had a special connection with their bodily remains on earth and the communities that possessed these relics. Evodio Nieberle reminded the crowd at Ranshofen in 1699 that "the blessed souls [of saints] still long for a part of their once suffering bodies; therefore, they cannot take their eyes off of their relics and finally from the place—this cloister church—where they rest."[41] Since their entire bodies were in one place rather than scattered in fragments, Marius's and Coelestinus's could focus on a single location from their perch in heaven.

The undivided attention of this pair of saints, Nieberle implied, would also result in exceptional protection for the Ranshofen community. Nieberle's assertions were based on the traditional Catholic belief that saints provided protection for the town or church in which their relics were housed. At Poxau, Wasserburg quoted Archbishop Charles Borromeo, who stated that relics were "solid doors, the strongest redoubts and ramparts of those cities and countries, indeed in all the places, where they are kept and venerated."[42] In Frontenhausen, Wasserburg further emphasized to the town the importance of possessing relics, explaining that "our saint Amantius is . . . precious before God in heaven, precious to men on earth, and especially precious in this church to the pious parishioners of this lucky place."[43] Like the saints at Ranshofen, Amantius's attention was not split among multiple locations due to bodily dispersal. He was free to focus solely on protecting Frontenhausen and its inhabitants.

At Taufkirchen, Michael Angelus Hochenzoll dramatized the special relationship between a saint and the place where his remains rested by conducting a conversation with Saint Victor about his exclusive connection with the community. Hochenzoll asked Victor, "Could it be, blessed Victor—you, who are glorified and venerated in heaven and on earth—could forget or will forget us here?" Victor replied, "Far from it!" Hochenzoll then expounded further on Victor's answer: "No one should imagine that Victor would not embrace us in our hardships; the theologians say that the saints in heaven pay special attention to those places in the world where their holy bodies and relics rest, especially where they are venerated with appropriate honor; those places are freed from divine punishment through their manifold intercession(s)."[44] Thus, with backing from church fathers and the saint himself, Taufkirchen's inhabitants were assured that they had a patron devoted exclusively to protecting them and their local community.

The exclusivity of the relationship between a whole-body catacomb saint and his or her resting place in Bavaria was further intensified by deploying and amplifying an older hagiographical trope in which a saint actively chose where to "live." In miracle stories and vitae, saints expressed the desire to have their earthly remains moved to another location in visions or via independent movements.[45] The presence of whole-body relics allowed this literary conceit to be brought to life in a vivid manner and had important consequences when it came to the relationship between a community and its new patron. To begin with, a saint's preference to reside in a community—when they could have picked anywhere else to be—singled out the community in a very flattering manner. Of all the places in the world, these saints chose—in many cases—to live in a small village or cloister in rural Bavaria. This decision alone helped to establish a relationship between a new saint and his or her new home; it gained further significance because the martyr's entire body was in a particular place.

Preachers emphasized that a saint had selected a particular community above all others for his or her final resting place. In Erding, "the holy martyr Placidus himself chose Bavaria, and *this* village, from thousands of other places as his resting place."[46] According to the devotional booklet printed after his arrival, Saint Antoninus in Landshut made a similar decision: "He no longer wanted to be in Italy, but rather in Germany; namely he wanted to rest and stay with the virgins at [the convent of] Seligenthal."[47] It was not always preachers who reported a saint's desire to reside in a community to audiences present for translation festivities. Using creative dialogue, the saints themselves were brought to life and expressed their fervent wishes to live in a town or village in the Electorate. In sermons at Raitenhaslach and Ranshofen, catacomb saints told the audiences—paraphrasing several lines of Psalm 131—"This is my resting place. I want to live here because I have chosen it."[48] For the translation of Saints Innocentius and Clemens to Rottenbuch in 1710, the same verse appeared on a large shield attached to a large, temporary double arch erected for the translation.[49] Whatever the medium, in sermon or through artwork, the message that Roman martyrs had actively selected to leave their resting places in the catacombs for Bavaria was repeatedly woven into arrival ceremonies.

Preachers further animated these saints' decisions by connecting a saint's choice of place to physical, bodily movement. At both Amberg and Pfettrach, preachers related a miraculous story about King Casimir II of Poland (r. 1177–90) and Pope Lucius III (r. 1181–85).[50] According to legend, King Casimir had requested saintly relics, and the pope went into the catacombs to fulfill the request. Once underground, Pope Lucius jokingly asked which saints wanted to go to Poland. To his surprise, several corpses sat up and raised their hands. Wasserburg told this story in Pfettrach and asked his audience, "Why shouldn't we think that saint Felicissimus, when the question was posed, 'which saint wants to go to Bavaria?' answered . . . 'I want to go, I want to make Bavaria my home'?"[51] Here, Felicissimus is brought vividly to life, and his ability to sit up and signal his desire to go to Bavaria is predicated on the presence of whole body, not a smaller fragment. The saints' physically demonstrated desire to move to another location is yet another example of how Bavarian preachers were able to personify catacomb saints in new ways due to the presence of their whole bodies. Through description, dialogue, and dramatic scenes, these whole-body saints became living persons with the agency to choose their final resting place.

Once transferred, the spotlight of whole-body saint's patronage shone like a narrow beam on a very specific domain. At Pfettrach, Saint Felicissimus provided comfort to the "the surrounding neighborhood," and in Erding, Placidus's patronage reached "the praiseworthy city of Erding together with the whole area."[52] The limited size of a catacomb saint's patronage net is especially evident in a description by Franz Valentin Fridl at the translation of Saint Porphyrius to Arschwang. Fridl stated that Porphyrius is "so affectionate and humble that he will not reject or spurn anyone in this tiny clod of earth."[53] Despite the fact that the area and the town were small and insignificant—just a "tiny clod of earth," in Fridl's words—they were precious in the eyes of the saint, and its inhabitants would receive his full attention. Even in the occasional case where a preacher mentioned a catacomb saint's patronage in relation to the well-being of the entire Electorate, the focus quickly narrowed to more local concerns. At Steingaden, Andreas von Sancta Theresia said he wished he could shout the name of Beninus across the whole of the state. But, he protested, with somewhat affected humility, he was too weak to accomplish such a feat. Instead, he planned to discuss how the saint would serve as a comfort for the "surrounding pious neighborhood."[54] The Carmelite's rhetoric reveals a clear understanding of how such holy bodies would function in a local religious environment.

The exclusive—but geographically limited—protection that whole-body catacomb saints conferred on a given location manifested itself in practice in the cults and rituals that developed around Roman holy bodies imported to Electorate. The cult of Saint Felix in Gars illustrates how a localized cult could develop in the rural Bavarian landscape. In 1675, just two months after the saint's arrival in town, a terrible fire broke out in the village. Desperate to prevent its spread, the villagers and monks paraded the saint's body through the streets along with a Eucharistic Host. Miraculously, the fire was contained, and Felix gained a reputation as an intercessor against deadly blazes.[55] After this incident, the martyr's reputation and veneration continued to grow among the local community. That same year, Johann Chrysostomos Hager, the monk who had organized the saint's translation festival, recorded in his *Tagebuch* (diary) how he had conducted a successful exorcism with the help of the saint, expelling seven thousand evil spirits from a local woman named Catherina Humplin. According to Hager, the saint also

FIGURE 49. Ceiling fresco of Saint Felix protecting the village and cloister of Gars from a thunderstorm, Felix chapel, Gars cloister, Anton Lichtenfurtner, 1752. (Photograph by author)

FIGURE 50. *Ex voto* painting of Saint Felix protecting the village of Gars am Inn from fire, Gars cloister, 1675. (Photograph by author)

miraculously helped save many villagers from a deadly fever afflicting the community in August 1675.[56]

In the years after 1675, the villagers celebrated the saint's arrival with an annual festival and continued to ask for his assistance in votive masses. Between 1689 and 1690 alone, more than one hundred petitioners paid to have their pleas for help read in front of the saint's altar.[57] Over the subsequent decades, the veneration of the saint continued. In 1754, nearly eighty years after the saint's translation, lay brother Anton Lichtenfurtner painted three frescoes in Felix's chapel in 1754 that depict the saint protecting the cloister and its hinterlands from fire, thunderstorms, and shipwrecks (fig. 49).[58] The cloister, the village of Gars, as well as the surrounding fields and forests are visible in each fresco as Felix turns a different danger away from the town's inhabitants and their crops. The town of Gars and its surroundings also appear in several *ex voto* paintings left to thank the saint for his intercession, including one from 1675, in which the saint is seen defending the town from a raging fire (fig. 50).

Both the frescoes as well as the *ex voto* images left for Felix demonstrate a continued veneration of the saint as well as his function as a local patron who protected and helped those in and around the town of Gars with various types of difficulties common to early modern life. The local nature of the devotion to the saint was also noted in the 1754 territory-wide survey of religious festivals commissioned by the duke: "The body of the wonder-working martyr St. Felix rests [in Gars] in a special chapel. He is highly venerated and the entire parish of Gars as well as the surrounding neighborhood considers him a particular helper in all types of accidents. His translation festival is celebrated most solemnly each year on the Sunday after St. Ulrich's [feast day] with a large crowd of people in attendance."[59] This entry illustrates how a once-foreign saint became a significant patron in a particular parish and neighborhood.

Many elements of the cult of Saint Felix are typical of the ways in which veneration of catacomb saints became a regular part of the religious ritual and practice of individual Bavarian communities in the decades and centuries following their arrival from Rome. Towns adopted the saints as patrons and held local festivals on the anniversary of their translations. Their shrines drew pilgrims seeking help from the immediate surroundings. Devotional images, printed miracle books, as well as baptismal records provide further evidence of the conception and function of catacomb saints as localized patrons whose reach remained limited to small areas. Unlike the opening page of *Bavaria Sancta*, which depicts the Archangel Michael and the Virgin Mary presiding over a map of the entire duchy (fig. 2), the *Andachtsbilder* and *ex voto* images of catacomb saints also show them as protectors of very specific towns and churches. In engravings produced for the cloisters of Geisenfeld, Landshut-Seligenthal, and St. Veit, catacomb saints appear hovering above cloister buildings (fig. 41). The images focus on the monasteries and their outbuildings but do not even include the nearby towns.

The same trend is evident in an *Andachtsbild* from the parish church at Ried, which shows Saints Jucundinus and Justina along with a *Gnadenbild* (wonder-working image) of the Virgin Mary above an outline of the church. In these cases, the saint's role as protector of a single location was implied iconographically as they appear protectively above each location. Sometimes the saint's role was made more explicit through visual or textual details. Images commissioned by the cloisters at Raitenhaslach and Indersdorf use beams of light to connect the saints to the cloister buildings below. In the engraving made by Johann Georg Dieffenbrunner for Indersdorf, these rays contain words that make up the sentence: "May the foundation of this house stand firm through our protection, help and support" (fig. 51). This statement clearly expresses the saints' roles both as intercessors and protectors of the cloister.[60] While one of the goals of such *Andachtsbilder* was likely to advertise

FIGURE 51. Engraving of the patron saints of Indersdorf cloister including catacomb saints Julius, Innocentius, Felix, and Lucius in Morhart, *Kurtze historische Nachricht,* Georg Dieffenbrunner, 1762. (Special Collections, The Sheridan Libraries, Johns Hopkins University)

the location of a saint at specific location to attract visitors and pilgrims, it also underscores the extremely tight connection between a whole-body catacomb saint and the single site of his or her display.

Naming patterns as well as miracle books further confirm the localized nature of catacomb saint cults. A survey of baptism records in the diocese of Freising, which covered a large part of the early modern Electorate, demonstrated that if children were named after catacomb saints, it was only in the town where the saints were present, not in the surrounding communities. These names typically experienced a high rate of popularity in the first ten years after a translation in communities where the saint rested in the local parish church. For example, when the town of Aufkirchen an der Maisach welcomed Saint Jucundinus to its parish church in 1757, parents in the town quickly began to use the previously unknown Latin name for their sons. In 1757, eight of the seventeen boys born in town were named Jucundinus. The name remained quite popular for the following decade, accounting for between 8 and 36 percent of the male baptismal names in the village each year.[61] A similar pattern can be observed after Saint Clemens arrived in Aufkirchen bei Erding in 1781. That year, seven of the twenty-two boys born in the village were named Clemens; in the following year, around a third of the village's sons were baptized Clemens (9/29).[62] After an initial burst of popularity, catacomb saint names often continued to circulate in towns over generations, often passing down from parent to child or borrowed from a godparent. Prosper, the name of a catacomb saint translated to Erding in 1675, remained in circulation for almost 125 years, indicating a continued awareness and veneration of the saint over a long period of time.[63]

A similarly localized pattern of veneration and patronage is evident in miracle books that survive for the cults of Saint Antoninus in Landshut and Saint Dionysius in Geisenfeld, both of which developed into pilgrimage sites. The pilgrimage to Saint Antoninus at the convent of Seligenthal in Landshut stemmed from the popularity of the miraculous healing oil taken from lamps that hung next to his shrine.[64] A handwritten miracle book records 154 miracles that occurred from 1667 to 1680. Based on its entries, which recorded the origin of the supplicants, the area of Saint Antoninus's influence was restricted to the city of Landshut and the Lower Bavarian countryside. Occasionally, there are vows from people hailing from towns farther away, but this is rare. Petitioners visited the saint and used his miracle-working oil to help with sickness, difficult childbirths, blindness, as well as falls and accidents. Few people of high rank are mentioned in the miracle book, just the abbess of the convent and one noble.[65] The limited catchment area of Saint Antoninus's cult as well as the social standing of his visitors indicate that this was a local patron—one that helped with day-to-day challenges and did not draw dignitaries or those of high rank from far away. In Taufkirchen, silver-plated *ex voto* gifts in the shapes of eyes, hearts, limbs, and a jaw left by pilgrims at the shrine of Saint Victor attest to the saint's role as a healer of a variety of types of physical ailments (fig. 5).

Similar traits also characterize the pilgrimage to Saint Dionysius in Geisenfeld. Miracle books printed in 1674 and 1715 catalog the saint's miracles and include the names, dates, hometowns, maladies, votive gifts, and the help granted by the saint.[66] In 1674, all of the people from the booklet—with one exception—hail from within a twelve-mile radius of the convent.[67] Most of those mentioned are citizens of Geisenfeld, Vohburg, and Pfaffenhofen and the surrounding farmland. The same is true for the 1715 book, which includes fifty-four miracles, a "tenth" of those that could have been recorded, according to the author, Jesuit Joseph Mayr. The supplicants are once again from a very small region, with all but one coming from within a ten-mile radius of Geisenfeld.[68]

This pattern of localized veneration was not necessarily foreseen or intended by church officials in Rome when they excavated and exported catacomb relics out of the Eternal City. For high church officials and historians believed the bones themselves provided testimony to the unbroken history of the Catholic Church and its doctrines. They could not have predicted how Bavarian communities would use the bodies of the ancient Roman martyrs to make age-old concepts like a saint's *domus* or role as *patronus* materially present in their hometowns. Lying in glass shrines on side altars, these *heilige Leiber* concretized the ancient idea that saints *lived* in their churches and made these intercessors and human role models constantly accessible to visitors. The bodily concentration of the ancient Roman martyrs also meant the cults they inspired were intense, but geographically circumscribed. Artwork, naming patterns, and the catchment areas of the pilgrimages the holy bodies inspired demonstrate how Bavarian communities constructed exclusive patronage relationship with catacomb saints, whose remains rested in one church and nowhere else. This singular relationship facilitated the particularization of the sacred landscape across the duchy and meant that the local pantheon of patron saints varied from village to village under the larger umbrella of Bavaria sancta.

Epilogue

CATACOMB SAINTS IN THE MODERN ERA

When Franz Xaver Schönhammer von Schöngau arrived in Rottenbuch in late 1803, he was on a mission: to liquidate the "useless cloister church" in the town and auction its furnishings for the benefit of the state. Appointed by Elector Max IV Joseph (r. 1799–1816) and his reform-minded minister Count Maximilian von Montgelas, Schönhammer quickly set to work. Though his state supervisors in Munich advised him to keep the building intact for later use as a parish church, they encouraged him to remove or sell the shrines holding "purportedly holy bodies, bones, heads" whose display on altars caused "offense and disgust."[1] By early December, Schönhammer had organized an auction for the possessions of the Augustinian monastery, including its relics.

At the sale, several priests from Reutte bei Tirol, just over the border into Austria, purchased the shrines holding the bodies of Primus and Felicianus, paying well over asking price. Encouraged by this success, Schönhammer organized another auction, this time offering the shrines of Roman catacomb saints Innocentius, Julius, and Florian from the cloister church as well as the bodies of Wenceslaus, Gaudentius, and Clara from the nearby pilgrimage church at Hohenpeißenberg, which the Augustinian canons had long supervised. As before, Austrian priests eagerly took advantage of the opportunity to bring the holy bodies back to their parishes in Tirol.

Though Schönhammer was quite pleased with his efforts, the citizens of Rottenbuch were not. When the first saints departed town in January 1804, a large procession of townspeople accompanied them on their way as the bells of the church tolled, a mirror image of their festive welcome in the previous centuries. The crowd accompanied the relics all the way to the Austrian border. The last choir director of the cloister, Raimund Pertl, recorded the events of the day in his *Tagebuch* (diary), describing how "old Bavaria bid farewell to its saints with tears and sobs" and lamenting, "Oh holy Bavaria, how far you have fallen!" Annoyed by this continued display of devotion to what he considered superstitious objects, Schönhammer issued a ban on any further processions or tolling of bells upon the departure of the rest of the saints, ordering that they leave town "in total silence." By the end of February, all the town's beloved holy bodies were gone.[2]

In the first decade of the nineteenth century, the remains of many other catacomb saints in cloisters across Bavaria suffered the same fate as those at Rottenbuch. Beginning in the 1750s, Bavarian electors Maximilian III Joseph (r. 1745–77) and Karl Theodor (r. 1777–99) attempted to centralize and modernize the administration of their state, often at the expense of ecclesiastical institutions.[3] Inspired by Enlightenment ideals as well as absolutist ambitions, the rulers targeted monasteries for reform for both economic and religious reasons.[4] The monasteries controlled more than a quarter of the land in the state, which the Electors wanted both to control and to tax as a means of consolidating power. Furthermore, the monks and nuns in the cloisters followed a form of religious life that many proponents of the German Catholic Enlightenment considered superstitious, backward, and nonproductive. Advocates for reform, who were often elite members of the clergy themselves, wanted to create a simpler, less elaborate form of Catholicism that dispensed with pilgrimages, processions, and other "traditional" forms of piety.[5]

Bavarian state efforts to reform monastic institutions culminated under Max IV Joseph in the nineteenth century. Max IV Joseph's reforms followed the secularization program plan laid out by his principal advisor, Count Montgelas, which specifically called for the incorporation of the church into the state by confiscating the property of ecclesiastical institutions. Over the course of 1802 and 1803, the Elector issued decrees suppressing almost all the territory's 160 monasteries.[6] Dissolution commissioners like Schönhammer fanned out across the region to close monasteries and convents and sell all their moveable goods. In some cases, they even had orders to deconsecrate the churches within the cloister complexes so the buildings could be used for secular purposes.

Whereas some cloisters like Altomünster, Indersdorf, Niederaltaich, and Waldsassen managed to keep their full complement of holy bodies intact, other communities watched as their relics—like the monks and nuns themselves—were dispersed to other locations. The cloisters in Munich, home to sixty-one catacomb saints, were particularly hard hit. Directly in the line of sight of secularization authorities, the city's cloisters saw all of their catacomb saints either sold or buried. Cloisters in Freising (ten) as well as those at Polling (four) and Gotteszell (three) also lost multiple saints.[7] Some of these holy bodies were stripped of their decorations and buried, but far more were offered up for sale along with other church furnishings. Since it was against canon law to sell relics, state officials appraised the value of the elaborate *Klosterarbeit* and the gilded shrines to set prices for the holy bodies at auction.

Although Max IV Joseph and his administrative officials viewed the bodies and shrines of catacomb saints as sources of revenue, local Bavarian Catholics—like the parishioners in Rottenbuch—were loath to allow their cherished intercessors and protectors to leave their communities. When given the opportunity, laypeople and parish churches across the region clamored to buy and rehouse the displaced saints who had become so rooted in the spiritual landscape of the territory. In multiple cases, local citizens purchased catacomb saints from cloisters in their own towns, ensuring that the holy bodies would not be allowed to leave the community. In Dingolfing, a merchant bought Saint Tigrinus's shrine from the dissolved Franciscan cloister in town and donated him to the parish church, where he joined catacomb saints Faustina and Martialis.[8] Parish churches in the areas surrounding rural cloisters also proved eager buyers for homeless catacomb saints. A farmer purchased Saint Honestus from the Augustinian cloister in Seemanshausen at auction and, after storing the holy body in his house for a short while, donated it to St. Michael's parish church in Wiesbach, just five miles down the road from the cloister.[9] Two Roman saints from the Gotteszell cloister ended up only two and eleven miles away from their original home in villages of Achslach and Viechtach, respectively; a few years later, in 1811, the village of Obing welcomed Saint Sabinianus from the nearby Augustinians at Herrencheimsee.[10]

Though communities like Rottenbuch mourned the loss of their patrons, for the villages that took them in, the arrival of catacomb saints provided cause for great celebration. In 1804, Binabiburg welcomed the martyrs Valerius and Victor from the church of the Munich Augustinians with a large procession. Once the festivities concluded, the two new heroes found homes on altars inside St. Johann Baptist parish church.[11] Despite the attitudes of the clerical and secular elite toward relics, the demand for displaced catacomb saints indicates the high value ordinary Bavarian Catholics continued to place on the intercessors and protectors whom they had come to know and rely upon in the decades and centuries since their arrival from Rome.

Repeated "overpayment" by bidders for holy bodies and their shrines at dissolution auctions held by commissioners like Schönhammer also attests to the importance catacomb saint relics had achieved across the former Electorate. In 1804, Franz Joseph Kerle, a parish priest from Weissenbach bei Reutte, bought the shrines containing the bodies of Saints Clara and Gaudentia from the pilgrimage church of Hohenpeißenberg. Though appraisal value for saints' decoration and shrines only totaled 96 Gulden, Kerle paid more than four times the asking price for the holy bodies (400 Gulden).[12] A similar situation occurred at the Pütrich cloister in Munich, where the appraiser noted the decorations on each of the five catacomb saints were "completely fake and the stones had no worth."[13] Still, the state official in charge of selling the convent's furnishings had multiple buyers lining up to compete for the five saints and their shrines. The interested parties included a shoemaker—who wanted to give two or three of the holy bodies to local villages—as well as an apothecary and a librarian. All five of the saints were eventually sold to various bidders; however, two—Dorothea and Hyacinth—mysteriously made their way to Reutberg cloister, where the sisters had been sent after the convent's dissolution. Just as they had circumvented the authority of their male supervisor to acquire Saint Dorothea in 1662, this time it seems the nuns outmaneuvered the state authorities by arranging a straw buyer for the beloved saints. Once purchased, the buyer subsequently sent the holy bodies to Reutberg for continued display and veneration.[14]

1804–1871: Continued Acquisitions, Festivities, and Decoration

The enthusiasm for catacomb saints among Catholic Bavarians was not limited to acquiring the holy bodies available from dissolved cloisters. Between 1804 and 1871, churches in Bavaria acquired twenty-seven additional catacomb saints from the Eternal City.[15] The notable pause in importation between 1805 and 1824 can be traced to the impact of monastic secularization as well as political upheaval caused by the dissolution of the Holy Roman Empire in 1806, and Bavaria's involvement in the Napoleonic Wars (1803–15).

In the Jubilee year of 1825, holy bodies from Rome once again flowed en masse over the Alps into the now-kingdom of Bavaria. Laypeople who wished to bring catacomb saints home to their hometown churches largely drove the acquisition of the catacomb saints during this period, though parish priests participated in the movement as well.[16] The prominence of parish and pilgrimage churches in the import of the martyrs continued a trend visible in the last three decades of the eighteenth century, when the number of saints going to cloisters had begun to decline, likely as a result of both Enlightenment influences within the cloisters themselves as well as the efforts of the Electors to implement control over these institutions.[17]

During the nineteenth century, lay Bavarians of various backgrounds—merchants, farmers, and craftsmen—all managed to procure bodies from the Eternal City. A hermit named Anna Maria Kreitner, known as the "Forest Sister" (Waldschwester), walked all the way from Pfeffenhausen to Rome on pilgrimage and back in 1825. She managed to bring eight catacomb saints back to her village, splitting them evenly between the town's parish church and the pilgrimage church next to her hermitage.[18] In 1842, farmer Josef Mayr von Egg traveled to Rome and returned with two holy bodies. For Mayr, the acquisition of the two saints in Rome was so significant that he chose to commemorate the achievement on his gravestone. Located in the local parish church in Waging am See, Mayr's memorial notes that he "brought the holy bodies of saints Fidelis and Viktor to Waging [am See] and Mühlberg" in 1842.[19]

As with their counterparts who arrived in the seventeenth and eighteenth centuries, the arrival of catacomb saints to Bavarian villages in the 1800s often prompted elaborate translation celebrations. They included processions, triumphal arches, music, gun salutes, and widespread community participation. The only major change in these festivities was the lack of actors playing the saints in plays or *tableaux vivant,* a practice that had been banned by church authorities.[20] Visual and written records of Saint Clemens's transfer festivities to Bad Endorf in 1825 highlight the effort and excitement Catholic communities still showed upon the arrival of the remains of ancient Roman martyrs into the nineteenth century. While on pilgrimage to Rome, two farmer's sons had managed to acquire a catacomb saint during the Jubilee year. Once back home, they sent the relics to the Benedictine nuns at Frauenchiemsee for decoration and construction into a holy body.[21] With the work complete, the time came to transfer Saint Clemens from the nun's island cloister to Bad Endorf. The translation began in the early morning hours with gunshots and music at the convent, followed by a Mass and then a procession around the island to the lake. There, a flotilla of forty-five boats carrying four hundred people waited to accompany Saint Clemens on his trip across the lake. A hand-drawn and -colored image of the waterborne procession depicts a fleet of small rowboats filled with families sailing across the Chiemsee to shore. The largest boat—festooned with garlands, flags, and pennants—carried the full-body saint and his shrine while another vessel carried musicians playing horns and drums (fig. 52). After the two-hour journey, a crowd of clergy and laypeople—along with another band—met the saint in the lakeside village of Prien. The day's events continued apace, with further stops in Rimsting and finally in Bad Endorf, where ten thousand people had gathered to hear an outdoor high Mass and watch as Saint Clemens took up his final resting place in the parish church of St. Jakobus.[22]

Twenty years later, another festive translation occurred on the Chiemsee after priest Franz Xaver Schöpfer returned from Rome with a catacomb saint he had acquired in the hope of reviving the pilgrimage to the "Kleine Madron" near Flintsbach.[23] Like the village of Bad Endorf, Schöpfer sent the relics to the nuns at Frauenchiemsee for decoration. As the nuns worked on the *Klosterarbeit,* Flintsbach and other villages along the shore of the Chiemsee once again prepared a multiday celebration to welcome the saint to the neighborhood.

FIGURE 52. Drawing of Saint Clemens's waterborne translation across the Chiemsee to Bad Endorf, Gasthaus Weingarten, Rimsting, 1825. (Photograph by author)

When the decoration was complete, two men from the town along with twelve boys retrieved the saint from the nuns and sailed it back to shore, where the villagers of Prien awaited. The party then set out on the eighteen-mile trek to its final destination. The trip included several processions from town to town, an overnight stay in Frasdorf, a ferry over the river Inn, and finally a festive entry into the parish church at Flintsbach. After two weeks of veneration, a final procession—attended by an "enormous throng of people"—took Saint Victor up the Petersburg to his final resting place in the pilgrimage church.[24] The size and scope of these translations is further testament to the enduring importance and appeal of catacomb saint relics and their role in the expression of Catholic identity in nineteenth-century Bavaria.

As the decades passed, the clerical elite once again began to display active support for the presence of catacomb saints in Bavarian churches. In the 1850s, the bishop of Regensburg had to step in to resolve a dispute over the display of a catacomb saint in the town of Oberpiebing. At the time, a wealthy farmer named Bartholomäus Englberger von Riedling decided to build a small church on his land and acquired a catacomb saint named Theodor for the chapel. Unfortunately, the saint did not fit on the existing church altar, and Englberger did not want to undertake renovations to accommodate the holy body. Englberger's friend Johann Fischer, an episcopal assistant (*Kooperator*) suggested a solution: the farmer could donate the holy body to the nearby parish church in Oberpiebing.

Convinced to make the donation, Englberger was shocked when the parish priest, Alois Zeidler (1819–1853), refused to accept his generous gift. Englberger found this especially galling since he had already paid to have the saint decorated in Regensburg and placed in a glass shrine; all the priest needed to do was put the saint on one of the church altars. In order to resolve the dispute, Englberger and Fischer turned to the bishop of Regensburg, who confirmed the authenticity of the saint's bones and ordered the obstinate priest to display the saint in the parish church. Ten months later, the saint was nowhere to be seen. Fischer wrote to the bishop again to complain, explaining that Father Zeidler "had, to the great annoyance of his parish, refused to introduce and display the holy body." The bishop's office replied, ordering Zeidler to stop refusing to transfer the saint into the church or to write back within eight days of receipt of the letter to explain his recalcitrance. One week later, the priest wrote back saying that he was not the only one opposed to bringing the saint into the church and that his parishioners did not want it there either. The installation of the saint's shrine, the priest explained, would block a painting of Saint Sebastian, who had long protected the town from the plague. Zeidler explained, "I and the majority of my parishioners do not have anything against holy body, but I could not agree to ruin one of their side altars." The new saint, he added, had not proved he could or had helped anyone. He ended his missive by noting: "We do not need these bones and they are not at all useful to us. . . . Englberger built his own church for himself in Riedling a few years ago: there is plenty of room for the saint and anyone can go venerate the saint there."

The bishop responded to Zeidler's letter tartly. He called the priest's refusal to put the saint in the parish chapel "baseless" and ordered Saint Theodor transferred into the church within four days. To add insult to injury, the bishop informed Zeidler that an *additional* holy body, that of Saint Victoria, would soon be placed on the other side altar. Should he choose not to comply with these orders, the bishop continued, a priest from another village would be called in to carry out the festive translation—at Zeidler's expense.

At this point in the saga, the records go quiet. Correspondence between Zeidler's successor, Anton Moosmüller, and the diocese reveals that both Theodor and Victoria had been installed in the town's parish church by 1861, though it is not clear whether this occurred during Zeidler's tenure.[25] In any case, the bishop's forceful support for the installation of the saints in Oberpiebing—as well as the provision of a second holy body along the way—demonstrates the Catholic Church hierarchy's renewed support for the display and veneration of catacomb saint bodies well into the nineteenth century. Decorated in *Klosterarbeit* and staged as intact bodies, Theodor and Victoria in Oberpiebing also demonstrate the persistence of this type of relic presentation into the 1850 and 1860s. Nuns in multiple convents in the region continued to practice the art form of cloister work, and at least seventeen of the twenty-seven saints translated between 1804 and 1871 were presented as intact bodies with sparkling décor.[26]

The bodies of catacomb saints translated during the early modern period also continued to receive care, attention, and veneration into the modern era. In Gars, pilgrims left *ex votos* to thank Saint Felix for relief from a variety of diseases and ailments as well as the safe delivery of children. Laywomen from parish congregations in Erding and Unterdiessen created new outfits for Saints Prosper and Peregrina respectively when the older ones needed repair.[27] In the 1870s, Maximiliana Wallner donated 700 Gulden to renovate the shrine and holy body of Saint Theodor, housed in the Heilig Kreuz church in Schönbrunn. A painter restored Saint Theodor's shrine, while the Servite nuns in Munich redecorated the saint's body with *Klosterarbeit.* On June 29, 1876, the village met the saint at the Röhrmoos train station and led him back to the parish church in a celebratory procession.[28]

As these cases demonstrate, the visual presentation of older saints did not remain static as the years passed. In addition to those removed from cloisters during secularization, holy bodies were modified, redecorated, covered up, moved to different altars, and occasionally even buried according to the preferences and needs of individual congregations. One of the major drivers of a change in presentation was the increasing popularity of the neo-Gothic architectural style, which entailed the removal of much baroque and rococo decoration. In some cases, catacomb saints found new homes in shrines that harmonized with the new design programs for the church. Sometimes the bodies remained intact and behind glass, whereas in other cases, the saints were dismembered and placed in Gothic-inspired casket reliquaries. Some scholars have suggested that changing sensibilities about death and worries about the "horror" the skeletons could provoke in viewers may have sometimes provided the impetus to cover or remove bodies; however, the continued staging and display of new saints as intact bodies suggests this was not a particularly widespread occurrence.[29]

Rather, in times of greatest need—including during some of the most difficult moments in modern German history—Bavarians returned to catacomb saints again and again for protection and intercession. Two *ex voto* paintings left for Saint Felix in Gars thank the saint for his protection during the wars of German unification. A small panel in the saint's chapel shows soldiers running into battle against the Prussians, the leader on horseback with a sword hoisted high in the air. The text in the corner states it was left to thank the saint for "rescuing the soldiers from the greatest danger in battle" on July 10, 1866. In another *ex voto,* soldiers from the town expressed their thanks to Felix and the mother of God "for their safe return from the war with France" in 1871. In Erding, the names of hometown soldiers who did not return from World War I and II flank a statue of Saint Prosper on the back wall of the parish church.

Catacomb Saints Today

Though their appearance may have changed in the centuries since they arrived from Rome, catacomb saints—still most often presented as sparkling skeletons—have remained on altars across the former Electorate. Despite the challenge posed by secularization and renovation programs, more than half of the saints transferred to cloisters before 1803 are still in situ (127 of the original 245). Retention rates at parish and pilgrimage churches are even higher, at 76 percent (67/88) and 83 percent (19/23), respectively. In the last several decades, some saints have even made their way back into parish churches after periods of being off display. At the behest of the local historical society, Pfreimd's two catacomb saints were taken out of storage, decorated, and returned to the parish church in new reliquaries in 1999.[30] Recent years have also seen an increase in appreciation for the saints as part of the region's cultural and artistic heritage. Congregations as well as local dioceses and individual churches have begun to invest significant amounts of money in the preservation of the holy bodies. In 2021, the diocese of Munich and Freising paid restorer Uta Ludwig, who has restored more than fifty catacomb saints in the last thirty years, €20,000 to return the bodies of Hilarius and Florentius from Maria Thalheim to their former glory.[31]

Traces of the saints' cultural, historical, and religious impact on civic identity and ritual also remain visible across the Bavarian landscape. In Erding, Saint Prosper's role as an ancient Roman soldier and the city's protector has continued to resonate into the modern era. In 1996, the city erected a bronze statue of the saint near the center of town in 1996, and every year a local brewery produces a stout (*Starkbier*) for Lent named after the ancient martyr. Maps of Kemnath, Erding, and Pfreimd feature streets, plazas, and even a wildlife refuge named after catacomb saints. The Maurus Verlag, a publishing house founded in 2005 in Miesbach, is named after the local catacomb saint who arrived in the village in 1725. The gift shop at St. Peter's in Munich sells prayer cards for Saint Munditia, still the patron saint of single women, and the congregation holds a Mass in her honor each November. In Waldsassen, the parish still observes the Holy Bodies Festival begun in 1756 to honor its ten catacomb saints.

In 2020, when the COVID-19 pandemic struck the region, the residents of Waldsassen once again turned to the ten familiar holy protectors housed in the former cloister church to help shield them from the coronavirus. Beginning on March 16, parish priest Thomas Vogl began holding a special devotion after Mass each day to "call on the holy bodies for their intercession with God so that the city, cloister and church, the entire *Stiftland,* all countries and people of the earth may be saved from this misery." He noted that the "long and good tradition [of praying to the saints] gained new meaning and important significance in these difficult times" and that "among Waldsasseners, their power is well known and treasured." Noted particularly over the centuries for sparing the town from bad weather, the saints had now been called upon to protect local worshippers from a growing global pandemic. With the church closed for months, Vogl asked parishioners to send prayer requests for the saints via text messages and email until the basilica could open its doors again. Daily prayer services, along with the ringing of the church bells for fifteen minutes each day, lasted through August 2, the annual celebration of the Holy Body Festival. Though the technology had changed dramatically over the centuries since these ancient Roman martyrs arrived in the village as representatives of the universal Catholic Church, their role as important local protectors and intercessors has persisted all the way into the twenty-first century.[32]

Appendix

WHOLE-BODY CATACOMB SAINTS TRANSLATED TO THE DUCHY/ELECTORATE OF BAVARIA, 1590–1871

Methodology

This appendix represents the first attempt to list all whole-body catacomb saints transferred to the Duchy/Electorate of Bavaria from the sixteenth to the nineteenth centuries. It contains two sets of data. The first lists catacomb saints transferred to Bavaria in the early modern period. Specifically, it covers the years between 1590—when the when the first *heilige Leiber* arrived in the territory—and 1803, when most Bavarian cloisters were secularized and the Reichskirche was dissolved. The second list covers the period between 1804 and 1871, when the final holy body arrived in the territory.

Compiling a complete list of all the whole-body Roman catacomb saints translated to Bavaria over the centuries was a challenging task for a variety of reasons. No contemporary inventory of these saints was compiled before 1803. In addition, the secularization of the monasteries as well as changing aesthetic tastes and attitudes toward relics resulted in the sale, removal, and displacement of some saints from their original locations. Furthermore, many churches were either destroyed, deconsecrated, or redecorated extensively in the nineteenth and twentieth centuries.

To create a comprehensive list of Bavarian catacomb saints, I relied on a wide variety of sources both early modern and modern. The core sources used to create the list were diocesan inventories and histories completed between the eighteenth and mid-twentieth centuries. These works included lists of catacomb saints or detailed descriptions of the altars and the relics in a particular diocese.[1] While helpful, these sources also had limitations. Some were created before the end of the early modern period and others as late as 1939. This left gaps in the records, which I filled in using a range of other sources. These included primary printed and archival sources; a wide range of modern secondary sources (academic journal articles and books, *Kirchenführer* etc.); images of church interiors; and nearly eighty site visits to churches across the former Electorate. I also consulted archives of the custodian of sacred relics at the Archivio storico del Vicariato di Roma.[2] The custodian, along with the papal sacristan, were the two officials responsible for granting catacomb saint relics in this era.[3] Unfortunately, both sets of Roman records are incomplete and do not cover the entire early modern era consistently. They also do not necessarily provide reliable information about where a saint's relics were ultimately housed since recipients were allowed to—and often did—sign over the holy bodies to third parties (see chapter 1). In the end, sources from and about Bavaria proved more useful in the creation of my catalog of whole-body saints.

Once the core of my list was established, I used primary and secondary sources to confirm that the saints listed in diocesan inventories and those I had added based on additional research were, in fact, Roman catacomb saints translated in the early modern period. These sources included a variety of secondary literature on individual cloisters and churches. If I could not corroborate a saint's origin in a second source—either primary or secondary—I did not include the saint in the comprehensive list below.

Notes on Appendix Entries

- The dioceses listed for each church are those in which they were located in the early modern period.
- The dates listed for the catacomb saints are translation dates, not necessarily the year the relics arrived at the church or cloister. Often it took several years to decorate the saint or build an altar where it could be displayed.
- When a range of dates is provided for a saint's translation, it is because I could not locate the exact date.
  - Those saints listed with a "before 1740" translation date were mentioned in the 1740 inventory of the diocese of Freising, indicating they were present in the church before the inventory was carried out.
  - When a saint was sent to a cloister and no translation date could be identified, I listed the date of translation as "before 1803." Many cloisters were secularized by this date and were no longer operating and/or acquiring relics; thus, it is logical to assume the saints were transferred before 1803.
  - The dates sometimes represent an abbot's tenure; in some cases, I knew a saint was acquired during an abbot's reign but could not find an exact date of translation.

—Some churches served multiple constituencies. For example, a collegiate church could also be used as a parish church. In these cases, I have listed the church's primary role first.

—The "other" label in the "Type of Church" category represents chapels and churches that were not parish, cloister, or noble churches. These include confraternity oratories, hospital churches, and private non-noble chapels.

Table 1. Roman catacomb saints translated to Bavaria from 1590 to 1803

Name	Date of translation	Town/city	Church	Order (if applicable)	Region	Diocese	Type of church
Caius	1590	Munich	St. Michael	Jesuit	Upper Bavaria	Freising	Cloister
Januarius	1591	Munich	St. Michael	Jesuit	Upper Bavaria	Freising	Cloister
Saturninus	1593	Munich	St. Michael	Jesuit	Upper Bavaria	Freising	Cloister
Euphebius	1593	Munich	St. Michael	Jesuit	Upper Bavaria	Freising	Cloister
Modestus	1610	Munich	Schlosskapelle Herzog-Max-Burg		Upper Bavaria	Freising	Noble
Serena	1620	Andechs	Kloster Andechs	Benedictine	Upper Bavaria	Augsburg	Cloister
Sylvanus	1623	Munich	Augustinerkirche (St. Johann Evg. und Bapt.)	Augustinian (OSA)	Upper Bavaria	Freising	Cloister
Vitalis	1623	Munich	Augustinerkirche (St. Johann Evg. und Bapt.)	Augustinian (OSA)	Upper Bavaria	Freising	Cloister
Romula	1623	Munich	Augustinerkirche (St. Johann Evg. und Bapt.)	Augustinian (OSA)	Upper Bavaria	Freising	Cloister
Concordia	1623	Munich	Augustinerkirche (St. Johann Evg. und Bapt.)	Augustinian (OSA)	Upper Bavaria	Freising	Cloister

Fortunatus	1624	Andechs	Kloster Andechs	Benedictine	Upper Bavaria	Augsburg	Cloister
Primenius	1626	Benediktbeuren	Kloster Benedikt-beuren	Benedictine	Upper Bavaria	Augsburg	Cloister
Antherus	1626	Polling	Kloster Polling	Augustinian Can-ons (CRSA)	Upper Bavaria	Augsburg	Cloister
Severina	1626	Polling	Kloster Polling	Augustinian Can-ons (CRSA)	Upper Bavaria	Augsburg	Cloister
Perpetua	1626	Polling	Kloster Polling	Augustinian Can-ons (CRSA)	Upper Bavaria	Augsburg	Cloister
Rogatus	1626	Seeon	Kloster Seeon	Benedictine	Upper Bavaria	Salzburg	Cloister
Honoratus	1654	Munich	St. Peter		Upper Bavaria	Freising	Parish
Faustus	1662	Munich	Kloster St. Antonius	Franciscan (OFM)	Upper Bavaria	Freising	Cloister
Dorothea	1662	Munich	Kloster Pütrich (St. Christopher)	Franciscan (ter-tiaries)	Upper Bavaria	Freising	Cloister
Perpetua	1663	Munich	Ridlerkloster (Johannes der Täufer und Johannes Evg.)	Franciscan (ter-tiaries)	Upper Bavaria	Freising	Cloister
Antigonus	1663	Munich	Angerkloster (St. Jakob)	Poor Clares (OSC)	Upper Bavaria	Freising	Cloister
Perpetua	1663	Munich	Kloster St. Elisabeth	Servite	Upper Bavaria	Freising	Cloister
Hyacinth	1664	Munich	Kloster Pütrich (St. Christopher)	Franciscan (tertiaries)	Upper Bavaria	Freising	Cloister

(*continues*)

Table 1 (*continued*)

Name	Date of translation	Town/city	Church	Order (if applicable)	Region	Diocese	Type of church
Faustinus	1664	Munich	Angerkloster (St. Jakob)	Poor Clares (OSC)	Upper Bavaria	Freising	Cloister
Beninus	1664	Steingaden	Kloster Steingaden	Premonstratensian	Upper Bavaria	Augsburg	Cloister
Demitrius	1665	Dietramszell	Kloster Dietramszell	Augustinian Canons (CRSA)	Upper Bavaria	Freising	Cloister
Marcellinus	1665	Dietramszell	Kloster Dietramszell	Augustinian Canons (CRSA)	Upper Bavaria	Freising	Cloister
Columbus	1666	Munich	Ridlerkloster (Johannes der Täufer und Johannes Evg.)	Franciscan (tertiaries)	Upper Bavaria	Freising	Cloister
Gregorius	1667	Munich	Kloster St. Cajetan (Theatinerkirche)	Theatines	Upper Bavaria	Freising	Cloister
Antonius	1668	Landshut	Kloster Seligenthal	Cistercian (women)	Lower Bavaria	Regensburg	Cloister
Crescentianus	1669	Amberg	St. Martin		Upper Palatinate	Regensburg	Parish
Victoria	1669	Munich	Kloster St. Antonius	Franciscan (OFM)	Upper Bavaria	Freising	Cloister
Laurentia	1670	Landshut	Kloster Heiligkreuz	Franciscan (tertiaries)	Lower Bavaria	Regensburg	Cloister

Pontianus	1670	Wessobrunn	Kloster Wessobrunn	Benedictine	Upper Bavaria	Freising	Cloister
Severus	1671	Klosterlechfeld	Maria Hilf auf dem Lechfeld		Swabia	Augsburg	Pilgrimage
Mitilla	1671	Munich	Kloster St. Antonius	Franciscan (OFM)	Upper Bavaria	Freising	Cloister
Justinus	1671	Munich	Angerkloster (St. Jakob)	Poor Clares (OSC)	Upper Bavaria	Freising	Cloister
Justina	1671	Munich	Angerkloster (St. Jakob)	Poor Clares (OSC)	Upper Bavaria	Freising	Cloister
Eugenia	1671	Wasserburg	St. Jakob		Upper Bavaria	Freising	Parish
Lucilla	1672	Freising	Kloster St. Franciscus Seraphicus	Franciscan (OFM)	Upper Bavaria	Freising	Cloister
Hyacinth	1672	Fürstenfeld-bruck	Kloster Fürstenfeld	Cistercian	Upper Bavaria	Freising	Cloister
Cassianus	1672	Landshut	Kloster Seligenthal	Cistercian (women)	Lower Bavaria	Regensburg	Cloister
Candidus	1672	Munich	Josephspitalkirche		Upper Bavaria	Freising	Other
Honoratus	1673	Bad Aibling	Mariä Himmelfahrt		Upper Bavaria	Freising	Parish
Dionysius	1673	Geisenfeld	Kloster Geisenfeld	Benedictine	Upper Bavaria	Regensburg	Cloister
Felix	1674	Gars am Inn	Kloster Gars	Augustinian Canons (CRSA)	Upper Bavaria	Salzburg	Cloister
Prosper	1675	Amberg	St. Georg		Upper Palatinate	Regensburg	Parish

(*continues*)

Table 1 (*continued*)

Name	Date of translation	Town/city	Church	Order (if applicable)	Region	Diocese	Type of church
Prosper	1675	Erding	St. Johann		Upper Bavaria	Freising	Parish
Eleutheria	1675	Munich	Angerkloster (St. Jakob)	Poor Clares (OSC)	Upper Bavaria	Freising	Cloister
Victoria	1675	Rosenheim	St. Nikolaus		Upper Bavaria	Freising	Parish
Victor	1676	Landshut	Kloster Seligenthal	Cistercian (women)	Lower Bavaria	Regensburg	Cloister
Eutychia	1676	Munich	Angerkloster (St. Jakob)	Poor Clares (OSC)	Upper Bavaria	Freising	Cloister
Felix	1677	Klosterlechfeld	Maria Hilf auf dem Lechfeld		Swabia	Augsburg	Pilgrimage
Munditia	1677	Munich	St. Peter		Upper Bavaria	Freising	Parish
Prosper	1679	Freising	St. Georg		Upper Bavaria	Freising	Parish
Felix	1679	Freising	St. Georg		Upper Bavaria	Freising	Parish
Felicitas	1679	Munich	Kloster Pütrich (St. Christopher)	Franciscan (ter- tiaries)	Upper Bavaria	Freising	Cloister
Theodorus	1680	Landshut	Kloster Seligenthal	Cistercian (women)	Lower Bavaria	Regensburg	Cloister
Fortunatus	1680	Landshut	Ursulinenkloster (St. Joseph)	Ursulines	Lower Bavaria	Regensburg	Cloister

Theodora	1680	Pfarrkirchen	St. Simon and St. Judas Thaddäus		Lower Bavaria	Passau	Parish
Amantius	1680	Wessobrunn	Kloster Wessobrunn	Benedictine	Upper Bavaria	Freising	Cloister
Concordius	1682	Ingolstadt	Kloster St. Johann im Gnadenthal	Franciscan (tertiaries)	Upper Bavaria	Eichstätt	Cloister
Vitus	1683	Bernried	Kloster Bernried	Augustinian Canons (CRSA)	Lower Bavaria	Augsburg	Cloister
Tigrinus	1683	Dingolfing	Kloster St. Oswald	Franciscan (OFM)	Lower Bavaria	Regensburg	Cloister
Leo	1685	Kühbach	Kloster Kühbach	Benedictine (women)	Swabia	Augsburg	Cloister
Vincentius	1685	Mindelheim	Jesuitenkirche (Mariä Verkündigung)	Jesuit	Swabia	Augsburg	Cloister
Maximian	1688	Altomünster	Kloster Altomünster	Bridgettine	Upper Bavaria	Freising	Cloister
Alexander	1688	Altomünster	Kloster Altomünster	Bridgettine	Upper Bavaria	Freising	Cloister
Valentinus	1688	Andechs	Kloster Andechs	Benedictine	Upper Bavaria	Augsburg	Cloister
Donatus	1688	Andechs	Kloster Andechs	Benedictine	Upper Bavaria	Augsburg	Cloister
Deodatus	1688	Waldsassen	Kloster Waldsassen	Cistercian	Upper Palatinate	Regensburg	Cloister
Benignus	1689	Polling	Kloster Polling	Augustinian Canons (CRSA)	Upper Bavaria	Augsburg	Cloister
Constantius	1689	Polling	Kloster Polling	Augustinian Canons (CRSA)	Upper Bavaria	Augsburg	Cloister

(*continues*)

Table 1 (*continued*)

Name	Date of translation	Town/city	Church	Order (if applicable)	Region	Diocese	Type of church
Victorinus	1691	Arnstorf	Schlosskapelle		Lower Bavaria	Passau	Noble
Innocentius	1691	Lenggries	St. Jakob		Upper Bavaria	Freising	Parish
Geminus	1691	Munich	Kloster Pütrich (St. Christopher)	Franciscan (tertiaries)	Upper Bavaria	Freising	Cloister
Euphrosina	1692	Munich	Kloster St. Elisabeth	Servite	Upper Bavaria	Freising	Cloister
Clemens	1692	Munich	Kloster St. Elisabeth	Servite	Upper Bavaria	Freising	Cloister
Columbus	1692	Munich	Kloster St. Elisabeth	Servite	Upper Bavaria	Freising	Cloister
Primianus	1693	Kemnath	Mariä Himmelfahrt		Upper Palatinate	Regensburg	Parish
Mercuria	1694	Altomünster	Kloster Altomünster	Bridgettine	Upper Bavaria	Freising	Cloister
Victoria	1694	Altomünster	Kloster Altomünster	Bridgettine	Upper Bavaria	Freising	Cloister
Fortunatus	1694	Altomünster	Kloster Altomünster	Bridgettine	Upper Bavaria	Freising	Cloister
Porphyrius	1694	Arnschwang	St. Martin		Upper Palatinate	Regensburg	Parish
Clarus	1694	Neuhaus am Inn	Kloster Vornbach	Benedictine	Lower Bavaria	Passau	Cloister
Victor	1695	Aufhausen	Kloster Aufhausen	Collegiate	Upper Palatinate	Regensburg	Cloister

Joannes	1695	Aufhausen	Kloster Aufhausen	Collegiate	Upper Palatinate	Regensburg	Cloister
Desiderius	1695	Aufhausen	Kloster Aufhausen	Collegiate	Upper Palatinate	Regensburg	Cloister
Lucius	1695	Neumarkt-Sankt Veit	Kloster St. Veit	Benedictine	Upper Bavaria	Salzburg	Cloister
Victor	1695	Taufkirchen	Schlosskapelle		Upper Bavaria	Freising	Noble
Theodora	1696	Hilgertshausen	St. Stephen		Upper Bavaria	Freising	Parish
Alexander	1696	Munich	Kloster St. Antonius	Franciscan (OFM)	Upper Bavaria	Freising	Cloister
Honestus	1696	Seemanshausen	Kloster Seemanshausen	Augustinian (OSA)	Lower Bavaria	Regensburg	Cloister
Vincentia	1697	Burghausen	Kloster Heilig Schutzengel	English Ladies	Upper Bavaria	Freising	Cloister
Asterius	1697	Straubing	Ursulinenkloster (Unbefleckte Empfängnis Mariens)	Ursulines	Lower Bavaria	Regensburg	Cloister
Felicissimus	1698	Munich	Kloster Englische Fräulein	English Ladies	Upper Bavaria	Freising	Cloister
Benedictus	1698	Raitenhaslach	Kloster Raitenhaslach	Cistercian	Upper Bavaria	Salzburg	Cloister
Ausanius	1698	Raitenhaslach	Kloster Raitenhaslach	Cistercian	Upper Bavaria	Salzburg	Cloister
Concordia	1698	Raitenhaslach	Kloster Raitenhaslach	Cistercian	Upper Bavaria	Salzburg	Cloister

(*continues*)

Table 1 (*continued*)

Name	Date of translation	Town/city	Church	Order (if applicable)	Region	Diocese	Type of church
Fortunata	1698	Raitenhaslach	Kloster Raitenhaslach	Cistercian	Upper Bavaria	Salzburg	Cloister
Fidelis	1699	Anzing	Högerkapelle		Upper Bavaria	Freising	Noble
Margarita	1699	Munich	Kloster Englische Fräulein	English Ladies	Upper Bavaria	Freising	Cloister
Mercurius	1699	Munich	Kloster Englische Fräulein	English Ladies	Upper Bavaria	Freising	Cloister
Coelestinus	1699	Ranshofen	Stift Ranshofen	Augustinian Canons (CRSA)	Innviertel	Passau	Cloister
Marius	1699	Ranshofen	Stift Ranshofen	Augustinian Canons (CRSA)	Innviertel	Passau	Cloister
Alexander	end 17th century	Ettal	Kloster Ettal	Benedictine	Upper Bavaria	Freising	Cloister
Marius	1700	Altenmarkt an der Alz	Kloster Baumburg	Augustinian Canons (CRSA)	Upper Bavaria	Salzburg	Cloister
Martha	1700	Altenmarkt an der Alz	Kloster Baumburg	Augustinian Canons (CRSA)	Upper Bavaria	Salzburg	Cloister
Felix	1700	Breitenbrunn	Mariä Himmelfahrt		Upper Palatinate	Eichstätt	Parish
Benedicta	1700	Breitenbrunn	Mariä Himmelfahrt		Upper Palatinate	Eichstätt	Parish

Claudius	1700	Griesstätt	Kloster Altenhohenau	Dominican (women)	Upper Bavaria	Salzburg	Cloister
Alexander	1700	Munich	Schlosskapelle Blutenberg		Upper Bavaria	Freising	Noble
Felicissimus	1700	Munich	Schlosskapelle Blutenberg		Upper Bavaria	Freising	Noble
Bonosa	1700	Munich	Schlosskapelle Blutenberg		Upper Bavaria	Freising	Noble
Valentina	1700	Munich	Schlosskapelle Blutenberg		Upper Bavaria	Freising	Noble
Martialis	1700	Niederaichbach	St. Nikola		Lower Bavaria	Regensburg	Parish
Peregrina	1700	Unterdießen	St. Nikolaus		Upper Bavaria	Augsburg	Parish
Martialis	1701	Dingolfing	St. Johannes		Lower Bavaria	Regensburg	Parish
Placidus	1701	Freising	Dom (St. Maria and St. Korbinian)		Upper Bavaria	Freising	Cloister (Cathedral)
Hilaria	1701	Niederschönenfeld	Abteikirche	Cistercian (women)	Swabia	Augsburg	Cloister
Innocentia	1702	Munich	Herzogspital	Franciscan (tertiaries)	Upper Bavaria	Freising	Cloister
Columbinus	1702	Munich	Herzogspital	Franciscan (tertiaries)	Upper Bavaria	Freising	Cloister
Amantius	1708	Frontenhausen	St. Jakob		Lower Bavaria	Regensburg	Parish

(*continues*)

Table 1 (*continued*)

Name	Date of translation	Town/city	Church	Order (if applicable)	Region	Diocese	Type of church
Pastor	1708	Griesstätt	Kloster Altenhohenau	Dominican (women)	Upper Bavaria	Salzburg	Cloister
Martyria	1708	Tegernsee	Kloster Tegernsee	Benedictine	Upper Bavaria	Freising	Cloister
Julia	1709	Poxau in Marklkofen	Schlosskapelle		Lower Bavaria	Regensburg	Noble
Claudius	1709	Reichersberg	Kloster Reichersberg	Augustinian Canons (CRSA)	Innviertel	Passau	Cloister
Lucidus	1710	Munich	Augustinerkirche (St. Johann Evg. und Bapt.)	Augustinian (OSA)	Upper Bavaria	Freising	Cloister
Clemens	1710	Rottenbuch	Kloster Rottenbuch	Augustinian Canons (CRSA)	Upper Bavaria	Freising	Cloister
Innocentius	1710	Rottenbuch	Kloster Rottenbuch	Augustinian Canons (CRSA)	Upper Bavaria	Freising	Cloister
Clemens (boy)	1710	Rottenbuch	Kloster Rottenbuch	Augustinian Canons (CRSA)	Upper Bavaria	Freising	Cloister
Julius	1712	Indersdorf	Kloster Indersdorf	Augustinian Canons (CRSA)	Upper Bavaria	Freising	Cloister
Innocentius	1712	Indersdorf	Kloster Indersdorf	Augustinian Canons (CRSA)	Upper Bavaria	Freising	Cloister

Hilarius	1712	Maria Thalheim	Maria Thalheim		Upper Bavaria	Freising	Pilgrimage
Paulina	1714	Freising	Franziskanerkloster (St. Franciscus Seraphicus)	Franciscan (OFM)	Upper Bavaria	Freising	Cloister
Floridus	1716	Vilsbiburg	Maria Hilf		Lower Bavaria	Regensburg	Pilgrimage
Clementia	1717	Altomünster	Kloster Altomünster	Bridgettine	Upper Bavaria	Freising	Cloister
Martha	1717	Altomünster	Kloster Altomünster	Bridgettine	Upper Bavaria	Freising	Cloister
Constans	1718	Habach	St. Ulrich	Collegiate	Upper Bavaria	Augsburg	Cloister
Sigismundus	1719	Dachau	St. Jakob		Upper Bavaria	Freising	Parish
Ernestus	1719	Dachau	St. Jakob		Upper Bavaria	Freising	Parish
Clara	1719	Hohenpeißenberg	Mariä Himmelfahrt		Upper Bavaria	Freising	Pilgrimage
Adrianus	1719	Schäftlarn	Kloster Schäftlarn	Benedictine	Upper Bavaria	Freising	Cloister
Candidus	1720	Munich	St. Cajetan (Theatinerkirche)	Theatines	Upper Bavaria	Freising	Cloister
Valentina	1722	Straubing	Franziskanerkloster (Schutzengelstift)	Franciscan (OFM)	Lower Bavaria	Regensburg	Cloister
Mauritia	1722	Straubing	Franziskanerkloster (Schutzengelstift)	Franciscan (OFM)	Lower Bavaria	Regensburg	Cloister
Longinus	1722	Tunzenberg	Schlosskapelle		Lower Bavaria	Regensburg	Noble

(*continues*)

Table 1 (*continued*)

Name	**Date of translation**	**Town/city**	**Church**	**Order (if applicable)**	**Region**	**Diocese**	**Type of church**
Valerius	1722	Tunzenberg	Schlosskapelle		Lower Bavaria	Regensburg	Noble
Lucius	1723	Beuerberg	Kloster Beuerberg	Augustinian Canons (CRSA)	Upper Bavaria	Freising	Cloister
Alexander	1723	Beuerberg	Kloster Beuerberg	Augustinian Canons (CRSA)	Upper Bavaria	Freising	Cloister
Albert	1723	Burgrain	St. Georg		Upper Bavaria	Freising	Noble
Innocentius	1723	Freising	St. Andreas	Collegiate	Upper Bavaria	Freising	Cloister
Modestus	1723	Freising	St. Andreas	Collegiate	Upper Bavaria	Freising	Cloister
Clemens	1723	Freising	St. Andreas	Collegiate	Upper Bavaria	Freising	Cloister
Julius	1723	Niederalteich	Kloster Niederaltaich	Benedictine	Lower Bavaria	Passau	Cloister
Maximilian	1724	Altomünster	Kloster Altomünster	Bridgettine	Upper Bavaria	Freising	Cloister
Sebastian	1724	Altomünster	Kloster Altomünster	Bridgettine	Upper Bavaria	Freising	Cloister
Ascania	1724	Freising	Kloster Neustift	Premonstratensian	Upper Bavaria	Freising	Cloister
Ascanius	1724	Freising	Kloster Neustift	Premonstratensian	Upper Bavaria	Freising	Cloister
Wenceslaus	1724	Hohenpeißenberg	Mariä Himmelfahrt		Upper Bavaria	Freising	Pilgrimage
Gaudentius	1724	Hohenpeißenberg	Mariä Himmelfahrt		Upper Bavaria	Freising	Pilgrimage

Claudius	1725	Beuerberg	Kloster Beuerberg	Augustinian Canons (CRSA)	Upper Bavaria	Freising	Cloister
Bonifatius	1725	Beuerberg	Kloster Beuerberg	Augustinian Canons (CRSA)	Upper Bavaria	Freising	Cloister
Maurus	1725	Miesbach	Mariä Himmelfahrt		Upper Bavaria	Freising	Parish
Severus	1725	Reisach	Schlosskapelle Urfahrn		Upper Bavaria	Freising	Noble
Florianus	1725	Rottenbuch	Kloster Rottenbuch	Augustinian Canons (CRSA)	Upper Bavaria	Freising	Cloister
Julius	1725	Rottenbuch	Kloster Rottenbuch	Augustinian Canons (CRSA)	Upper Bavaria	Freising	Cloister
Marcellus	1727	Grafing	Marktkirche zur Allerheiligsten Dreifaltigkeit		Upper Bavaria	Freising	Parish
Claudius	1728	Großschwindau	St. Wolfgang	Collegiate	Upper Bavaria	Freising	Cloister
Benedictus	1728	Großschwindau	St. Wolfgang	Collegiate	Upper Bavaria	Freising	Cloister
Mauritius	1728	Königsdorf	St. Laurentius		Upper Bavaria	Freising	Parish
Martinus	1729	Gotteszell	Kloster Gotteszell	Cistercian	Lower Bavaria	Regensburg	Cloister
Dulcissimus	1729	Gotteszell	Kloster Gotteszell	Cistercian	Lower Bavaria	Regensburg	Cloister
Hilarius	1729	Gotteszell	Kloster Gotteszell	Cistercian	Lower Bavaria	Regensburg	Cloister
Julia	1729	Wasserburg	St. Jakob		Upper Bavaria	Freising	Parish

(*continues*)

Table 1 (*continued*)

Name	Date of translation	Town/city	Church	Order (if applicable)	Region	Diocese	Type of church
Pius	1730	Hirschau	Mariä Himmelfahrt		Upper Palatinate	Regensburg	Parish
Julia	1731	Niederalteich	Kloster Niederaltaich	Benedictine	Lower Bavaria	Passau	Cloister
Antoninus	1731	Niederalteich	Kloster Niederaltaich	Benedictine	Lower Bavaria	Passau	Cloister
Aurelia	1731	Niederalteich	Kloster Niederaltaich	Benedictine	Lower Bavaria	Passau	Cloister
Magnus	1731	Niederalteich	Kloster Niederaltaich	Benedictine	Lower Bavaria	Passau	Cloister
Athanasius	1732	Rinchnach	Kloster Rinchnach	Benedictine	Lower Bavaria	Passau	Cloister
Barbara	1732	Rinchnach	Kloster Rinchnach	Benedictine	Lower Bavaria	Passau	Cloister
Justinus	1733	Seeon	Kloster Seeon	Benedictine	Upper Bavaria	Salzburg	Cloister
Liberata	1733	Sielenbach	Unserer Lieben Frau im Birnbaum		Swabia	Freising	Pilgrimage
Casta	1735	Kirchdorf b. Haag	Mariä Himmelfahrt		Upper Bavaria	Freising	Parish
Justus	1736	Munich	Kloster St. Antonius	Franciscan (OFM)	Upper Bavaria	Freising	Cloister
Hirena	1736	Polling	Kloster Polling	Augustinian Canons (CRSA)	Upper Bavaria	Augsburg	Cloister
Klara	1738	Aldersbach	Kloster Aldersbach	Cistercian	Lower Bavaria	Passau	Cloister

Aurelius	1738	Munich	Angerkloster (St. Jakob)	Poor Clares (OSC)	Upper Bavaria	Freising	Cloister
Victor	1738	Munich	Angerkloster (St. Jakob)	Poor Clares (OSC)	Upper Bavaria	Freising	Cloister
Felix	1738	Munich	Angerkloster (St. Jakob)	Poor Clares (OSC)	Upper Bavaria	Freising	Cloister
Victor	1738	Wasserburg	St. Jakob		Upper Bavaria	Freising	Parish
Markus	1740	Hohenwart	Kloster Hohenwart	Benedictine (women)	Upper Bavaria	Augsburg	Cloister
Maximinus	1740	Waldsassen	Kloster Waldsassen	Cistercian	Upper Palatinate	Regensburg	Cloister
Felix	1741	Indersdorf	Kloster Indersdorf	Augustinian Canons (CRSA)	Upper Bavaria	Freising	Cloister
Lucius	1741	Indersdorf	Kloster Indersdorf	Augustinian Canons (CRSA)	Upper Bavaria	Freising	Cloister
Faustus	1741	Indersdorf	Kloster Indersdorf	Augustinian Canons (CRSA)	Upper Bavaria	Freising	Cloister
Fortunatus	1741	Indersdorf	Kloster Indersdorf	Augustinian Canons (CRSA)	Upper Bavaria	Freising	Cloister
Olympia	1742	Raitenhaslach	Kloster Raitenhaslach	Cistercian	Upper Bavaria	Salzburg	Cloister
Clemens	1743	Berg am Laim	St. Michael		Upper Bavaria	Freising	Noble/Other
Benedikt	1743	Berg am Laim	St. Michael		Upper Bavaria	Freising	Noble/Other

(*continues*)

Table 1 (*continued*)

Name	Date of translation	Town/city	Church	Order (if applicable)	Region	Diocese	Type of church
Timotheus	1753	Freising	St. Georg		Upper Bavaria	Freising	Parish
Clara	1753	Freising	St. Georg		Upper Bavaria	Freising	Parish
Bonifacia	1743	Munich	Kloster St. Antonius	Franciscan (OFM)	Upper Bavaria	Freising	Cloister
Deodatus	1745	Mühldorf am Inn	St. Nikolaus	Collegiate	Upper Bavaria	Salzburg	Cloister
Constantius	1745	Schongau	Mariä Himmelfahrt		Upper Bavaria	Augsburg	Parish
Valerius	1746	Aldersbach	Kloster Aldersbach	Cistercian	Lower Bavaria	Passau	Cloister
Valerius	1746	Weyarn	Kloster Weyarn	Augustinian Canons (CRSA)	Upper Bavaria	Freising	Cloister
Clemens	1747	Arrach	St. Valentin		Upper Palatinate	Regensburg	Parish
Domitius Alexander	1747	Munich	Kloster St. Antonius	Franciscan (OFM)	Upper Bavaria	Freising	Cloister
Coelestina	1748	Altötting	St. Philippus and Jakobus		Upper Bavaria	Passau	Parish
Benedictus	1749	Speinshart	Kloster Speinshart	Premonstratensian	Upper Palatinate	Regensburg	Cloister
Jucundinus	1750	Freising	Kloster Weihenstephan	Benedictine	Upper Bavaria	Freising	Cloister

Constantius	1750	Freising	Kloster Weihen-stephan	Benedictine	Upper Bavaria	Freising	Cloister
Maximus	1750	Munich	Bürgersaalkirche		Upper Bavaria	Freising	Other
Victor	1750	Munich	Asamkirche		Upper Bavaria	Freising	Other
Gratianus	1750	Waldsassen	Kloster Waldsassen	Cistercian	Upper Palati-nate	Regensburg	Cloister
Vitalianus	1750	Waldsassen	Kloster Waldsassen	Cistercian	Upper Palati-nate	Regensburg	Cloister
Marcellus	1751	Freising	St. Andreas	Collegiate	Upper Bavaria	Freising	Cloister
Constantia	1751	Freising	St. Andreas	Collegiate	Upper Bavaria	Freising	Cloister
Julius	1751	Prien	Taufkapelle St. Johann		Upper Bavaria	Chiemsee	Parish
Innocenz	1752	Altötting	St. Philippus and Jakobus		Upper Bavaria	Passau	Parish
Laurentia	1752	Langquaid	St. Jakob		Lower Bavaria	Regensburg	Parish
Pius	1752	Munich	Kloster St. Antonius	Franciscan (OFM)	Upper Bavaria	Freising	Cloister
Constanti-nus	1753	Amberg	Frauenkirche/Hofka-pelle		Upper Palati-nate	Regensburg	Noble
Clemens	1753	Amberg	Frauenkirche/Hofka-pelle		Upper Palati-nate	Regensburg	Noble
Florentius	1753	Maria Thalheim	Maria Thalheim		Upper Bavaria	Freising	Pilgrimage

(*continues*)

Table 1 (*continued*)

Name	Date of translation	Town/city	Church	Order (if applicable)	Region	Diocese	Type of church
Clemens	1754	Fürstenfeld-bruck	Kloster Fürstenfeld	Cistercian	Upper Bavaria	Freising	Cloister
Auxilius	1754	Kühbach	Kloster Kühbach	Benedictine (women)	Swabia	Augsburg	Cloister
Silvanus	1754	Tirschenreuth	Mariä Himmelfahrt		Upper Palati-nate	Regensburg	Parish
Urbanus	1754	Tirschenreuth	Mariä Himmelfahrt		Upper Palati-nate	Regensburg	Parish
Victor	1754	Bad Tölz	Heilig Kreuz (Kalvarienberg)		Upper Bavaria	Freising	Pilgrimage
Paulina	1755	Andechs	Kloster Andechs	Benedictine	Upper Bavaria	Augsburg	Cloister
Illuminatus	1755	Freystadt	Mariahilfbasilika		Upper Palati-nate	Eichstätt	Pilgrimage
Saturninus	1755	Niederaschau in Chiemgau	Pfarrkirche Darstel-lung des Herrn		Upper Bavaria	Chiemsee	Parish
Felix	1756	Ottengrün	Kleine Kappl (St. Sebastian)		Upper Palati-nate	Regensburg	Pilgrimage
Asteria	1757	Amberg	St. Martin		Upper Palati-nate	Regensburg	Parish

Jucundinus	1757	Aufkirchen an der Maisach	St. Georg		Upper Bavaria	Freising	Parish
Innocentius	1757	Oberaudorf	Mariä Himmelfahrt		Upper Bavaria	Freising	Parish
Theophilus	1757	Pfreimd	Mariä Himmelfahrt		Upper Palati-nate	Regensburg	Parish
Victor	1757	Pfreimd	Mariä Himmelfahrt		Upper Palati-nate	Regensburg	Parish
Albanus	1758	Freising	Dom (St. Maria and St. Korbinian)		Upper Bavaria	Freising	Cloister (Cathedral)
Jucundinus	1758	Ried	St. Walburga		Swabia	Augsburg	Parish
Julia	1759	Lenggries	St. Jakob		Upper Bavaria	Freising	Parish
Nicasius	1760	Amberg	Schulkirche (St. Augustinus)	Salesians	Upper Palati-nate	Regensburg	Cloister
Coelestinus	1760	Amberg	Schulkirche (St. Augustinus)	Salesians	Upper Palati-nate	Regensburg	Cloister
Innocenz	1760	Mammendorf	St. Jakob		Upper Bavaria	Freising	Parish
Amandus	1760	Oberammergau	St. Peter and Paul		Upper Bavaria	Freising	Parish
Clemens	1760	Rott am Inn	Kloster Rott	Benedictine	Upper Bavaria	Freising	Cloister
Constantius	1760	Rott am Inn	Kloster Rott	Benedictine	Upper Bavaria	Freising	Cloister
Felicissima	1761	Munich	Kloster auf dem Lil-ienberg (Au)	Benedictine (women)	Upper Bavaria	Freising	Cloister

(*continues*)

Table 1 (*continued*)

Name	Date of translation	Town/city	Church	Order (if applicable)	Region	Diocese	Type of church
Felicis	1761	Munich	Kloster auf dem Lilienberg (Au)	Benedictine (women)	Upper Bavaria	Freising	Cloister
Felix	1761	Raitenhaslach	Marienberg (Maria Königin des hl. Rosenkranzes)		Upper Bavaria	Salzburg	Pilgrimage
Justus	1762	Raitenhaslach	Marienberg (Maria Königin des hl. Rosenkranzes)		Upper Bavaria	Salzburg	Pilgrimage
Vinzentius	1762	Raitenhaslach	Marienberg (Maria Königin des hl. Rosenkranzes)		Upper Bavaria	Salzburg	Pilgrimage
Vincentius	1763	Oberalteich	Kloster Oberalteich	Benedictine	Lower Bavaria	Regensburg	Cloister
Felicianus	1765	Metten	Kloster Metten	Benedictine	Lower Bavaria	Regensburg	Cloister
Candidatus	1765	Wolfratshausen	St. Andreas		Upper Bavaria	Freising	Parish
Benigna	1766	Dietfurt a.d. Altmühl	Kloster Dietfurt	Franciscan (OFM)	Upper Palatinate	Eichstätt	Cloister
Benedicta	1766	Freystadt	Maria Hilf		Upper Palatinate	Eichstätt	Pilgrimage
Benedikt	1766	Ingolstadt	St. Moritz		Upper Bavaria	Eichstätt	Parish

Innocenz	1766	Michelfeld	Kloster Michelfeld	Benedictine	Upper Palatinate	Bamberg	Cloister
Maximus	1766	Waldsassen	Kloster Waldsassen	Cistercian	Upper Palatinate	Regensburg	Cloister
Fortunatus	1767	Metten	Kloster Metten	Benedictine	Lower Bavaria	Regensburg	Cloister
Justina	1767	Ried	St. Walburga		Swabia	Augsburg	Parish
Florianus	1768	Munich	Bürgersaal		Upper Bavaria	Freising	Other
Victorius	1768	Reutberg	Kloster Reutberg	Franciscan (tertiaries)	Upper Bavaria	Freising	Cloister
Clemens	1768	Sandizell (Schrobenhausen)	Wasserschlosskapelle (St. Peter)		Upper Bavaria	Augsburg	Noble
Maximus	1768	Sandizell (Schrobenhausen)	Wasserschlosskapelle (St. Peter)		Upper Bavaria	Augsburg	Noble
Felicissimus	1769	Straubing	St. Jakob	Collegiate	Lower Bavaria	Regensburg	Cloister
Illuminatus	1769	Suben	Kloster Suben	Augustinian Canons (CRSA)	Lower Bavaria	Passau	Cloister
Honoratius	1769	Vilsbiburg	Mariä Himmelfahrt		Lower Bavaria	Regensburg	Parish
Desiderius	1770	Dingolfing	Kloster St. Oswald	Franciscan (OFM)	Lower Bavaria	Regensburg	Cloister
Faustina	1770	Dingolfing	St. Johannes		Lower Bavaria	Regensburg	Parish
Desiderius	1770	Kollbach	St. Martin		Upper Bavaria	Regensburg	Parish

(*continues*)

Table 1 (*continued*)

Name	Date of translation	Town/city	Church	Order (if applicable)	Region	Diocese	Type of church
Benedikt	1770	Wasserburg	St. Jakob		Upper Bavaria	Freising	Parish
Felix	1771	Hahnbach	St. Jakob		Upper Palatinate	Regensburg	Parish
Alexander	1773	Westenhofen bei Schliersee	St. Martin		Upper Bavaria	Freising	Parish
Donatus	1775	Oberaudorf	Mariä Himmelfahrt		Upper Bavaria	Freising	Parish
Vinzentius	1777	Schäftlarn	Kloster Schäftlarn	Benedictine	Upper Bavaria	Freising	Cloister
Theodor	1780	Bad Tölz	Maria Hilf (Mühlfeldkirche)		Upper Bavaria	Freising	Pilgrimage
Theodor	1780	Wemding	Maria Brünnlein		Swabia	Eichstätt	Pilgrimage
Clemens	1781	Aufkirchen bei Erding	St. Johann Baptist		Upper Bavaria	Freising	Parish
Clemens	1781	Freising	Dom (St. Maria und St. Korbinian)		Upper Bavaria	Freising	Cloister (Cathedral)
Generosus	1781	Halsbach	St. Martin		Upper Bavaria	Passau	Parish
Placidus	1782	Hirschau	Mariä Himmelfahrt		Upper Palatinate	Regensburg	Parish
Juliana	1803	Tiefenbach	St. Vitus		Upper Palatinate	Regensburg	Parish

Felicianus	1669–83	Aldersbach	Kloster Aldersbach	Cistercian	Lower Bavaria	Passau	Cloister
	1669–1803	Freising	Altöttinger Kapelle		Upper Bavaria	Freising	Other
	1669–1803	Freising	Altöttinger Kapelle		Upper Bavaria	Freising	Other
Faustus	1674–1724	Schlehdorf	Kloster Schlehdorf	Augustinian Canons (CRSA)	Upper Bavaria	Freising	Cloister
Marcus	1674–1724	Schlehdorf	Kloster Schlehdorf	Augustinian Canons (CRSA)	Upper Bavaria	Freising	Cloister
Constantius	1674–1724	Schlehdorf	Kloster Schlehdorf	Augustinian Canons (CRSA)	Upper Bavaria	Freising	Cloister
Fortunatus	1690–1739	Griesbach im Rottal	Kloster Sankt Salvator	Premonstratensian	Lower Bavaria	Passau	Cloister
Felicissimus	1690–1739	Pfettrach	Schlosskapelle		Lower Bavaria	Regensburg	Noble
Felicissimus	1691–1803	Schwarzhofen	Kloster Schwarzhofen	Dominican (women)	Upper Palatinate	Regensburg	Cloister
Maximilianus	1701–26	Schleißheim	Schlosskapelle Schleißheim		Upper Bavaria	Freising	Noble
Stephanus	1725–28	Donauwörth	Heilig Kreuz	Benedictine	Swabia	Augsburg	Cloister
Benedictus	1725–28	Donauwörth	Heilig Kreuz	Benedictine	Swabia	Augsburg	Cloister
Alexander	1735–40	Waldsassen	Kloster Waldsassen	Cistercian	Upper Palatinate	Regensburg	Cloister
Theodosius	1735–40	Waldsassen	Kloster Waldsassen	Cistercian	Upper Palatinate	Regensburg	Cloister

(*continues*)

Table 1 (*continued*)

Name	Date of translation	Town/city	Church	Order (if applicable)	Region	Diocese	Type of church
Valentinus	1735–40	Waldsassen	Kloster Waldsassen	Cistercian	Upper Palatinate	Regensburg	Cloister
Ursa	1735–40	Waldsassen	Kloster Waldsassen	Cistercian	Upper Palatinate	Regensburg	Cloister
Maximus	1741–1803	Freising	Kollegiatsstift St. Johann Baptist	Collegiate	Upper Bavaria	Freising	Cloister
Valerius	1741–1803	Munich	Augustinerkirche (St. Johann Evg. und Bapt.)	Augustinian (OSA)	Upper Bavaria	Freising	Cloister
Victor	1741–1803	Munich	Augustinerkirche (St. Johann Evg. und Bapt.)	Augustinian (OSA)	Upper Bavaria	Freising	Cloister
Columba	1748–1803	Straubing	Kloster Azlburg	Franciscan (tertiaries)	Lower Bavaria	Regensburg	Cloister
Coelestinus	1748–1803	Straubing	Kloster Azlburg	Franciscan (tertiaries)	Lower Bavaria	Regensburg	Cloister
Victoria	1750–1810	Ingolstadt	Kloster St. Georg	Ursulines	Upper Bavaria	Eichstätt	Cloister
Prosper	1761–62	Raitenhaslach	Marienberg (Maria Königin des hl. Rosenkranzes)		Upper Bavaria	Salzburg	Pilgrimage

Viktorius	1765–66	Waldsassen	Kloster Waldsassen	Cistercian	Upper Palatinate	Regensburg	Cloister
Columba	18th century	Schwarzhofen	Kloster Schwarzhofen	Dominican (women)	Upper Palatinate	Regensburg	Cloister
Abundus	Before 1704	Habach	St. Ulrich	Collegiate	Upper Bavaria	Augsburg	Cloister
Aurelia	Before 1740	Ettal	Kloster Ettal	Benedictine	Upper Bavaria	Freising	Cloister
Victor	Before 1740	Ettal	Kloster Ettal	Benedictine	Upper Bavaria	Freising	Cloister
Marcellinus	Before 1740	Ettal	Kloster Ettal	Benedictine	Upper Bavaria	Freising	Cloister
Antoninus	Before 1740	Ettal	Kloster Ettal	Benedictine	Upper Bavaria	Freising	Cloister
Felix/Felicis	Before 1740	Ettal	Kloster Ettal	Benedictine	Upper Bavaria	Freising	Cloister
Paulilus	Before 1740	Ettal	Kloster Ettal	Benedictine	Upper Bavaria	Freising	Cloister
Saturnius	Before 1740	Ettal	Kloster Ettal	Benedictine	Upper Bavaria	Freising	Cloister
Lena	Before 1740	Ettal	Kloster Ettal	Benedictine	Upper Bavaria	Freising	Cloister

(*continues*)

Table 1 (*continued*)

Name	Date of translation	Town/city	Church	Order (if applicable)	Region	Diocese	Type of church
Bonifatius	Before 1740	Ettal	Kloster Ettal	Benedictine	Upper Bavaria	Freising	Cloister
Valentia	Before 1740	Munich	Augustinerkirche (St. Johann Evg. und Bapt.)	Augustinian (OSA)	Upper Bavaria	Freising	Cloister
Alexander	Before 1740	Munich	Augustinerkirche (St. Johann Evg. und Bapt.)	Augustinian (OSA)	Upper Bavaria	Freising	Cloister
Bonossa	Before 1740	Munich	Augustinerkirche (St. Johann Evg. und Bapt.)	Augustinian (OSA)	Upper Bavaria	Freising	Cloister
Alexander (2)	Before 1740	Munich	Augustinerkirche (St. Johann Evg. und Bapt.)	Augustinian (OSA)	Upper Bavaria	Freising	Cloister
Valentina	Before 1740	Munich	Augustinerkirche (St. Johann Evg. und Bapt.)	Augustinian (OSA)	Upper Bavaria	Freising	Cloister
Placidus	Before 1740	Munich	Augustinerkirche (St. Johann Evg. und Bapt.)	Augustinian (OSA)	Upper Bavaria	Freising	Cloister

Deodata	Before 1740	Munich	Augustinerkirche (St. Johann Evg. und Bapt.)	Augustinian (OSA)	Upper Bavaria	Freising	Cloister
Pulcheria	Before 1740	Munich	Karmelitenkloster (St. Nikolaus)	Discalced Carmelites	Upper Bavaria	Freising	Cloister
Secundinus	Before 1740	Munich	Karmelitenkloster (St. Nikolaus)	Discalced Carmelites	Upper Bavaria	Freising	Cloister
Laurentia	Before 1740	Munich	Karmelitenkloster (St. Nikolaus)	Discalced Carmelites	Upper Bavaria	Freising	Cloister
Expurantia	Before 1740	Munich	Karmelitenkloster (St. Nikolaus)	Discalced Carmelites	Upper Bavaria	Freising	Cloister
Constantius	Before 1740	Munich	St. Anna	Salesians	Upper Bavaria	Freising	Cloister
Christina	Before 1740	Munich	Frauenkirche (Dom zu Unserer Lieben Frau)	Collegiate	Upper Bavaria	Freising	Cloister/ Parish
Pamphilius	Before 1740	Tegernsee	Kloster Tegernsee	Benedictine	Upper Bavaria	Freising	Cloister
Placidus	Before 1742	Erding	Kloster Erding	Capuchin	Upper Bavaria	Freising	Cloister
Benignus	Before 1784	Suben	Kloster Suben	Augustinian Canons (CRSA)	Lower Bavaria	Passau	Cloister

(continues)

Table 1 (*continued*)

Name	Date of translation	Town/city	Church	Order (if applicable)	Region	Diocese	Type of church
Hyacinth	Before 1803	Gars am Inn	Kloster Au	Augustinian Canons (CRSA)	Upper Bavaria	Salzburg	Cloister
Sabinianus	Before 1803	Herrenchiemsee	Domstiftskirche (St. Sixtus und St. Sebastian)	Augustinian Canons (CRSA)	Upper Bavaria	Chiemsee	Cloister
Benedictus	Before 1803	Mallersdorf	Kloster Mallersdorf	Benedictine	Lower Bavaria	Regensburg	Cloister
Clemens	Before 1803	Mallersdorf	Kloster Mallersdorf	Benedictine	Lower Bavaria	Regensburg	Cloister
Victorinus	Before 1803	Munich	Kloster Pütrich (St. Christopher)	Franciscan (tertiaries)	Upper Bavaria	Freising	Cloister
Clementina	Before 1803	Neuhaus am Inn	Kloster Vornbach	Benedictine	Lower Bavaria	Passau	Cloister
Pius	Before 1803	Oberalteich	Kloster Oberalteich	Benedictine	Lower Bavaria	Regensburg	Cloister
Vincentius	Before 1803	Osterhofen	Kloster Osterhofen	Premonstratensian	Lower Bavaria	Passau	Cloister
Urbanus	Before 1803	Rohr	Kloster Rohr	Augustinian Canons (CRSA)	Lower Bavaria	Regensburg	Cloister

Lucianus	Before 1803	Rohr	Kloster Rohr	Augustinian Canons (CRSA)	Lower Bavaria	Regensburg	Cloister
Secundus	Before 1803	Rottenbuch	Kloster Rottenbuch	Augustinian Canons (CRSA)	Upper Bavaria	Freising	Cloister
Coelestinus	Before 1803	Rotthalmünster	Kloster Asbach	Benedictine	Lower Bavaria	Passau	Cloister
Theodor	Before 1803	Schönbrunn	Heilig Kreuz		Upper Bavaria	Freising	Parish
Norbertus	Before 1803	Speinshart	Kloster Speinshart	Premonstratensian	Upper Palatinate	Regensburg	Cloister
Hyazinth	Before 1803	Steingaden	Kloster Steingaden	Premonstratensian	Upper Bavaria	Augsburg	Cloister
Sabinus	Before 1803	Windberg	Kloster Windberg	Premonstratensian	Lower Bavaria	Regensburg	Cloister
Bonifacius		Altdorf	Mariä Heimsuchung		Lower Bavaria	Regensburg	Parish
Orphila		Altheim	St. Peter		Lower Bavaria	Regensburg	Parish
Romanus		Adlkofen (Essenbach)	St. Michael		Lower Bavaria	Regensburg	Parish
Felix		Deggendorf	Mariä Himmelfahrt		Lower Bavaria	Regensburg	Parish
Justinus		Essenbach	Mariä Himmelfahrt		Lower Bavaria	Regensburg	Parish
Joannes		Feldkirchen	St. Joannes		Lower Bavaria	Regensburg	Parish
Desiderius		Haindlfing	St. Laurentius		Upper Bavaria	Freising	Parish

(continues)

Table 1 (*continued*)

Name	Date of translation	Town/city	Church	Order (if applicable)	Region	Diocese	Type of church
Vitalis		Hebertsfelden	St. Emmeram		Lower Bavaria	Regensburg	Parish
Gratus		Laaberberg	Mariä Opferung		Lower Bavaria	Regensburg	Parish
Pacificus		Laaberberg	Mariä Opferung		Lower Bavaria	Regensburg	Parish
Innocentius		Loizenkirchen	St. Dionysius		Lower Bavaria	Regensburg	Parish
Justinus		Luhe	St. Martin		Upper Palatinate	Regensburg	Parish
Hilaria		Luhe	St. Martin		Upper Palatinate	Regensburg	Parish
Coelestinus		Mötzing	Maria Immaculata		Upper Palatinate	Regensburg	Parish
Confidentia		Munich	Josephspital		Upper Bavaria	Freising	Other
Felicianus		Nabburg	St. Johannes Baptist		Upper Palatinate	Regensburg	Parish
Clara		Neukirchen b. hl. Blut	Mariä Geburt		Upper Palatinate	Regensburg	Pilgrimage
Fortunatus		Oberviechtach	St. John the Baptist		Lower Bavaria	Regensburg	Parish
Basilius		Oberviechtach	St. John the Baptist		Lower Bavaria	Regensburg	Parish
Pulcheria		Offenstetten	Schlosskapelle		Lower Bavaria	Regensburg	Noble

Justus		Offenstetten	Schlosskapelle		Lower Bavaria	Regensburg	Noble
Fortunatus		Regendorf (in Zeitlarn)	Schlosskapelle		Upper Palati-nate	Regensburg	Noble
Donatus		Reichlkofen	St. Michael		Lower Bavaria	Regensburg	Parish
Generosus		Schnaitsee	Mariä Himmelfahrt		Upper Bavaria	Freising	Parish
Victoria		Traunstein	St. Oswald		Upper Bavaria	Salzburg	Parish
Calavella		Vilsbiburg	Maria Hilf		Lower Bavaria	Regensburg	Pilgrimage
Donatus		Vilsbiburg	Maria Hilf		Lower Bavaria	Regensburg	Pilgrimage
Hilarilla		Vilsbiburg	Maria Hilf		Lower Bavaria	Regensburg	Pilgrimage
Peregrinus		Weißenregen	Mariä Himmelfahrt		Upper Palati-nate	Regensburg	Pilgrimage

Table 2. Roman catacomb saints translated to Bavaria from 1804 to 1871

Name	Date of translation	Town/city	Church	Order (if applicable)	Region	Diocese	Type of church
Geminus	1804	Lohkirchen	Mariä Himmelfahrt		Upper Bavaria	Freising	Parish
Clemens	1825	Bad Endorf	St. Jakob		Upper Bavaria	Freising	Parish
Innocentia	1825	Pfeffenhausen	St. Martin		Lower Bavaria	Regensburg	Parish
Vincentius	1825	Pfeffenhausen	St. Martin		Lower Bavaria	Regensburg	Parish
Theodora	1825	Pfeffenhausen	St. Martin		Lower Bavaria	Regensburg	Parish
Reparatus	1825	Pfeffenhausen	St. Martin		Lower Bavaria	Regensburg	Parish
Benignus	1825	Pfeffenhausen	Wallfahrtskirche zu Unserer Lieben Frau		Lower Bavaria	Regensburg	Pilgrimage
Victoria	1825	Pfeffenhausen	Wallfahrtskirche zu Unserer Lieben Frau		Lower Bavaria	Regensburg	Pilgrimage
Columba	1825	Pfeffenhausen	Wallfahrtskirche zu Unserer Lieben Frau		Lower Bavaria	Regensburg	Pilgrimage
Blasius	1825	Pfeffenhausen	Wallfahrtskirche zu Unserer Lieben Frau		Lower Bavaria	Regensburg	Pilgrimage
Innocentius	1827	Bad Heilbrunn	St. Kilian		Upper Bavaria	Augsburg	Parish
Honorata	1828	Gnadenberg	St. Birgitta		Upper Palatinate	Eichstätt	Parish

Viktor	1840	Altötting	St. Magdalena	Redemp-torist	Upper Bavaria	Passau	Cloister
Felizitas	1842	Gerolsbach	St. Andreas		Upper Bavaria	Freising	Parish
Bonifazia	1842	Gerolsbach	St. Andreas		Upper Bavaria	Freising	Parish
Victor	1842	Mühlberg	Maria Mühlberg		Upper Bavaria	Freising	Pilgrimage
Fidelis	1842	Waging am See	St. Martin		Upper Bavaria	Freising	Parish
Placidus	1842	Zorneding	St. Martin		Upper Bavaria	Freising	Parish
Felix	1844	Grassau	Wallfahrtskirche Mariä Himmelfahrt		Upper Bavaria	Freising	Parish
Victor	1845	Flintsbach	St. Peter (Kleine Madron)		Upper Bavaria	Freising	Pilgrimage
Aurelius	1845	Moosbach	St. Peter and Paul		Upper Palatinate	Regensburg	Parish
Modestinus	1845	Oberschneiding	Mariä Himmelfahrt		Lower Bavaria	Regensburg	Parish
Theophilus	1846	Sandharlanden	St. Gallus		Lower Bavaria	Regensburg	Parish
Theodorus	1847	Reißing	Mariä unbeleckte Empfängnis		Lower Bavaria	Regensburg	Parish
Victoria	1861	Oberpiebing	St. Nikolaus		Lower Bavaria	Regensburg	Parish
Theodorus	1861	Oberpiebing	St. Nikolaus		Lower Bavaria	Regensburg	Parish
Irenäus	1871	Cham	Franziskanerkirche	Franciscan	Upper Palatinate	Regensburg	Cloister

NOTES

Abbreviations

AEM	Archiv des Erzbistums München und Freising
ASVR	Archivio storico del Vicariato di Roma
BayHStA	Bayerisches Hauptstaatsarchiv München
—Fasz	Faszikel
—GR	General Register
—KL	Klosterliteralien
BLfD	Bayerisches Landesamt für Denkmalpflege
FÖWAH	Fürstlich Oettingen-Wallersteinsches Archiv Harburg
STAA	Staatsarchiv Amberg
UBM	Universitätsbibliothek der LMU München

Introduction

1. The territory of Bavaria was a duchy until 1628. As a result of the Catholic forces' victory at the Battle of White Mountain, the Bavarian dukes took over the territory of the Upper Palatinate as well as its electoral title. From 1623 to 1806, the state was known as the Electorate of Bavaria (Kurfürstentum Bayern).
2. Duhamelle and Baciocchi, "Les reliques romaines," 5.
3. Oryshkevich, "History of the Roman Catacombs," 3. Oryshkevich demonstrates that the catacombs were not as forgotten as contemporary writers claimed. At least five catacombs had been accessible and frequented throughout the Middle Ages and Renaissance, and the names and locations of several dozen catacombs appeared throughout this period in guides to Rome.
4. Julia M. H. Smith, "Portable Christianity," 152.
5. Legner, "Vom Glanz," 96; Evangelisti, "Material Culture."
6. Forster, *Catholic Germany from the Reformation to the Enlightenment,* 154; Harries, *Bavarian Rococo Church,* 48–72; Pötzl, "Volksfrömmigkeit," 901, 956.
7. Forster, *Catholic Germany from the Reformation to the Enlightenment,* 164.
8. Melion, "Introduction: The Jesuit Engagement," 1–40; Jeffrey Chipps Smith, *Sensuous Worship,* 35–52.
9. Bynum, *The Resurrection of the Body,* 105.
10. Copeland, "Sanctity," 239; Johnson, *Magistrates, Madonnas and Miracles,* 270.
11. Delfosse, "Les reliques des catacombs de Rome aux Pays-Bas," 263; Ticchi, "Mgr Sacriste," 190; Baciocchi, Bonzon, and Julia, "De Rome au royaume de France," 413–15; Bonzon, "Autour de Montpellier," 459–60; Achermann, *Die*

Katakombenheiligen, 47; Duhamelle and Baciocchi, "Des Guardes Suisses," 390–98.

12. Duhamelle and Baciocchi, "Les reliques romaines," 5.
13. Ditchfield, "Thinking with Saints," 575.
14. Guazzelli, "Cesare Baronio and the Roman Catholic Vision of the Early Church," 62; Oryshkevich, "History of the Roman Catacombs," 331–32.
15. Walsham, "Introduction: Relics and Remains," 14–15.
16. Bartlett, *Why Can the Dead Do Such Great Things?*, 85–89.
17. One of the fiercest critiques in this vein came from the Protestant reformer John Calvin (see Calvin, *A Treatise on Relics*, 217–82).
18. *Decrees of the Ecumenical Councils*, 2:775.
19. Ibid., 2:775–76.
20. For concise overviews of research in each of these areas, see Ditchfield, "Tridentine Worship and the Cult of Saints"; Copeland, "Sanctity"; and Lepage, "Art and the Counter-Reformation."
21. Delooz, "Towards a Sociological Study of Canonized Sainthood," 194–95; Burke, "How to Become a Counter-Reformation Saint," 130; Ditchfield, "Martyrs on the Move"; Ditchfield, *Liturgy, Sanctity and History*.
22. Bouley, *Pious Postmortems*, 13–57; Harris, "Gift, Sale, and Theft"; Olds, "The Ambiguities of the Holy."
23. Ditchfield, "How Not to Be a Counter-Reformation Saint"; Gentilcore, *From Bishop to Witch*, 162–202; Haliczer, *Between Exaltation and Infamy;* Gotor, *I Beati del papa;* Schutte, *Aspiring Saints*; Zarri, "Living Saints."
24. This trend began with the following foundational works: Christian, *Local Religion in Sixteenth-Century Spain;* Burke, "How to Become a Counter-Reformation Saint," 130. For an overview of more recent scholarship, see Copeland, "Sanctity."
25. Worcester, "Saints and Baroque Piety," 851; Laven, introduction to *The Ashgate Research Companion to the Counter-Reformation*, 9.
26. Hills, "How to Look like a Counter-Reformation Saint," 208.
27. Walsham, "Introduction: Relics and Remains," 15n13, 16n19. The literature on medieval relics and reliquaries is extensive. Some of the most important works include Angenendt, *Heilige und Reliquien;* Beissel, *Die Verehrung der Heiligen und ihrer Reliquien;* Bagnoli, *Treasures of Heaven;* Braun, *Die Reliquiare;* Brown, *The Cult of the Saints;* Diedrichs, *Vom Glauben zum Sehen;* Geary, *Furta Sacra;* Geary, "Sacred Commodities"; Hahn, *Strange Beauty;* Herrmann-Mascard, *Les reliques des saints;* Reudenbach, "Visualizing Holy Bodies"; Julia M. H. Smith, "Saints and Their Cults"; Toussaint, *Kreuz und Knochen;* and van Os, "Seeing Is Believing," 103–62.
28. Louthan, "Tongues, Toes, and Bones," 168n2.
29. This edited collection of articles focuses exclusively on the use of relics in the sixteenth through the twentieth centuries: Boutry, Fabre, and Julia, *Reliques modernes*.

30. Johnson, "Holy Fabrications"; Lazure, "Possessing the Sacred," 58; Louthan, "Tongues, Toes, and Bones"; Jeffrey Chipps Smith, "Repatriating Sanctity"; Jeffrey Chipps Smith, "Salvaging Saints"; Walsham, "Skeletons in the Cupboard."
31. Hahn, *Reliquary Effect,* 150–211; Hills, "Nuns and Relics"; Hills, *Matter of Miracles;* Ulčar, "Saints in Parts."
32. Baciocchi and Duhamelle, *Reliques romaines;* Ghilardi, "Auertendo"; Ghilardi, "Quae signa erant illa."
33. John, ". . . mit Behutsambkeit vnd Referentz zu tractieren"; Krausen, "Das heilbringende Öl," 58–62; Krausen, "Die Verehrung römischer Katakombenheiliger"; Lechner, "Der heilige Martyrer Lucius"; Liebhart, "'doch sagt mir her'"; Markmiller, "Die Übertragung zweier Katakombenheiliger"; Mois, "Reliquien und Verehrung der Heiligen Primus und Felicianus"; Pötzl, "Bruderschaften, Wallfahrten und Katakombenheilige"; Pötzl, "Katakombenheiliege als 'Attribute' von Gnadenbildern"; Pötzl, "Volksfrömmigkeit," 919–28; Ritz, "Katakombenheiligen der Klosterkirche zu Altomünster"; Ritz, "Katakombenheiligen S. Sigismund und S. Ernest"; Ritz, "Heiligen Leiber St. Stephanus und St. Benedictus"; Wenhardt, "Felix-Wallfahrt."
34. Johnson, "Holy Fabrications"; Strasser, "Bones of Contention"; Harris, "A Known Holy Body."
35. Geraerts, "Early Modern Catholicism"; Laven, introduction to *The Ashgate Research Companion to the Counter-Reformation.*
36. Reinhard, "Pressures towards Confessionalization?"; Reinhard, "Reformation, Counter-Reformation, and the Early Modern State"; Lotz-Heumann, "Confessionalization," 33–36.
37. Forster, *Counter-Reformation in the Villages;* Forster, *Catholic Revival;* François, *Die unsichtbare Grenze;* Freitag, *Die Reformation in Westfalen;* Freitag, *Volks- und Elitenfrömmigkeit in der frühen Neuzeit;* Holzem, *Religion und Lebensformen;* Christian, *Local Religion in Sixteeenth-Century Spain;* Gentilcore, *From Bishop to Witch;* Kamen, *The Phoenix and the Flame;* Nalle, *God in La Mancha.*
38. Forster, "Catholic Confessionalism," 228; Forster, "With and without Confessionalization"; François, *Die unsichtbare Grenze,* 221; Holzem, *Religion und Lebensformen,* 455–70; Lotz-Heumann, "Confessionalization," 37–38.
39. Reinhard, "Was ist katholische Konfessionalisierung?"; Hsia, *Social Discipline in the Reformation;* Veit and Lenhart, *Kirche und Volksfrömmigkeit im Zeitalter des Barock;* Hubensteiner, *Vom Geist des Barock,* 20, 51, 64, 201.
40. Ziegler, "Bayern," 49–53, 56–57, 63.
41. Forster, *Catholic Germany from the Reformation to the Enlightenment,* 49.
42. Albrecht V established Jesuit branches in Altötting, Biburg, Ebersburg, Regensburg, and Münchmunster. For a detailed analysis of St. Michael's church and its iconography, see Jeffrey Chipps Smith, *Sensuous Worship,* 57–102.
43. Müller, "Der Versuch Herzog Wilhelms V," 117–35; Jeffrey Chipps Smith, "Salvaging Saints," 23–38; Jeffrey Chipps Smith, "Repatriating Sanctity," 1084–88.

44. Steiner, "Der gottselige Fürst," 254. For more on the Wittelsbachs' policies on the regulation of gender and sexuality in the early modern period, see Strasser, *State of Virginity.*
45. Johnson, "Holy Dynasts and Sacred Soil"; Schmid, "Bavaria Sancta et Pia."
46. For a detailed overview of Bavarian political and religious history in early modern period, see Albrecht, *Das alte Bayern,* 289–533; and Ziegler, "Reformation und Gegenreformation 1517–1648." For a detailed examination of the re-Catholicization process in the Upper Palatinate, see Johnson, *Magistrates, Madonnas and Miracles.*
47. Woeckel, *Pietas Bavarica,* 33–36. For more on the revitalization of pilgrimages and shrines in Bavaria during this period, see Soergel, *Wondrous in His Saints.*
48. Herzig, *Der Zwang zum wahren Glauben,* 176–77.
49. Woeckel, *Pietas Bavarica,* 95.
50. Schmid, "Altbayern 1648–1803," 355.
51. Steiner, "Der gottselige Fürst," 262.
52. Johnson, *Magistrates, Madonnas and Miracles,* 6; Pentzlin, "The Cult of Corpus Christi," 5–6.

1. Creating Bavaria sancta from the Ground Up

1. Rader, *Bavaria Sancta et Pia,* 4r–5r. Cited passage translated in Johnson, "Defining the Confessional Frontier," 161.
2. Steiner, "Der gottselige Fürst," 253.
3. Jeffrey Chipps Smith, "Salvaging Saints," 30.
4. Eisengrein, *Ein Christliche predig,* 22–55.
5. For more information on Johannes Nas and his career, see Remigius Bärmer, "Nas, Johannes," in *Neue Deutsche Biographie* 18, ed. Franz Menges (Berlin: Duncker and Humblot, 1997).
6. Nas, *Ein tröstliche Creützpredig,* Aiiij–r.
7. Burkardt, "Zur aller antiquitet lieb und naigung," 644; Jeffrey Chipps Smith, "Salvaging Saints," 23–38; Jeffrey Chipps Smith, "Repatriating Sanctity," 1084–88.
8. Jeffrey Chipps Smith, "Repatriating Sanctity," 1085.
9. Luther, *Widder den newen Abgott.*
10. Ibid., 68.
11. Steiner, "Der gottselige Fürst," 258.
12. Jeffrey Chipps Smith, "Repatriating Sanctity," 1085; Jeffrey Chipps Smith, "Salvaging Saints," 30; Seelig, "Dieweil wir dann nach dergleichen Heiltumb."
13. Herbert Brunner and Albrecht Miller, *Die Kunstschätze der Münchner Residenz* (Munich: Süddeutscher Verlag, 1977), 183.
14. For more on the relic collection at St. Michael's, see *Trophaea Bavarica;* and Seelig, "Dieweil wir dann nach dergleichen Heiltumb."
15. *Trophaea Bavarica,* 220n239.

16. Burkardt, "Zur aller antiquitet lieb und naigung," 653.
17. Krausen, "Schicksale römischer Katakombenheiliger," 165.
18. Dreher, *Die Augustiner-Eremiten,* 424; Pötzl, "Katakombenheiliege als 'Attribute' von Gnadenbildern," 173–74; Hemmerle, *Die Benediktinerabtei Benediktbeuern,* 513.
19. For a detailed study of the re-Catholicization process in the Upper Palatinate, see Johnson, *Magistrates, Madonnas and Miracles.*
20. Johnson, "Holy Fabrications," 282.
21. Burkardt, "Zur aller antiquitet lieb und naigung," 653.
22. For more information on the role of the Jesuits in Bavaria, see Baumstark, *Rom in Bayern;* and Rummel, "Jesuiten," 842–57. For more information on the role of the Capuchins in Bavaria, see Sprinkart, "Kapuziner."
23. Monastic orders founded after the outbreak of the Reformation that were active in Bavaria include the Jesuits, the Capuchins, the Theatines, the Oratorians, the Discalced Carmelites, the English Ladies, the Ursulines, and the Salesians/Visitandines.
24. BayHStA, KL Fasz. 1069 172, Elector Maximilian II Emmanuel to Geisenfeld cloister, letter requesting list of holy bodies acquired in last century, February 4, 1701.
25. Ibid., Duke Maximilian to Geisenfeld cloister, letter requesting a list of all relics held at the cloister church, 1601.
26. *Saeculum octavum,* 4 (Beschreibung).
27. Ferrua, "Corpi Santi," 587.
28. Segni, *Reliquiarum,* 128–29.
29. Dooley, *Church Law on Sacred Relics,* 4–5.
30. For more on forging authentication certificates for stolen relics, as well one rather notorious practitioner of such illegal activities, see Ghilardi, "Auertando"; Harris, "Gift, Sale, and Theft," 10; and Herklotz, "Wie Jean Mabillon," 201–3.
31. "Diversae Ordinationes circa extractionem reliquiarum ex Coemeteriis Urbis, & Locorum, circumvincinorum, illarumque custodiam, & distributionem," in *Bullarium Romanum seu novissima et accuratissima collectio apostolicarum constitutionum ex autographis, quæ in Secretiori Vaticano, aliisque Sedis Apostolicæ scriniis asservantur: cum rubricis, summariis, scholiis, & indice quadruplici* (Rome: Hieronymi Mainardi, 1733), 161–62.
32. For more information on the position and responsibilities of the custodian of sacred relics, see Cuggiò, *Della giurisdittine,* 112–20; and Ghilardi, "Il Custode delle Reliquie."
33. Ticchi, "Mgr Sacriste," 197–98, 205–6; Boutry, "Les corps saints des catacombes," 230.
34. Cuggiò, *Della giurisdittione e prerogative,* 114.
35. Achermann, *Die Katakombenheiligen,* 35–36.
36. ASVR, Fondo Reliquie 77, "Custodia d. SS. Reliquie dell' Emo Sig Card. Vicario di N.S. Corpi, Reliquie de'SS. Martiri donate, Tom. I," 1737–83; ASVR, Fondo

Reliquie 78, "Custodia delle SS. Reliquie dell'Emo Signor Cardinale Vicario di N.S. Corpi, e Reliquie de' SS. Martiri donate, Tomo II," 1783–86; ASVR, Fondo Reliquie 79, "Corpi e reliquie de'SS Martiri donate Tom. III," 1786–1800.

37. ASVR, Fondo Reliquie 77, Francesco Saverio Morthl to Custodian of Sacred Relics, January 18, 1782.
38. ASVR, Fondo Reliquie 78, Giuseppe König and Antonio Wipenberger to the Custodian of Sacred Relics, October 22, 1785.
39. Cuggiò, *Della giurisdittione e prerogative,* 113–14.
40. Ibid., 117.
41. Boldetti, *Osservazioni,* 248–49.
42. Baciocchi and Duhamelle, "Les reliques romaines," in Duhamelle and Baciocchi, *Reliques romaines,* 6; Boutry, "Les corps saints des catacombes," ibid., 230.
43. Cuggiò, *Della giurisdittione e prerogative,* 114; Archiv der Münchener Provinz der Redemptoristen zu Gars, Dokumente betreffend die Echtheit u. Überfuhurng der Gebeine des Hl. Martyrer Felix nach Gars v. Jahr 1671–74, authentication certificate.
44. Achermann, *Die Katakombenheiligen,* 20–21.
45. Ibid., 30–31; Strasser, "Bones of Contention," 273–80.
46. *Translatio oder Erheb- und uberbringung deß H. Antonini Martyrers,* A7r–8r.
47. Bosl, "Heilige Leiber," 117.
48. Andreas Hobmayer, *Die Verehrung der schmerzhaften und wunderthätighen Gnadenmutter Maria in der Pfarrkirche zu Miesbach* (Miesbach, Germany: J. Mayer, 1857), 12–13; "Der Heilige Maurus," http://www.maurusverlag.de/maurus_von_miesbach.htm; *Translation oder feyerliche und herrliche Ubersetzung des Heil. Leibs S. Maximi,* Bericht.
49. Pichler, "Reisebeschribung des Schumacherssohnes." Pichler's account was transcribed by J. Obermayer and appeared in serialized form over several months in the *Audorfer Heimgarten* in 1925.
50. Thomas Führer, "P. Matthäus Ludwig, letzter Prior des Klosters der Birgittiner in Altomünster," *Amperland* 4 (1969): 20.
51. Archiv der Münchener Provinz der Redemptoristen zu Gars, Dokumente betreffend die Echtheit u. Überfuhurng der Gebeine des Hl. Martyrer Felix nach Gars v. Jahr 1671–74, authentication certificate.
52. Pfarrarchiv St. Peter in München, Urkunde 398A, authentication certificate for catacomb saint relics, including Saint Honoratus, given to Thomas Candidus by the Cardinal Vicar Marzio Ginetti, October 20, 1646.
53. Pfarrarchiv St. Peter in München, Urkunde 406, notarized donation of Saint Honratus's holy body to Stephan Höck from Thomas Candidus, June 25, 1650.
54. Pfarrarchiv St. Peter in München, Urkunde 408A, Stephan Höck's donation of Saint Honoratus's holy body to St. Peter's parish church in Munich, June 15, 1653.
55. Malgaritta, *Jahrs- und kurtze Beschreibung,* 5; Weinberger, *Glorwürdiges Sechstes Jubel-Jahr,* 240–41; Bosl, "Heilige Leiber," 120.
56. ASVR, Editta vicarii Urbis, 1566–1609, 217r.

57. Landucci, "Pratica per estrarre li corpi," 123–24.
58. Ibid., 128–29. See also Ghilardi, "Quae signa erant illa," 90–92.
59. Strasser, "Bones of Contention," 262.
60. Ibid., 274.
61. Ibid., 275.
62. Ibid., 280–82.
63. Stadtarchiv Dingolfing, B VIII Nr. 10, *Anmerckhung wie undt wass Weiss die Gepeiner der heiligen Jungfrau undt Marterin Faustina von Rom aus piss Dingolfing jberpracht undt den 4. Juni amb Pfingstmontag prozessinallider in die Pfahrkirchen getragen undt zuhr St. Anna Capellen, so denen petten Handtwerchen der Mauerern undt Zimerleiten zuehgeherig, jbersetzt wordten,* entries for the year 1766.
64. Stadtarchiv Dingolfing, B VIII Nr. 10, entries for 1768.
65. Ibid., notes for 1769–70.
66. Meychel, *Erhebung des H. Martyrers Honorat,* B6r and Cr.
67. *Prototypon Munditiae.*
68. STAA, Geistliche Sachen 681, Letter of May 1, 1668.
69. STAA, Gestliche Sachen 681, Letters of May 3 and June 8, 1668.
70. Geppert, *Schatz und Schutz,* 16.
71. Erlmeier, *Chronik von Frontenhausen,* 6.
72. Heidtmann, "Der Heilige mit dem zuckenden Fuß," 49–50.
73. Between 1804 and 1871, parish and pilgrimage churches in Bavaria acquired twenty-seven more Roman catacomb saints. Cloisters obtained two.
74. Burkardt, "Zur aller antiquitet lieb und naigung," 631.
75. *Saeculum nostrum,* 179.
76. Augustinian Canons (16/19 cloisters), Benedictines (24/35 cloisters), Cistercians (8/12 cloisters), Premonstratensians (6/6 cloisters), and collegiate foundations (11/17 cloisters). For information on the old orders and their building projects, see Forster, *Catholic Germany from the Reformation to the Enlightenment,* 128–30.
77. Catacomb saints were transferred at the anniversary celebrations of the cloisters at Aldersbach (600th anniversary); Gotteszell (100th anniversary of rebuilding of the church after a fire); Hohenpeißenberg (anniversary of consecration, Rottenbuch's 600th anniversary); Ridlerkloster (400th anniversary); Raitenhaslach (600th anniversary); Ranshofen (800th anniversary); Vornbach (600th anniversary).
78. Mannhardt, *Stamm- und Blut-rothes Rothenbuch,* E2v.
79. *Kurze Beschribung von der feyerlich-und herlichen Uberseßung,* 2.
80. Wenhardt, "Felix-Wallfahrt," 6.
81. Krausen, "Heilige 'zweiter Klasse,'" 4.
82. Haeckhl, *Der geistliche von dem Feuer,* 13.
83. BayHStA, KL Raitenhaslach 114, letters of response from abbots and parish priests to Abbot Candidus's invitation to attend the translation festivities for

Saints Ausanius, Concordia, and Fortunatus; dates range from May 18 to August 15, 1698.

84. Bosl, "Heilige Leiber," 121.
85. BayHStA, Bayer. Franziskanerprovinz Lit. 281, description of translation festivities for Saint Tigrinus including guest list, fol. 176, January 1683.
86. Fridl, *Freundlicher Willkomb oder Jubel- und Freudenfest,* 7.
87. Geppert, *Schatz und Schutz,* C1L.
88. Adolf Hochholzer, *300 Jahre Wallfahrtskirche Gartlberg: 1688–1988* (Pfarrkirchen, Germany: Förderverein Gartlberg-Pfarrkirchen, 1988), 21.
89. Ibid., 21–22.
90. Thomas Daller, "Taufkirchen: Als die Maß Bier nur rund 90 Cent kostete," *Süddeutsche Zeitung,* April 27, 2011, http://www.sueddeutsche.de/muenchen/erding/taufkirchen-als-die-mass-bier-nur-rund-cent-kostete-1.962363; Bodo Gsedl, Josef Heilmaier, and Hubert Kemper, *Das Wasserschloss Taufkirchen* (Taufkirchen an der Vils, Germany: Heimat- und Verschönerungsverein, 2008), 102–3.

2. Some Assembly Required

1. Geppert, *Schatz und Schutz,* 8.
2. *Translation oder feyerliche und herrliche Ubersetzung deß Heil. Leibs S. Maximi,* 5.
3. Angenendt, "Corpus incorruptum," 130–31.
4. *The Vulgate Bible,* vol. 6: *The New Testament Douay-Rheims Translation,* Dumbarton Oaks Medieval Library, ed. Angela M. Kinney (Cambridge, MA: Harvard University Press, 2013), 691.
5. Ibid., 441.
6. Angenendt, "Corpus incorruptum," 124.
7. Angenendt, "Zur Ehre der Altäre erhoben," 222–26.
8. Bynum, *The Resurrection of the Body,* 106.
9. Schmitz-Esser, *Der Leichnam im Mittelalter,* 153.
10. Abou-El-Haj, *The Medieval Cult of Saints,* 31.
11. Bynum, *The Resurrection of the Body,* 202.
12. Hahn, "The Voices of Saints," 20. This type of reliquary was originally categorized as a "speaking" (*redende*) reliquary by Joseph Braun in his 1940 encyclopedic study of reliquaries (Braun, *Reliquiare des christlichen Kultes,* 380–458). Braun believed these reliquaries "spoke" or expressed their contents through their shapes. For more information on the historiographical treatment of these reliquaries, see Boehm, "Body-Part Reliquaries: The State of Research."
13. Hahn, "What Do Reliquaries Do for Relics?," 305.
14. Toussaint, "Die Sichtbarkeit des Gebeins im Reliquiar," 97–98.
15. For more information on relic festivals in late medieval Germany, see Kühne, *Ostensio reliquiarum.*

16. Soergel, *Wondrous in His Saints,* 25.
17. Klosterarchiv Grafrath, Mirakelbuch III (1692–1728), 1004.
18. Saint Caius's relics were buried under the main altar in the church.
19. The full title of the *Schatzbuch von St. Michael* is *Liber Sacrarum Reliquiarum et Supellectilis Argenteae Templi St. Michaelis Collegii Societatis Iesu.* The manuscript includes two volumes, the first of which was compiled and illustrated between 1591 and 1607. The second volume contains images of reliquaries acquired in the seventeenth century. For more information on the *Schatzbuch* and St. Michael's collection of relics, see Seelig, "Dieweil wir dann nach dergleichen Heiltumb."
20. *Schatzbuch von St. Michael,* fol. 60.
21. Ibid., fol. 53.
22. Ibid., fol. 54.
23. *Heiliger Schatz oder hochschätzbare hochheilige Reliquien,* B2v.
24. Ibid., Br.
25. Ibid., B2v.
26. Strasser, "Bones of Contention," 255–67, 273–86.
27. *Bittrich voll deß himmlischen Manna,* 188–89; John, ". . . mit Behutsambkeit vnd Reverentz zu tractieren," 17.
28. John, ". . . mit Behutsambkeit vnd Reverentz zu tractieren," 19.
29. *Chronik deß hochberümbten Closters und Gottshauses heiligen Berg Andechs S. Benedicten Ordens Augsburger Bisthumbs in Obern Bayrn gelegen* (Munich: Johann Jäcklin, 1657), 88; *Mons Sanctus Andechs: Das ist kurtzer Begriff oder Innhalt von dem gnadenrichen Heil. Berg Andechs* (Augsburg: Jacob Koppmayer, 1691), 46; *Mons Sanctvs Andechs in Svperiori Boiaria: Das ist kurtzer Begriff, oder Innhalt von dem gnadenreichen heiligen Berg Andechs, deß heiligen Vatters Benedicti Ordens, Augspurger Bistumbs in obern Bayrn* (Munich: Johann Lucas Straub, 1715), 46; *Mons Sanctus das ist kurzer Begriff von dem gnadenreichen Heiligen Berg Andechs* (Augsburg: Joseph Domenicus Gruber, 1745), 46.
30. Alois Schmid, "Zwischen Reformationszeit und Aufklärung," in *Andechs der heilige Berg: Von der Frühzeit bis zur Gegenwart,* ed. Karl Bosl, Odilo Lechner, Wolfgang Schüle, and Josef Othmar Zöller (Munich: Prestel, 1993), 70 and Tafel 33.
31. BayHStA KL Fasz. 626 No. 1; Alexander Heisig, *Rott am Inn* (Rott am Inn, Germany: Katholisches Pfarramt St. Peter und Paul, 2005), 30.
32. Borromeo and Voelker, "Charles Borromeo's *Instructiones,*" 207–8.
33. Müller, *Kirchen-Geschmuck,* 71–81.
34. *Decrees of the Ecumenical Councils,* 2:776.
35. Achermann, *Die Katakombenheiligen,* 71.
36. Legner, "Vom Glanz," 133.
37. Achermann, *Die Katakombenheiligen,* 96.
38. Pfeiffer, "Auferweckt in Herrlichkeit!," 16.

39. Ibid., 49.
40. Uta Ludwig, "Dokumentation: Skelettreliquie Hl. Fidelis" (unpublished manuscript, August 13, 2001), Microsoft Word file, 3.
41. AEM, Pfarrakten, Freising-St. Georg 08.05/7, account book of donations and costs for the decoration of Saints Timotheus and Clara, March 8, 1751.
42. The Gulden was a gold or silver coin used in Bavaria, and across the southern and western Holy Roman Empire, until 1873. It was the equivalent of the Italian florin and therefore was often abbreviated as "Fl." or "fl." in account books. One Gulden was equal to 60 Kreuzer, and 1 Kreuzer was worth 8 Heller (hl.).
43. AEM, Pfarrakten, Freising-St. Georg 08.05/7, account book of donations and costs for the decoration of Saints Timotheus and Clara, March 8, 1751.
44. Ibid.
45. Uta Ludwig, email message to author, April 22, 2014.
46. Pfeiffer, "Auferweckt in Herrlichkeit!," 66–118.
47. BLfD, Hahnbach, "Restaurierung, Reliquie Hl. Felix: Konservierungsprotokoll," 3–4, 2011; BLfD, Berg am Laim-München, "Ganzkörperreliquie Hl. Clemens: Restaurierungsbericht mit Fotodokumentation," 2, 2011; BLfD, Berg am Laim-München, "Ganzkörperreliquie Hl. Benedict: Restaurierungsbericht mit Fotodokumentation," 2, 2011.
48. BLfD, Unterdießen/Lkr. Landsberg a. L/OB, "St. Nikolaus, Hl. Peregrina," 2–4, 1996.
49. Sitting saints are present at Gars am Inn, Altenhohenau, and Altomünster, all former cloister churches. Standing saints can be found in Altomünster, Osterhofen, Tirschenreuth, and Waldsassen.
50. FÖWAH, K16. 2a. Nr. 38, 1, Magdalena Fletting to Abbot Amandus Röls, October 4, 1725.
51. Ibid., Abbot Amandus Röls to Magdalena Fletting, October 15, 1725.
52. For more information on Eder, see Gläßel, *Adalbert Eder.*
53. Johann Baptist Sparrer, *Der Reliquienschatz in der ehemaligen Stifts- und Klosterkirche zu Waldsassen* (Regensburg, Germany: Habbel, 1892), 62–63.
54. Pfeiffer, "Auferweckt in Herrlichkeit!," 54.
55. BayHStA GR 513 65x.
56. Uta Ludwig, "Dokumentation—Skelettreliquie Hl. Albano" (unpublished manuscript, January 29, 2010), Microsoft Word file, 2–7.
57. Schiedermair, "Klosterarbeiten," 9.
58. Ibid., 17.
59. Ibid., 10.
60. Ibid., 19–20.
61. Legner, "Vom Glanz," 129.
62. Achermann, *Die Katakombenheiligen,* 84; John, ". . . mit Behutsambkeit vnd Reverentz zu tractieren," 8; Schiedermair, "Klosterarbeiten," 19.
63. Schiedermaier, "Klosterarbeiten," 12.
64. Pfeiffer, "Auferweckt in Herrlichkeit!," 13.

65. Schiedermaier, "Klosterarbeiten," 12.
66. Rita Hoidn, "Kloster Reutberg 1606–1802: Geschichte, Kunst und Frömmigkeit mit besonderer Berücksichtigung der 'Schönen Arbeiten'" (PhD diss, Universität Bamberg, 2001), 313.
67. Pfeiffer, "Auferweckt in Herrlichkeit!," 51.
68. Schiedermair, "Die Waldsassener Heiligen Leiber," 359.
69. Ibid., 364.
70. Weinberger, *Glorwürdiges Sechstes Jubel-Jahr,* 99.
71. Achermann, *Die Katakombenheiligen,* 103; Legner, "Vom Glanz," 35; Ritz, "Die Katakombenheiligen S. Sigismund und S. Ernest," 226.
72. Wasserburg, *Fluenta Jordanis,* 403.
73. Ritz, "Die Katakombenheiligen S. Sigismund und S. Ernest," 227.
74. Stadtarchiv Dachau, Kirchenrechnungen 1719, fol. 39f.
75. "Loth" was a unit of measurement equal to 1/32 of a pound.
76. Stadtarchiv Dachau, Kirchenrechnungen 1719, fol. 39f.
77. Ibid.
78. Margareta Edlin-Thieme, *Studien zur Geschichte des Münchner Handelsstandes im 18. Jahrhundert* (Stuttgart: G. Fischer, 1969), 86.
79. Strasser, *State of Virginity,* 52; Ritz, "Die Katakombenheiligen S. Sigismund und S. Ernest," 279.
80. Stadtarchiv Dachau, Kirchenrechnungen 1719, fol. 39f. Wilhelm Jocher von Eggersberg (1565–1636) was a Bavarian statesman who served at the court of Maximilian I as a jurist and member of the privy council. He left money in his will for the creation of the Jocherschen Spitalstiftung—a hospital foundation—to serve the inhabitants of Dachau. For more information on von Eggersberg, see Felix Stieve, "Wilhlem Jocher von Ebersperg," in *Allgemeine Deutsche Biographie* 14 (Leipzig: Duncker & Humblot, 1881), 102–3.
81. Stadarchiv Dingolfing, B VIII Nr. 10, entry for February 7, 1784.
82. Markmiller, "Die Übertragung zweier Katakombenheiliger," 133.
83. AEM, Pfarrakten, Freising-St. Georg 150, Joseph Krimmer to Freising Cathedral chapter, August 28, 1736.
84. AEM, Pfarrakten, Freising-St. Georg 08.05/7, account book of donations and costs for the decoration of Saints Timotheus and Clara, March 8, 1751.
85. AEM, Pfarrakten, Freising-St. Georg 151, Joseph Krimmer to Freising Cathedral chapter, April 18, 1743.
86. Mannhardt, *Stamm- und Blut-rothes Rothenbuch,* 2.
87. Kurz, *Blutschaumendes der Welt zur Nachfolge,* 30.
88. BayHStA KL Fasz. 971, Rechnungsbücher 1740–48, 17r–19r. The total income for the cloister in 1741 was 20,620 Gulden, 23 Kreuzer, and 3½ Heller, while the total costs related to the catacomb saints was 2,226 Gulden and 16 Kreuzer.
89. FÖWAH, K16. 2a. Nr. 38, 1, Abbot Amandus Röls to Magdalena Fletting, October 15, 1725.
90. Fischer, *Neuer Meer- und Glücksstern,* 2.

91. BayHStaA, KL Fasz. 390/1705, Joachim von Empacher to Abbess Maria Eleonora, September 24, 1681; Zwingler, *Das Klarissenkloster bei St. Jakob am Anger,* 594.
92. BayHStA, KL Fasz. 424.
93. BayHStA, KL Fasz. 1069–72.

3. Whole-Body Saints and Eucharistic Doctrine

1. *Decrees of the Ecumenical Councils,* 2:695.
2. Ibid., 2:734.
3. Ambrose of Milan, "Letter XXI," in *A Select Library of Nicene and Post-Nicene Fathers of the Christian Church, Second Series: Saint Ambrose, Select Works and Letters,* ed. and trans. Philip Schaff and Henry Wace (New York: Christian Literature Company, 1896), 10:438.
4. Angenendt, "Zur Ehre der Altäre erhoben," 221–23.
5. *Decrees of the Ecumenical Councils,* 1:145; Geary, *Furta Sacra,* 18, 37; Snoek, *Medieval Piety from Relics to the Eucharist,* 175–202.
6. Geary, *Furta Sacra,* 23.
7. Snoek, *Medieval Piety from Relics to the Eucharist,* 5.
8. *Decrees of the Ecumenical* Councils, 2:734.
9. For a detailed treatment of the different confessional interpretations of the Eucharist during the Reformation, see Wandel, *The Eucharist in the Reformation.*
10. *Decrees of the Ecumenical* Councils, 2:695.
11. Ibid., 2:732.
12. Ibid., 2:733.
13. Soergel, *Wondrous in His Saints,* 86–98.
14. Johnson, *Magistrates, Madonnas and Miracles,* 209. For examples of Catholic German theologians defending the Eucharist, see Eck, *De Sacrificio Missae Libri Tres (1526).*
15. For more on the Corpus Christi procession in early modern Bavaria, see Mitterwieser, *Geschichte der Fronleichnamsprozession in Bayern,* 33–63; Pentzlin, "The Cult of Corpus Christi," 116–60; and Soergel, *Wondrous in His Saints,* 87–94.
16. Pentzlin, "The Cult of Corpus Christi," 167.
17. Ibid., 189.
18. For an assessment of the "active role of the populace" in creating Catholic confessional identity through the celebration of the feast of Corpus Christi in early modern Bavaria, see Pentzlin, "The Cult of Corpus Christi," 16, 47–70, 136–60, 209–14.
19. Orban, *Ramus Aureus,* 22.
20. Malgaritta, *Jahrs- und kurtze Beschreibung,* Bericht. The pages of this miracle book are not numbered. The cited passage appears on the sixth page of the section entitled "Kurz und gründlich bestellter Bericht uber den zu Rom

erhebten und in hiesig: weit beriembten hochLöbl: Gotts=Hauß / und Jungkfraw Kloster deß ChurFürstl: Marckts Geisenfeldt den 30. Julij im 1673. Jahr beygesetzt / und ruehenden gantzen Heiligen Leib S. DIONYSII M."

21. Wasserburg, *Fluenta Jordanis*, 395.
22. Later it was discovered that the substance in the vases was not blood but perfume (see Herklotz, "Antonio Bosio und Carlo Bascapè," 93). For more on the history of the debate on the contents of these "blood vases," see de Rossi and Ferrua, *Sulla questione del vaso di sangue.*
23. *St. Beninus Martyrer*, 16.
24. Weinberger, *Glorwürdiges Sechstes Jubel-Jahr*, 46; Hamilton, *Die glorwürdige Blutzeugen*, 10.
25. Wasserburg, *Fluenta Jordanis*, 387.
26. Weinberger, *Glorwürdiges Sechstes Jubel-Jahr*, 34.
27. Wasserburg, *Fluenta Jordanis*, 401.
28. Hamilton, *Die glorwürdige Blutzeugen*, 17; *Decrees of the Ecumenical Councils*, 2:733. In chapter 2 of Session 22 of the decrees of the Council of Trent (September 17, 1562), the Council declared: "In this divine sacrifice which is performed in the mass, the very same Christ is contained and offered in bloodless manner who made a bloody sacrifice of himself once for all on the cross."
29. Wandel, *The Eucharist in the Reformation*, 223.
30. Wasserburg, *Fluenta Jordanis*, 430.
31. Ibid., 384.
32. *Saeculum octavum*, 189.
33. Wasserburg, *Fluenta Jordanis*, 437.
34. *Saeculum octavum*, 181.
35. V. M. Oberhauser, "Lamb of God," in *New Catholic Encyclopedia*, 2nd ed., ed. Berard Marthaler (Detroit, MI: Thomson/Gale, 2003).
36. *Prototypon Munditiae*, 9.
37. Weinberger, *Glorwürdiges Sechstes Jubel-Jahr*, 105.
38. Rubin, *Corpus Christi*, 310–12.
39. Weinberger, *Glorwürdiges Sechstes Jubel-Jahr*, 59–60.
40. Mannstorff, *Epitome Chronicorum Alderspacensium*, 56.
41. *St. Beninus Martyrer*, 31.
42. *The Vulgate Bible*, vol. 3: *The Poetical Books Douay-Rheims Translation*, Dumbarton Oaks Medieval Library, ed. Edgar Swift (Cambridge, MA: Harvard University Press, 2011), 237.
43. Ibid., 531.
44. Johnson, "*Trionfi* of the Holy Dead," 42.
45. Rubin, *Corpus Christi*, 245.
46. This occurred in processions at Aldersbach, Amberg (Hofkapelle), Arnschwang, Arnstorf, Benediktbeuren, Dingolfing (Faustina), Gars, Geisenfeld, Kühbach, Munich (Pütrichkloster), Munich (Angerkloster), Marienberg, Ranshofen, St. Veit, Steingaden, Straubing (Uruslines), and Vornbach.

47. *Translation oder feyerliche und herrliche Ubersetzung des Heil. Leibs S. Maximi Martyrers*, frontispiece; "Die Zerstörung 1944," Marianische Männerkongregation: Mariä Verkündigung am Bürgersaal zu München, accessed May 4, 2021, https://www.mmkbuergersaal.de/buergersaalkirche/oberkirche/die-zerstoerung-1944.html.
48. Braun, *Die Reliquiare*, 490.
49. Müller, *Kirchen-Geschmuck*, 123–25.
50. Hamm, *Barocke Altartabernakel*, 284–86.
51. Weinberger, *Glorwürdiges Sechstes Jubel-Jahr*, 102.
52. Frederick McManus and J. B. O'Connell, "Tabernacle," in *New Catholic Encyclopedia*, 2nd ed., ed. Berard Marthaler (Detroit, MI: Thomson/Gale, 2003).
53. Ibid.
54. Müller, *Kirchen-Geschmuck*, 17.
55. Hamm, *Barocke Altartabernakel*, 179–84; *Dictionary of Subjects and Symbols in Art*, ed. James Hall (London: J. Murray, 1974), s.v. "Flame."
56. E. Sauser, "Anker," in *Lexikon der christlichen Ikonographie*, ed. Engelbert Kirschbaum and Wolfgang Braunfels (Rome: Herder, 1968).
57. Ebermann, "300 Jahre St. Felix in Gars," 78.
58. E. Sauser, "Schmerzen Marians," in *Lexikon der christlichen Ikonographie*, ed. Engelbert Kirschenbaum and Wolfgang Braunfels (Rome: Herder, 1968). The iconography of the Mater Dolorosa is based on Luke 2:34–35. When Mary and Joseph presented Jesus in the Temple, the seer Simeon told Mary: "This child is set for the fall and resurrection of many in Israel and for a sign which shall be contradicted; and thy own soul a sword shall pierce, that out of many hearts thoughts may be revealed" (*The Vulgate Bible*, volume 6: *The New Testament Douay-Rheims Translation*, 307). The reference to the sword piercing Mary's soul was interpreted as an illusion to her son's future Crucifixion and Mary's empathetic suffering with him.
59. Pentzlin, "The Cult of Corpus Christi," 59.
60. Weinberger, *Glorwürdiges Sechstes Jubel-Jahr*, 67.
61. Kurz, *Blutschaumendes der Welt zur Nachfolge*, 23–24.

4. *Semper eadem*

1. For more information on the paleo-Christian revival in Rome, see Ditchfield, "Text before Trowel"; Ditchfield, "Reading Rome as a Sacred Landscape"; Guazzelli, "Cesare Baronio and the Roman Catholic Vision of the Early Church," 52–71; Guazzelli, "Antiquarianism and Christian Archaeology"; Guazzelli, "Roman Antiquities and Christian Archaeology"; Herklotz, "Antonio Bosio und Carlo Bascapè," 93–104; and Herklotz, "Wie Jean Mabillon." For additional scholarship that focuses on the reception of paleo-Christian texts by scholars outside Rome, see Guazzelli, Michetti, and Scorza Barcellona,

eds., *Cesare Baronio tra santità e scrittura storica* (Rome: Viella, 2012), 249–389; and Olds, "The 'False Chronicles.'"

2. This thesis is clearly articulated by Baronio in the *Apparatus ad annales ecclesiasticos ad lectorem* section at the beginning of first volume of his twelve-volume history of the church (see Cesare Baronio, *Annales ecclesiastici: Tomus primus* [Antwerp: Christopher Plantin, 1588], 33).
3. For a concise overview of the confessional debates around church history in the early modern period, see Grafton, "Church History in Early Modern Europe."
4. Ditchfield, "Thinking with Saints," 555.
5. Gregory, *Salvation at Stake,* 272.
6. Ditchfield, "*Romanus* and *Catholicus,*" 134.
7. Baronio, *Martyrologium Romanum,* i–xiv. For more information on the importance of martyrdom in the early modern period, see Burschel, *Sterben und Unsterblichkeit;* Gregory, "Persecutions and Martyrdom"; and Gregory, *Salvation at Stake,* 139–314.
8. Johnson, "Holy Fabrications," 294.
9. Münchner, *Neues Liecht oder Neuschein,* 19.
10. In areas north of the Alps, Gallonio's Italian treatise was often consulted and read in its cheaper Latin edition, *De ss. Martyrum cruciatibus liber.* There were far fewer illustrations in the Latin edition, though an adaptation of the image with Roman soldiers demonstrating the tools used for defleshing martyrs does appear in the 1594 translation (p. 137). For more information on Gallonio's *Trattato* and its illustrations, see Opher Mansour, "Not Torments, but Delights: Antonio Gallonio's *Trattato de gli instrumenti di martirio* of 1591 and Its Illustrations," in *Roman Bodies: Antiquity to the Eighteenth Century,* ed. Andrew Hopkins and Maria Wyke (London: British School at Rome, 2005), 167–83; and Touber, *Law, Medicine and Engineering,* 222–47. Roman soldiers as persecutors can also be seen in large graphic martyrdom cycles commissioned by the Jesuits for their German-Hungarian (St. Stefano Rotondo) and English (St. Thomas of Canterbury) Colleges in Rome in the early 1580s. These images were further propagated in printed reproductions of the frescoes that circulated across Europe.
11. Rader, *Bavaria Sancta,* 1:25 and 38; Rader, *Heiliges Bayer-Land,* 19, 75.
12. UBM ms 357, *Secretum meum misi,* entry for May 25, 1675.
13. Karl Christl, *300 Jahre barocke Pfarrkirche in Kühbach* (Kühbach, Germany: Pfarrgemeinde Kühbach, 1989), 22.
14. *Kurze Beschreibung der solennen Translation oder Einführung vier heiliger Leiber,* A4r–Br, B2r.
15. *Saeculum octavum,* foldout image after page 20. The engraving label describes boys dressed in "Roman" clothing in the seventy-first, seventy-fourth, and eighty-sixth positions in the procession.

16. *Dictionary of Subjects and Symbols in Art,* ed. James Hall (London: J. Murray, 1974), s.v. "Palm"; Engelbert Kirschenbaum and Wolfgang Braunfels, "Lorbeer," in *Lexikon der christlichen Ikonographie,* ed. Kirschenbaum and Braunfels (Rome: Herder, 1968); J. Flemming, "Palme," ibid.
17. Bosio, *Roma sotterranea,* 197.
18. Congregatio indulgentiarum et sacrarum, *Decreta authentica sacrae Congregationis indulgentiis sacrisque reliquiis praepositae: Ab anno 1668 ad annum 1882* (Regensburg, Germany: F. Pustet, 1883), 1.
19. Boldetti, *Osservazioni,* 125–212.
20. Geppert, *Schatz und Schutz,* 3.
21. Ibid., 4.
22. Weinberger, *Glorwürdiges Sechstes Jubel-Jahr,* 67.
23. Bosio, *Roma sotterranea,* 196–97. For the extended debate among early modern Catholic scholars about which of these signs were acceptable as markers of a martyr's grave, see Herklotz, "Wie Jean Mabillon," 203–28.
24. Bosio, *Roma sotterranea,* 197.
25. Geppert, *Schatz und Schutz,* 11.
26. The gravestone text reads: "DDM Mundicie Protocenie Benemerenti Quae vixit annos LX Quae ibit in Pace XV KAL D APC."
27. *Prototypon Munditiae,* 2.
28. Replica grave goods were also produced in Rome and shipped with saintly bodies. For more information on this practice, see Ghilardi, "Quae signa erant illa," 92–94.
29. For more information on early modern imitations of ancient Roman epitaphs, see Maria Letizia Caldelli, "Forgeries Carved in Stone," in *The Oxford Handbook of Roman Epigraphy,* ed. Christer Bruun and Jonathan Edmondson (Oxford, UK: Oxford University Press, 2014), 48–54; and Lewis, *Early Modern Invention of Late Antique Rome,* 8–11.
30. Herklotz, "Wie Jean Mabillon," 198.
31. *Translatio oder Erheb- und uberbringung deß H. Antonini Martyrers,* 4–10.
32. Ibid., 15.
33. Bozio's *Annales Antiquitatem* was a work intended to be a revision of Baronio's *Annales.* The first two volumes—of a planned ten-volume series—were published posthumously by Bozio's brother Francesco in 1637. For further information, see Piero Craveri, "Tommaso Bozio," in *Dizionario Biografico degli Italiani* 13, ed. Alberto M. Ghisalberti (Rome: Istituto dell'Enciclopedia Italiana, 1971).
34. Brückner, "Die Katakomben im Glaubensbewusstsein," 291–93; Carell, "Die Wallfahrt zu den sieben Hauptkirchen Roms," 126–27; Schudt, *Le Guide di Roma,* 347–53.
35. Weinberger, *Glorwürdiges Sechstes Jubel-Jahr,* 31.
36. Wasserburg, *Fluenta Jordanis,* 386.
37. Kurz, *Blutschaumendes der Welt zur Nachfolge,* 9.

38. Ibid., 14.
39. Ibid., 18–19.
40. Pichler, "Reisebeschribung des Schuhmacherssohnes," *Audorfer Heimgarten* 2, no. 1 (May 2, 1925): 3.
41. Ibid., 2.
42. *Saeculum octavum*, 75.
43. Weinberger, *Glorwürdiges Sechstes Jubel-Jahr*, 68.
44. Lechner, "Der heilige Martyrer Lucius," 74–75.
45. Wasserburg, *Fluenta Jordanis*, 395.
46. Ebermann, "300 Jahre St. Felix in Gars," 77.
47. Ibid.
48. Ibid., 78.

5. Welcoming the Saints Home

1. Austriacus, *Memoria Sexcentenaria*, frontispiece.
2. Ibid., 50–54
3. Ibid., 18.
4. Ibid., 14–15.
5. Arnold van Gennep, *Les rites de passage* (Paris: Émile Nourry, 1909), 266–67.
6. An octave was a period of eight days (usually a Sunday to a Sunday) during which major feasts such as Easter, Christmas, Corpus Christi, saints' days, and church consecrations were celebrated (see F. Cabrol, "Octave," in *The Catholic Encyclopedia*, ed. Charles G. Herbermann, Edward A. Pace, Condé B. Pallan, and Thomas J. Shahan [New York: Appleton, 1911]).
7. Achermann, *Die Katakombenheiligen*, 79.
8. Ibid., 75.
9. Ibid., 75–77.
10. Austriacus, *Memoria Sexcentenaria*, 33.
11. Ibid., 34–35.
12. Bosl, "Heilige Leiber," 121; BayHStA, KL Fürstenfeld, 193½, Abbot Martin to neighboring parish priests inviting them and their parishioners to the translation of Saint Hyacinth, October 13, 1672.
13. *Saeculum octavum*, Beschreibung, 8.
14. Mannhardt, *Stamm- und Blut-rothes Rothenbuch*, D4r.
15. Ibid., D4v.
16. Mannstorff, *Epitome Chronicorum Alderspacensium*, 60; Morhart, *Kurtze historische Nachricht*, 60; Kurz, *Blutschaumendes der Welt zur Nachfolge*, 6; Valentin Limmer, "Überführung der Reliquien des h. Viktorinus in die Schlosskapelle Arnstorf am 19. Oktober 1695," *Heimatblätter: Monatsbeilage zum Rottaler Anzeiger* 2, no. 15 (1925): 2; *S. Beninus Martyrer*, 3v.
17. Christl, *300 Jahre barocke Pfarrkirche in Kühbach*, 21; *Saeculum nostrum*, 17; Lothar Altman, "Aus der Geschichte von Kongregation und Bürgersaal," in

400 Jahre Marianische Männerkongregation am Bürgersaal zu München, ed. Horst Esterer (Regensburg, Germany: Schnell & Steiner, 2010), 41.

18. Spindler, *Handbuch der bayerischen Geschichte: Das alte Bayern*, 569, 572.
19. Johnson, "Trionfi of the Holy Dead," 49. For more on these processions, see Burkardt, "Les fêtes de translation."
20. Heinzelmann, *Translationsberichte*, 47–50.
21. Helmuth Stahleder, *Chronik der Stadt München*, vol. 2: *Belastung und Bedrückung, Die Jahre 1506–1705* (Ebenhausen, Germany: Dölling and Galitz, 2005), 210.
22. BayHStA KL Benediktbeuren 2/1, Archivi Benedioburani, Tomus I . . . Daß ist Erster Thail des Benedictbeürischen Archivs, 1730, 363r–v.
23. For information on the translation of Saint Castulus, see Appl, *Die Kirchenpolitik Herzog Wilhelms V*, 315–45. For information on Saint Benno's translation, see Jeffrey Chipps Smith, "Salvaging Saints," 36.
24. Harriet Rudolph, "Entreé [Festliche, Triumphale]," in *Höfe und Residenzen im spätmittelalterlichen Reich: Eindynastisch-topographisches Handbuch*, ed. Werner Paravicini, Jan Hirschbiegel, and Jörg Wettlaufer, vol. 2 (Ostfildern, Germany: Thorbecke, 2005), 318–23.
25. For more on the role of soldiers in these processions, see Burkardt, "Les fêtes de translation," 92–93.
26. Christl, *300 Jahre barocke Pfarrkirche in Kühbach*, 19.
27. Ibid., 21.
28. Ibid., 22–25.
29. Ibid., 21.
30. For more information on Jesuit theater in Bavaria, see Burschel, *Sterben und Unsterblichkeit*, 264–80; Fidel Rädle, "Jesuit Theatre in Germany, Austria and Switzerland," in *Neo-Latin Drama in Early Modern Europe*, ed. Jan Bloemendal and Howard Norland, Drama and Theatre in Early Modern Europe (Leiden, Netherlands: Brill, 2016), 185–292; and Kevin J. Wetmore Jr., "Jesuit Theater and Drama," Oxford Handbooks Online, July 7, 2016, https://doi.org/10.1093/oxfordhb/9780199935420.013.55. For more on the celebration of Corpus Christi in early modern Bavaria, see Mitterwieser, *Geschichte der Fronleichnamsprozession in Bayern*, 33–80; and Pentzlin, "The Cult of Corpus Christi," 116–60.
31. Fridl, *Freundlicher Willkomb oder Jubel- und Freudenfest*, 30.
32. Stadtarchiv Dingolfing, B VIII Nr. 10, translation procession order from June 4, 1770; Markmiller, "Die Übertragung zweier Katakombenheiliger," 146–47.
33. *Kurze Beschreibung der solennen Translation oder Einführung vier heiliger Leiber*, A4v–B2r.
34. Beissel, *Die Verehrung der Heiligen und ihrer Reliquien*, 3.
35. BayHStA, KL Benediktbeuren 2/1, Archivi Benedioburani, Tomus I, 1730, 364v.

36. Achermann, *Die Katakombenheiligen,* 142.
37. Stadtarchiv Dingolfing, B VIII Nr. 10, translation procession order from June 4, 1770; Markmiller, "Die Übertragung zweier Katakombenheiliger," 146.
38. *Kurze Beschreibung der solennen Translation oder Einführung vier heiliger Leiber,* A4v; *Bittrich voll deß himmlischen Manna,* 166.
39. Mändl, *Himmelwürdiges Kleinod,* 21–22.
40. Ibid., 22.
41. Ibid.
42. Fridl, *Freundlicher Willkomb oder Jubel- und Freudenfest,* D2r–v.
43. Lechner, "Der heilige Martyrer Lucius," 70.
44. For more information on these types of plays in the Swiss context, see Achermann, *Die Katakombenheiligen,* 185–218.
45. Ibid., 191.
46. *St. Beninus Martyrer,* 34.
47. Mannhardt, *Stamm- und Blut-rothes Rothenbuch,* 29.
48. Ibid., 37–39.
49. Ibid., 38.
50. Ibid., 39.
51. *Translation oder feyerliche und herrliche Ubersetzung des Heil. Leibs S. Maximi,* 5.
52. BayHStA, Clm 27048, Annales rerum notabilium in monasterio S. Altonis, a. 1691–1698, 79–80.
53. Ibid., 80–82.
54. Ibid., 82.
55. Ibid., 83.
56. Ibid., 86
57. Ibid., 87.
58. Ibid., 88.
59. Ibid.
60. Ibid., 84–117.
61. Ibid., 97–99.
62. Ibid., 99–100.
63. Ibid., 104.
64. Ibid., 105.
65. Ibid., 108.
66. Geppert, *Schatz und Schutz,* A4R; Wasserburg, *Fluenta Jordanis,* 388; Meychel, *Erhebung des H. Martyrers Honorat,* Lobgesang von dem H. Martyrer Honorat, verses 2 and 7.
67. Wasserburg, *Fluenta Jordanis,* 389; Wasserburg, *Willkomm und geistliche Begrüssung, S. Juliae,* D[1]r.
68. Wasserburg, *Fluenta Jordanis,* 389.
69. Ibid., 388.

70. Hochenzoll, *Frühzeitiger Sig, und glorwürdiger Triumph*, 8.
71. Wasserburg, *Fluenta Jordanis*, 430.
72. Ibid.
73. Wasserburg, *Willkomm und geistliche Begrüssung*, D4v.
74. Today, Iringsburg is known as Eurasburg, Upper Bavaria.
75. *Renovata Post Sexcentos Annos*, A3v–A4r.

6. Roman Catacomb Saints as Local Residents and Patrons

1. Wasserburg, *Fluenta Jordanis*, 384.
2. Beissel, *Verehrung der Heiligen und ihrer Reliquien*, 18; Brown, *The Cult of the Saints*, 88.
3. Brown, *The Cult of the Saints*, 50.
4. Ibid., 88.
5. *Saeculum octavum*, 75.
6. Fischer, *Neuer Meer- und Glücksstern*, 4.
7. *S. Beninus Martyrer*, 32.
8. Kurz, *Blutschaumendes der Welt zur Nachfolge*, 6–7.
9. Wasserburg, *Willkomm und geistliche Begrüssung*, A3v, D3r.
10. Hochenleutner, *Das Glorreiche Burg-Rain*, 11.
11. Archiv der Münchener Provinz der Redemptoristen zu Gars, Dokumente betreffend die Echtheit u. Überfuhurng der Gebeine des Hl. Martyrer Felix nach Gars v. Jahr 1671–74, authentication certificate.
12. "Diversae Ordinationes circa extractionem reliquiarum," 161. The bull did grant leeway to "great princes and prelates" when it came to the public display of their relics, saying that clerical authorities should be generous to them.
13. Wasserburg, *Fluenta Jordanis*, 430.
14. Ibid.
15. Marcia B. Hall, introduction to *The Sensuous in the Counter-Reformation Church*, ed. Hall and Tracy E. Cooper (Cambridge, UK: Cambridge University Press, 2013), 3–4.
16. Borromeo and Voelker, "Charles Borromeo's *Instructiones*," 143–44.
17. Brossette, "Theatrum virtutis et gloriae," 1:145.
18. Achermann, *Die Katakombenheiligen*, 97; Snoek, *Medieval Piety from Relics to the Eucharist*, 220.
19. Julia M. H. Smith, "Portable Christianity," 158. During the later Middle Ages, relics and reliquaries began to be incorporated more commonly into winged altarpieces as well as retables with predellas. Though these reliquaries remained permanently in their places, the winged altarpieces could be closed and the relics in the predella were usually blocked partially from view by grilles or decorative tracery. As Cynthia Hahn has noted: "Throughout the

Middle Ages, . . . the faithful almost never had an unobstructed view of relics: grilles, intervened, distances were maintained, containers with sheets of gold like mirrors deflected the gaze from the relics" (Hahn, "What Do Reliquaries Do for Relics?," 305). This stands in sharp contrast to the visibility of the catacomb saints, whose bodies were presented directly to the viewer behind large sheets of glass.

20. Münchner, *Neues Liecht oder Neuschein,* 8.
21. Ignatius Bonschab, *Thron der Liebe, und Barmherzigkeit Gott, dem Heiligen Blut-Zeugen Christi Mauritio, und seiner gantzen Legion* [. . .] *durch eine Ehren-Rede* [. . .] *angerühmet* (Augsburg: Johann Jacob Mauracher, 1760), 19.
22. Pfarrarchiv St. Peter in München, Urkunde 408A, Stephan Höck to St. Peter's church, letter regarding St. Honoratus's shrine, June 15, 1653.
23. Several historians have asserted that all catacomb saints were displayed only periodically (see Achermann, *Die Katakombenheiligen,* 249; Ursula Brossette, "Die Einholung Gottes und der Heiligen," 451; Legner, "Vom Glanz," 83–85; and Pötzl, "Volksfrömmigkeit," 928).
24. A third type of these *Verschlußtafel* survives outside of the former Electorate of Bavaria. These shrine covers depict the martyrdom of the saint, often in several scenes. Examples of this type of shrine cover can be found at Pfarrkirche St. Martin, Biberach (Baden-Württemberg), Candidusaltar; Kloster Schussenried (Baden-Württemberg), Josef und Valentinsaltar, Marian- und Vinzentiusaltar.
25. Legner, "Vom Glanz," 85.
26. Uta Ludwig, "Restaurierungsdokumentation—Ganzkörperreliquie Hl. Felix" (unpublished manuscript, August 20, 2010), Microsoft Word file, 3.
27. Kurz, *Blutschaumendes der Welt zur Nachfolge,* 34.
28. Museum Dingolfing, Abt. Bilder und Zeichen der Völksfrömmigkeit, Inv. Nr. 2567.
29. Hochenzoll, *Frühzeitiger Sig, und glorwürdiger Triumph,* frontispiece.
30. BayHStA, KL Fasz. 347/11, Johann Barbier's written account of the miracle performed by Saint Eleutheria, October 28, 1736. Barbier also notes that several years after his initial dream, he lost the hearing in his left hear. He tried several home remedies to no avail, and it finally occurred to him to look for help from Saint Eleutheria. Again, he promised monthly veneration and to double his small contribution.
31. van Os, "Seeing Is Believing," 147; Toussaint, "Die Sichtbarkeit des Gebeins im Reliquiar," 97–98.
32. Wasserburg, *Willkomm und geistliche Begrüssung,* B2r.
33. Ibid., D3v.
34. Wasserburg, *Fluenta Jordanis,* 393.
35. Gregory, *Salvation at Stake,* 313.
36. Geppert, *Schatz und Schutz,* 26.

37. Hochenleutner, *Das glorreiche Burg-Rain,* 21.
38. Ibid., 33.
39. *St. Beninus Martyrer,* 16–17.
40. Wasserburg, *Fluenta Jordanis,* 438.
41. *Saeculum octavum,* 222.
42. Wasserburg, *Willkomm und Geistliche Begrüssung,* C4r–v.
43. Wasserburg, *Fluenta Jordanis,* 388.
44. Hochenzoll, *Frühzeitiger Sig, und glorwürdiger Triumph,* 16.
45. Geary, *Furta Sacra,* 152.
46. Wasserburg, *Fluenta Jordanis,* 407.
47. *Translatio oder Erheb- und uberbringung deß H. Antonini Martyrers,* 17.
48. *Saeculum octavum,* 57; Weinberger, *Glorwürdiges Sechstes Jubel-Jahr,* 44–45.
49. Mannhardt, *Stamm- und Blut-rothes Rothenbuch,* 122.
50. Geppert, *Schatz und Schutz,* 15; Wasserburg, *Fluenta Jordanis,* 432. Both authors cite the *Annalium Baronii continuatio ab a. 1197 quo is desinit ad a. 1622* by Henri Spondanus (1568–1643) as the source of this anecdote. Spondanus, a Catholic bishop and historian, was one of the continuators of Cesare Baronio's *Annales Ecclesiastici.*
51. Wasserburg, *Fluenta Jordanis,* 431.
52. Ibid., 432 and 406.
53. Fridl, *Freundlicher Willkomb oder Jubel- und Freudenfest,* 43.
54. *St. Beninus Martyrer,* 2.
55. UBM ms 357, *Secretum meum misi,* entry for September 3, 1675; Ebermann, "300 Jahre St. Felix in Gars," 76.
56. UBM ms 357, *Secretum meum misi,* entries for July 25, 1675, and August 1676.
57. Ebermann, "300 Jahre St. Felix in Gars," 76.
58. Wenhardt, "Felix-Wallfahrt," 8.
59. *Chur-Bayrisch geistlicher Calender auf daß Jahr MDCCLIIII:* [. . .] *Rentamt München* (Munich: Joseph Anton Zimmermann, 1754), 451.
60. Morhart, *Kurtze historische Nachricht,* engraving entitled *Imago V.V.M. Auxiliatricis hic beneficiis Clara, SS: Iulius, Innocentius, Felix, Lucius MM: specialies Patroni, quorum SS: Corpora hic venerationi publicae sunt expositus.*
61. AEM, Matrikeln, Aufkirchen a.d. Maisach–St. Georg 4, CB027, M549—Taufen—1742–1781, 83–150.
62. AEM, Matrikeln, Aufkirchen bei Erding–St. Johann Baptist, CB028, M586—Taufen, obere Pfarrei (Aufkirchen, Notzing und Moosinning) 1698–1804, 350–58.
63. AEM, Matrikeln, Erding–St. Johann Baptist, CB082, M1584—Taufen—1675–1726, 1–546; AEM, Matrikeln, Erding–St. Johann Baptist CB082, M1586—Taufen—1727–1802, 1–936.
64. Krausen, "Das heilbringende Öl," 59.
65. Ibid., 61.
66. Malgaritta, *Jahrs- und kurtze Beschreibung,* D4v–Fv.

67. Ibid., section entitled "Wundersambe Werckh und Guetthaten S. Dionysii," 1–24.
68. *Wundersame Guetthaten,* D4v–Fv.

Epilogue

1. Mois, "Reliquien und Verehrung der Heiligen Primus und Felicianus," 45.
2. Ibid., 45–47.
3. For more on these reforms, see Schmid, "Altbayern, 1648–1803," 313–15.
4. Weis, *Die Säkularisation der bayerischen Klöster 1802/03,* 21; Beales, *Prosperity and Plunder,* 282–90.
5. Forster, *Catholic Germany from the Reformation to the Enlightenment,* 184–85, 194.
6. Weis, *Die Säkularisation der bayerischen Klöster 1802/03,* 10.
7. See the appendix for a list of saints in cloisters in each location.
8. Krausen, "Schicksale römischer Katakombenheiliger," 161.
9. Peter Käser, *1000 Jahre Binabiburg 1011–2011, 750 Jahre Pfarrei Binabiburg 1261–2011, 300 Jahre Sankt Salvator 1710–2010* (Binabiburg, Germany: Peter Käser, 2011), 152.
10. Anton Eberl, *Geschichte des ehemaligen Zisterzienserklosters Gotteszell im bayerischen Wald auf Grund eingehender archivalischer Studien* (Deggendorf, Germany: Nothhaft, 1935), 104–8; Karen Schaelow-Weber, *Viechtach* (Passau, Germany: Kunstverlag Peda, 1994), 11; Georg Brenninger, *Die Kirchen der Pfarrei Obing, Lkr. Traunstein, Obb., Erzbistum München-Freising* (Munich: Schnell & Steiner, 1990), 6–7. Other examples of parish churches acquiring catacomb saints from nearby cloister churches includes Wessobrunn to Hagenheim, Freising cathedral to Hohenkammer (1838).
11. Käser, *1000 Jahre Binabiburg,* 152.
12. Krausen, "Schicksale römischer Katakombenheiliger," 163.
13. John, ". . . mit Behutsambkeit vnd Reverentz zu tractieren," 12.
14. Ibid., 12–13.
15. For more information on catacomb saint distribution in the nineteenth century, see Boutry, "Les corps saints des catacombes"; and Boutry, "Les saints des Catacombes: Itinéraires français d'une piété ultramontaine (1800–1881)."
16. Between 1804 and 1871, nineteen catacomb saints went to parish churches, six to pilgrimage churches, and two to cloister churches.
17. For more information on the influence of the Enlightenment in Bavarian cloisters, see Philipp Schäfer, "Katholische Theologie in der Zeit der Aufklärung," in *Handbuch der Bayerischen Kirchengeschichte: Von der Glaubensspaltung bis zur Säkularisation,* ed. Walter Brandmüller (St. Ottilien: Germany: EOS Verlag, 1993), 506–31. For Enlightenment attitudes toward popular religion, see Pötzl, "Volksfrömmigkeit," 957–61.

18. Günter Müller, *Ein Wegweiser für die Kirchen der Pfarreiengemeinschaft Pfeffenhausen, Niederhornbach, Pfaffendorf, Rainertshausen* (Pfeffenhausen, Germany: Pfarrei Pfeffenhausen, 2013), 17.
19. Harvolk, "Die Translation eines Katakombenheiligen im Jahre 1825."
20. Ibid., 92.
21. The cloister at Frauenchiemsee was secularized in 1803, but the nuns were allowed to remain as the Bavarian government could not find a buyer for the buildings. The cloister was reestablished in 1836 under King Ludwig I.
22. Harvolk, "Die Translation eines Katakombenheiligen im Jahre 1825," 88–89.
23. Ibid., 87.
24. Ibid.
25. Gerhard Schormann Lecker, *Pfarrchronik Oberpiebing—Salching* (Oberpiebing, Germany: Kath. Pfarramt Oberpiebing, 1981), 56–58.
26. Bavarian cloisters that continued to decorate holy bodies after 1803 include the Servites in Munich, the English Ladies in Altötting, the Poor Clares at St. Maria Magdalena in Regensburg, the Dominicans at Kloster Strahlfeld bei Roding, and the Benedictines at Frauenchiemsee. Several of these cloisters survived dissolution, whereas others were reestablished after 1817 with permission from King Ludwig I. In other parts of Europe during the nineteenth century, it became customary to cover catacomb saints in wax, though this never became very popular in Bavaria. For more information on this type of presentation, see Hernández, "El cuerpo relicario"; Hernández, "The *Corpi Santi*"; and Ghilardi, *Il santo con due piedi sinistri.*
27. Georg Brenninger, *Gnadenstätten im Erdinger Land* (Munich: Schnell & Steiner, 1986), 26; BLfD, Unterdießen/Lkr. Landsberg a. L/OB, "St. Nikolaus, Hl. Peregrina," 5, 1996.
28. Sabine John, "Zwei barocke Passionsgruppen in der Hl.-Kreuz-Kirche in Schönbrunn: Streiflichter zu religiös-künstlerischem Umfeld und denkmalpflegerischer 'Entdeckung,'" *Bayerisches Jahrbuch für Volkskunde* (2004): 66; Hans Schertl, "Hofmarkkirche Heiliges Kreuz in Schönbrunn," Kirchen und Kapellen im Dachauer Land, http://kirchenundkapellen.de/kirchenpz/schoenbrunn.php.
29. For an alternate interpretation, see Krausen, "Schicksale römischer Katakombenheiliger," 45; and Koudounaris, *The Empire of Death,* 166.
30. Heidtmann, "Der Heilige mit dem zuckenden Fuß," 50.
31. Rita Kohlmaier, "Heiliger Geist: Liebe zum Detail und Bewunderung für die Handwerskunst vergangner Zeiten: Restauratorin Uta Ludwig verhilft Reliquien zu alter Schönheit," *Vogue Deutsch,* October 2016, 55; Thomas Obermaier, "Zwei Heilige auf Reisen," merkur.de, June 1, 2021, https://www.merkur.de/lokales/erding/fraunberg-ort377220/zwei-heilige-auf-reisen-90783160.html.
32. "Waldsassen: Tägliche Anbetung der heiligen Leiber zu Zeiten von Corona," Oberpfalz TV video, May 19, 2020, https://www.otv.de/waldsassen-heilige

-leiber-und-corona-432043/; Pfarrei Waldsassen, "Täglich Glockengeläut und eine Andacht—Pfarrei Waldsassen," March 17, 2020, https://www.pfarrei-waldsassen.de/taglich-glockengelaut-und-eine-andacht/.

Appendix

1. Deutinger, *Die älteren Matrikeln des Bisthums Freysing,* vols. 1–3; Hartig, *Die Errichtung des Bistums Freising im Jahre 739,* 62–63; *Matrikel des Bisthums Regensburg;* Buchner, *Das Bistum Eichstätt: historisch-statistische Beschreibung;* Pötzl, "Volksfrömmigkeit," 924–25.
2. ASVR, Fondo Reliquie, 77–79.
3. The records of the papal sacristan on the distribution of catacomb relics are held at the Biblioteca Apostolica Vaticana, Vat.lat. 14455–14462, 1737–1894.

BIBLIOGRAPHY

Archives

Archiv der Pfarrei St. Peter, München
Archiv des Erzbistums München und Freising
Archivio storico del Vicariato di Roma
Bayerisches Hauptstaatsarchiv München
Bayerisches Landesamt für Denkmalpflege
Bibliothek der Redemptoristen, Kloster Gars
Bischöfliches Zentralarchiv Regensburg
Fürstlich Oettingen-Wallersteinsches Archiv Harburg
Münchner Stadtmuseum
Museum Dingolfing
Staatsarchiv Amberg
Stadtarchiv Dingolfing
Pfarrarchiv Dachau
Universitätsbibliothek der LMU München

Printed Primary Sources

Austriacus, Romanus. *Memoria Sexcentenaria. Das ist: Sechshundert jährige Gedächtnuß der beständigen Verharnuß deß hochlöblichen Gotthauß und Closters Ordinis S. Benedicti zu Formbach in Underlands Bayrn, Wie auch Triumphalis Introductio, oder Triumphirliche Erheb- und Beysetzung des heiligen Martyrers Clari, welchem Ihro Päbstliche Heiligkeit Innocentius deß namens der XI. hochseeligster Gedächtnuß Dem hochwürdigen Herrn Wolffgango Abbten deß obbenenten Stiffts und Closters Formbach, verehret und allda in dessen Ehr, neukostbahr auffgerichten Altar beygesetzt worden. Welches alles unter herrlichen Freuden-Fest-Begängnuß den 26. Septembris Dominica 17. post pentecosten, im Jahr 1694 nach obligender besten Vermögenheit einer Volkreichen Versamblung in einer Lob-Predig hat vorgetragen.* Passau: Georg Adam Höller, 1694.

Baronio, Cesare. *Annales ecclesiastici: Tomus primus.* Antwerp, Belgium: Christopher Plantin, 1588.

———. *Martyrologium Romanum.* Rome: Dominici Basae, 1586.

Bittrich voll deß himmlischen Manna, und Süssen Morgen-Thau. Das ist: Historischer Discurs, von dem Ursprung, Fundation, Auffnamb, glücklichen Fortgang, Tugend-Wandel, und andern denckwürdigen Sachen deß löbl. Frauen-Closters, Ordens der dritten Regul deß Heil. Francisci, bey Sanct Christophen im Bittrich genannt, in der Chur-Fürstlichen Residentz-Stadt München. Munich: Johann Lucas Straub, 1721.

Boldetti, Marc' Antonio. *Osservazioni sopra i cimiterj de' santi martiri, ed antichi Cristiani di Roma*. Rome: G. M. Salvioni, 1720.

Borromeo, Carlo, and Evelyn Carole Voelker. "Charles Borromeo's *Instructiones fabricae et supellectilis ecclesiasticae, 1577*: A Translation with Commentary and Analysis." PhD diss., Syracuse University, 1977.

Bosio, Antonio. *Roma sotterranea: Opera postuma*. Rome: Appresso G. Facciotti, 1635.

Calvin, John. *A Treatise on Relics*. Translated by Valerian Krasinski. Edinburgh: Johnstone and Hunter, 1854.

Congregatio indulgentiarum et sacrarum. *Decreta authentica sacrae Congregationis indulgentiis sacrisque reliquiis praepositae: Ab anno 1668 ad annum 1882*. Regensburg, Germany: F. Pustet, 1883.

Cuggiò, Nicolò Antonio. *Della giurisdittione e prerogative del Vicario di Roma: Opera del canonico Nicolò Antonio Cuggiò segretario del triubunale di Sua Eminenza*. Edited by Domenico Rocciolo. Rome: Carocci, 2004.

Decrees of the Ecumenical Councils: Nicaea I to Lateran V. Vol. 1. Edited and translated by Norman P. Tanner. London: Sheed and Ward, 1990.

Decrees of the Ecumenical Councils: Trent to Vatican II. Vol 2. Edited and translated by Norman P. Tanner. London: Sheed and Ward, 1990.

Eck, Johannes. *De Sacrificio Missae Libri Tres (1526)*. Edited by Erwin Iserloh, Vinzenz Pfnür, and Peter Fabisch. Münster, Germany: Aschendorff, 1982.

Eisengrein, Martin. *Ein Christliche predig, was vom Heilthumb, so im Papstum in so grossen ehren, zuhalten sey, vnd ob ain frommer Christ mit guttem gewissen, zu disem oder jaenem Heiligen walfarten gehen künde*. Ingolstadt: Weyssenhorn, 1564.

Fischer, Michael. *Neuer Meer- und Glücks-Stern: So durch den Römischen heiligen Marter-Helden Asterium Dem Schiff der Gesellschafft der H. Ursulae zu Straubingen vorzuleuchten auffgangen. Observiert, und außgelegt an dem Fest-Tag der Translation seines von Rom überbrachten H. Leichnambs, da solcher mit grosser Solennitet in das werthe Gottshauß benändter Wohl-Ehrwürdigen Geistlichen Jungfrauen bey der unbefleckten Empfängnuß Mariae eingeholet und beygesetzt worden*. Regensburg, Germany: Johann Egidi Raith, 1698.

Fridl, Franz Valentin. *Freundlicher Willkomb oder Jubel- und Freudenfest, angestellt zu Ehren des Edlen Römers und heiligen Martyrers Porphyrii, als dessen gantzer Heil. Leib in die Pfarrkirch zu Arnschwang einbegleittet, auch einer Volkreichen Menge und zur offentlichen Verehrung das erste mal ausgesetzt und vorgestellt wurde im Jahr 1694, den 27 Juliij*. Regensburg, Germany: Johann Egidi Raith, 1694.

Geppert, Ernst. *Schatz und Schutz einer zweymahl beglückter Stadt Amberg bey feyerlicher Ubersetzung zweyer H. H. Leiber der Glorwürdigen Martyrer Constantii, und Clementis*. Amberg, Germany: Koch, 1753.

Haeckhl, Wolfgang. *Der geistliche von dem Feuer des heiligen Lieb- und Tugends-Eyfer gegen Gott [. . .] verzehrte und annoch lebende Phoenix Eugenius in einer Leich-, Lob- und Ehren-Predig vorgestellet.* Waldsassen, Germany: Witz, 1744.

Hamilton, Amadeus. *Die glorwürdige Blutzeugen der allerheiligsten Dreyfaltigkeit: oder Lob-rede der Martyrer Alexandri, Felicissimi, Bonosae, Valentinae, und Deodatae, in ihrer Versetzung in die Freyherrliche Berckemische-Schloß-Capellen Bluedenburg zu Mentzing.* Munich: Johann Jäcklin, 1700.

Heiliger Schatz oder hochschätzbare, hochheilige Reliquien, welche in dem uralten hochlöblichen Stüfft der Regulierten Lateranensischen Chor-Herren S. Augustini zu Pollingen in Ober-Bayren Augspurger-Bistumbs halten und verehrt werden. In Kupffer abgebildet und kürzlich beschriben, denen Christ-Catholischen Wallfahrteren zu Angedencken vorgestellt und in Druck gegeben. Munich: Johann Lucas Straub, 1729.

Hochenleutner, Gelasius. *Das glorreiche Burg-Rain in ihrem Gottshauß: das ist: schuldigiste Lob-Red bey solen. Translation des kostbar-gefasten Leibs des Heil. Blut-Zeugen Alberti, in das löbl. Neu-erbaute Gottshauß des hochfürstlichen Schloß Burg-Rain in höchster Gegenwart des hochwürdigist- und hochgeborenen Herrn / Herrn Joannis Francisci, Bischoffens und des H. Röm. Reichs Fürsten zu Freysing und einer grossen Volks-Menge vorgetragen.* Freising, Germany: Johann Christian Carl Immel, 1723.

Hochenzoll, Michael Angelus. *Frühzeitiger Sig, und glorwürdiger Triumph, welchen der heilige Victor ein edler Römer von dreyzehen Jahren wider die Verfolger deß Christlichen Glaubens in seiner standhafftigen Marter erhalten, dessen heiliger Leib von Rom gebracht [. . .] und in der Schloß-Capellen zu Tauff-Kirchen mit schöner Solemnitet Anno 1695, den 18. May 1695 ist beygesetzt worden.* Munich: Johann Jäcklin, 1695.

Kurz, Maximilian Emanuel. *Blutschaumendes der Welt zur Nachfolge, dem Himmel zur Belohnung abgespieltes Spectacul, das ist: Lob- und Ehren-Predig, von denen zwey heiligen Blut-Zeugen Christi Maximo und Clementi [. . .] deren zwey heiligen Leiber von [. . .] in das löbl. Pfarr-Gottshauß zu Sandizell daselbst hochfeyerlich übersetzt wurden den 25. September 1768.* Augsburg, Germany: Huggele, 1768.

Kurze Beschreibung der solennen Translation oder Einführung vier heiliger Leiber, als des H. Felix Martyrers, H. Victor Mart. H. Aurelius Mart. und der H. Eleutheria Martyrin. Munich: Johann Jacob Vötter, 1738.

Kurze Beschreibung von der feyerlich-und herrlichen Uberseßung der zweyen Heil. Heil. Leiber Constantii und Clementis Martyrer in die sogenannte hof-Capellen oder unser Lieben Frauen Kirchen der Churfürstlichen Ober-Pfalzischen Haupt und Regierungs-Stadt Amberg den 8 Julii im Jahr 1757 mit dem Anhang der darbey gehaltenen so trostreich-als nutzbahren Predig. Amberg, Germany: Johann Georg Koch, 1753.

Landucci, Ambrogio. "Pratica per estrarre li corpi de' santi martiri da sagri cimiteri di Roma." In *Sulla questione del vaso di sangue: Memoria inedita con introduzione storica e appendici di documenti,* edited by Giovanni Battista de Rossi, 99–129. Rome: Pontificio Istituto di Archeologia Cristiana, 1944.

Luther, Martin. *Widder den newen Abgott und allten Teuffel der zu Meyssen sol erhaben werden.* Wittenberg, Germany: Lufft, 1524.

Malgaritta, Stephan. *Jahrs- und kurtze Beschreibung etwelcher denkwürdig- wundersamer Werk* [. . .] *bey der 200 jährg. wundersamber Bildnuß S. Annae [. . .] in Geisenfeld.* Ingolstadt, Germany: Johann Ostermayr, 1674.

Mändl, Kaspar. *Himmelwürdiges Kleinod, in die irrdische Engel-burg übersetzt. Das ist Lob- und Ehren-Predig bei der Einbegleitung deß heiligen leibs deß glorwürdigen Blut-Zeugens und Martyrers Christi in die Behausung der Engelländischen Gesellschaft.* Munich: Johann Lucas Straub, 1698.

Mannhardt, Anselm. *Stamm- und Blut-rothes Rothenbeuch, das ist: kurtze Beschreibung des [. . .] Closters Rothenbeuch.* Mindelheim, Germany: Adolph Joseph Ebel, 1724.

Mannstorff, Michael von. *Epitome Chronicorum Alderspacensium: oder kurtzer Auszug aus denen Geschichts-Büchern des nunmehro 600. Jahr beständig unter dem Heil. und befreyten Cisterzer-Orden stehenden Closters Alderspach.* Stadt am Hof nächst Regensburg, Germany: Gastl, 1746.

Meychel, Hanns Georg. *Erhebung des H. Martyrers Honorat welche in der Churfürstl: Hauptstatt München hochfeyrtäglich begangen worden den 28. Weinmonat im Jahr 1654.* Munich: Lucas Straub, 1654.

Morhart, Gelasius Klauber. *Kurtze historische Nachricht von dem Ursprung und Fortgang deß Stifft- und Closters Ünderstorff Can. Reg. S. Aug. Congreg. Lateranensis in Ober-Bayrn, Rent-Amts München, Bisthumbs Freyßing. Herausgezogen aus den alt und neueren Closter-Chronicis.* Augsburg, Germany: Maximilian Simon Pingitzer, 1762.

Müller, Jakob. *Kirchen-Geschmuck das ist: kurtzer Begriff der fürnembsten Dingen, damit ein jede recht und wol zugerichte Kirchen, geziert vnd auffgebutzt seyn solle allen Prelaten vnd Pfarrherren durch das ganze Bistumb Regenspurg sehr notwendig.* Munich: Adam Berg, 1591.

Münchner, Josephus. *Neues Liecht oder Neuschein welches zu Neumarckt in Unter-Bayrn auffgangen als der durchleuchtige heilige Martyrer Lucius allda den 23. Septembris 1696 in das hochlobliche Closter Sancti Viti solemnissime ist transferirt worden.* Salzburg, Austria: Johann Baptist Mayr, 1696.

Nas, Johannes. *The Corpus Christi Sermons of Johannes Nas (1534–1590): An Edition with Notes and Commentary,* edited and translated by Richard Ernest Walker. Göppingen, Germany: Kümmerle, 1988.

———. *Ein tröstliche Creützpredig darin von vilerlay H. Bergen, auch von mancherlay Creützen vnd Leyden gehandelt wirdt.* Ingolstadt, Germany: Weißenhorn, 1574.

Orban, Ferdinand. *Ramus Aureus: Das guldene Zweig: Außgelegt in der hochfeyerlichen Einholung deß edlen Römers vnd heiligen Blutzeugen Christi, Victorini.* Landshut, Germany: Simon Golowitz, 1696.

Pichler, Sebastian. "Reisebeschribung des Schuhmacherssohnes Sebastian Pichler vom 'Schuster am Graben' von Oberaudorf nach Rom und Loretto im Jubeljahre 1775." *Audorfer Heimgarten* 1, no. 19–22 (1925): 75–76, 79–80, 83–84, 87–88.

———. "Reisebeschribung des Schumacherssohnes Sebastian Pichler vom 'Schuster am Graben' von Oberaudorf nach Rom und Loretto im Jubeljahre 1775." *Audorfer Heimgarten* 2, no. 1–5 (1925): 1–3, 5–7, 13–15, 17–20.

Prototypon Munditiae emblematico-morali penicillo delineatum in S. et glor. martyre Munditia. Munich: Johann Jäcklin, 1677.

Rader, Matthäus. *Bavaria Sancta et Pia.* Vol. 1. Munich: Raphael Sadeler, 1615.

———. *Heiliges Bayer-Land.* Augsburg, Germany: Johann Caspar Bencard, 1714.

Renovata Post Sexcentos Annos Mirabilis Sanctorum Apparitio in Canonia Beyrberg. Das ist: nach sechshundert Jahren erneuert wunderbahrliche Erscheinung der Heiligen, deren ehrwürdige Heyligthumber vnd Reliquien vom ersten Probsten Hainrich nach Beyrberg in die Stüffts-Kirchen seynd übersetzet worden, in einem anmuthigen Schau-Spihl, sambt allen sechshundert-jährigen Begebenheiten, vorgestellet bey angesetzter Translation, oder hochfeyrlicher Einführung deß glorwürdigen Leibs, eines heiligen Martyrers Claudii, deß eygnen Namens. Munich: Johann Lucas Straub, 1725.

Saeculum nostrum, etc: Unser erstes Jubel-Jahr der in mitten dess Feuers erleuchten aber wunderbahr unbeschädigten höltzernen Bildnuss der heiligen Gross-Mutter Annae celebriert in Stifft und Closter Gotteszell in Unter-Bayer. Straubing, Germany: J. Gottl. Rädlmayr, 1730.

Saeculum octavum, oder 8-tägiges Jubel-Fest zu schuldigister Danckbarkeit deß Aller-Höchsten ungemeinen Kirchen-gepräng, Pontificalischen Gotts-Diensten, kost- und scheinbahren Processionen, triumphierlicher Einholung der heiligen zweyen Römischen Martyer Marii u. Caelestini. [. . .] *In dem Hochlöbl. Gotts-Haus und Closter Ranshoven der Regulierten Chor-Herren deß H. Augustini Ordens der Lateranensischen Congregation in dem 1699. Jahr vom 23. tag Augustmonats als eilften Sonntag nach Pfingsten bis 30. inclusive gehalten.* Augsburg, Germany: Mar. Magdalena Utzschneiderin, 1702.

Segni, Giovanni Battista. *Reliquiarium, sive de reliquiis, et veneratione sanctorum in quo multa de necessitate, praestantia, usu, ac fructibus reliquiarum pertractantur.* Bologna, Italy: Apud haeredes Ioannis Rossii, 1610.

St. Beninus Martyrer welchen in einer schuldigen Lob- und Ehrnred auf einem Syg-fahnen bey überbringung vnnd großansehnlicher Einbegleitung seines zu Rom newlich erfundenen vnnd erhebten heiligen Leibs mit hochfeyrtäglicher Frewdenfest-Begängnuß (wie zu end diser Predig mit mehreren denckwürdigen Umbständ beschriben wird) in dem weitberühmbten hoch-lobwürdigen Gottshauß vnnd Premonstratenser-Abbtey der regulierten Chorherren St. Norberti zu Steingaden, den 10. Augusti im Jahr 1664 [. . .] *vorgestellt hat.* Munich: Lucas Straub, 1664.

Translatio oder Erheb- und uberbringung deß H. Antonini Martyrers glorwürdigen Gebain auß der Römischen Kirchen Haupt-Statt Rom in das Churft. Hochlobl.Gottshauß und Frawen Closter Seelligenthal Cistercienser Orden bey Landshuet, so mit gebührender Solennitet beygesetzt worden den 22. Aprill Anno 1668. Mit beygesetztem Lebensbegriff obgedachten H. Martyers und angehengten schönen Gebettelein und Letaneyen zu demselben andächtig zusprechen. Munich: Johann Jäcklin, 1669.

Translation oder feyerliche und herrliche Ubersetzung des Heil. Leibs S. Maximi Martyrers in dem Marianischen Saal der Löbl. Teutschen Congregation derer Herren und Burger in der Churfürstl. Haupt- und Residentz-Stadt München. Munich: Vötter, 1750.

Trophaea Bavarica—Bayerische Siegeszeichen: faksimilierter Nachdruck der Erstausgabe München 1597, mit Übersetzung und Kommentar. Edited and translated by Thomas Breuer, Günter Hess, and Klaus Wittstadt. Regensburg, Germany: Schnell & Steiner, 1997.

Wasserburg, Jordan von. *Fluenta Jordanis: Jordanische Flüß und Ausgueß. Das ist: Lob- und Ehr- Geist- und Lehrreich-fliessende Extraordinari-Concept, oder: ausser der Ordinari-Cantzel in verschidenen Gottes-Häuseren bey sonderbahren Festivitäten und Zuhöreren vernommene Predigen.* Landshut, Germany: Schmidt, 1742.

———. *Willkomm und geistliche Begrüssung, einer edlen Römerin und Blut-Zeugin Christi, S. Juliae, dero heiliger Leib in die hochfreyherrliche fraunhoverische Schloß-Capellen zu Poxau soleniter ward einbegleittet: und mit folgender Lob- und Ehren-Red empfangen.* Landshut, Germany: Golowitz, 1710.

Weinberger, Benedikt. *Glorwürdiges Sechstes Jubel-Jahr, oder Sechs-hundert-Jähriger Welt-Gang, Deß Heiligen und befreyten Cistercienser Ordens celebriert in dem Hochlöbl. Gotts-Hauß deß gemelten Ordens Raiten-Haßlach; So im Jahr 1698. den 17. Augusti, mit einer herrlichen Procession und Translation der Heiligen Römischen Martyrer und Blut-Zeugen Christi Ausanii, Concordiae und Fortunatae, Angefangen, und durch eine solemne Octav von einer Hoch- und Wol-Ehrwürdigen Geistlichkeit aus allen benachbarten Ordens-Ständen bey einer Volckreichen Versamblung, mit außerlesenen Lob- und Ehren-Predigen herrlichist geziehret, und den 24. Augusti glücklich beschlossen.* Salzburg, Austria: Mayr, 1699.

Wundersame Guetthaten, so die biß 300 Jahr in allhisigen Jungfräulichen hochadelichen Stüfft und Gottshauß Geisenfeldt ruhende Gnadenvolle Anfrau Jesu und Mutter Mariae h. Anna, wie nit minder der Sigprangende H. Priester und Martyrer Dionysius. Ingolstadt, Germany: Thomas Gratz, 1715.

Secondary Sources

Abou-El-Haj, Barbara Fay. *The Medieval Cult of Saints: Formations and Transformations.* Cambridge, UK: Cambridge University Press, 1997.

Achermann, Hansjakob. *Die Katakombenheiligen und ihre Translationen in der schweizerischen Quart des Bistums Konstanz.* Stans, Switzerland: Verlag Historischer Verein Nidwalden, 1979.

Albrecht, Dieter, ed. *Das alte Bayern: Der Territorialstaat vom Ausgang des 12. Jahrhunderts bis zum Ausgang des 18. Jahrhunderts.* Munich: Beck, 1988.

Angenendt, Arnold. "Corpus incorruptum. Eine Leitidee der mittelalterlichen Reliquienverehrung." In *Die Gegenwart von Heiligen und Reliquien,* edited by Angenendt and Hubertus Lutterbach, 109–43. Münster, Germany: Aschendorff, 2010.

———. *Heilige und Reliquien: Die Geschichte ihres Kultes vom frühen Christentum bis zur Gegenwart.* Munich: Beck, 1994.

———. "Zur Ehre der Altäre erhoben: Zugleich ein Beitrag zur Reliquienteilung." *Römische Quartalschrift für christliche Altertumskunde und Kirchengeschichte* 89 (1994): 221–44.

Appl, Tobias. *Die Kirchenpolitik Herzog Wilhelms V. von Bayern: Der Ausbau der bayerischen Hauptstädte zu geistlichen Zentren.* Munich: Beck, 2011.

Baciocchi, Stéphane, Anne Bonzon, and Dominique Julia. "De Rome au royaume de France: Patronages, inscriptions spatiales et médiations sociales (XVIe–XVIIIe s.). Introduction au dossier 'France.'" In *Reliques Romaines: Invention et circulation des corps saints des catacombes à l'époque moderne,* edited by Baciocchi and Christophe Duhamelle, 413–58. Rome: École française de Rome, 2016.

Baciocchi, Stéphane, and Christophe Duhamelle, eds. *Reliques romaines: Invention et circulation des corps saints des catacombes à l'époque modern.* Rome: École française de Rome, 2016.

Bagnoli, Martina, ed. *Treasures of Heaven: Saints, Relics, and Devotion in Medieval Europe.* New Haven, CT: Yale University Press, 2010.

Bartlett, Robert. *Why Can the Dead Do Such Great Things? Saints and Worshippers from the Martyrs to the Reformation.* Princeton, NJ: Princeton University Press, 2013.

Baumstark. Reinhold, ed. *Rom in Bayern: Kunst und Spiritualität der ersten Jesuiten.* Munich: Hirmer, 1997.

Beales, Derek. *Prosperity and Plunder: European Catholic Monasteries in the Age of Revolution, 1650–1815.* Cambridge, UK: Cambridge University Press, 2003.

Beissel, Stephan. *Die Verehrung der Heiligen und ihrer Reliquien in Deutschland im Mittelalter.* Darmstadt: Wissenschaftliche Buchgesellschaft, 1988.

Boehm, Barbara Drake. "Body-Part Reliquaries: The State of Research." *Gesta* 36 (1997): 8–19.

Bonzon, Anne. "Autour de Montpellier: reliques romaines et reconquête catholique aux XVIIe et XVIIIe siècles." In *Reliques romaines: Invention et circulation des corps saints des catacombes à l'époque moderne,* edited by Stéphane Baciocchi and Christophe Duhamelle, 459–84. Rome: École française de Rome, 2016.

Bosl, Inge. "Heilige Leiber." In *Seligenthal.de: Anders leben seit 1232,* edited by Franz Niehoff, 117–23. Landshut, Germany: Museen der Stadt Landshut, 2008.

Bouley, Bradford A. *Pious Postmortems: Anatomy, Sanctity, and the Catholic Church in Early Modern Europe.* Philadelphia: University of Pennsylvania Press, 2017.

Boutry, Philippe. "Les corps saints des catacombes." In *Reliques romaines: Invention et circulation des corps saints des catacombes à l'époque moderne,* edited by Stéphane Baciocchi and Christophe Duhamelle, 225–59. Rome: École française de Rome, 2016.

———. "Les saints des Catacombes: Itinéraires français d'une piété ultramontaine (1800–1881)." *Mélanges de l'École française de Rome. Moyen Age-Temps modernes* 91, no.1 (1979): 875–930.

Boutry, Philippe, Pierre-Antoine Fabre, and Dominique Julia, eds. *Reliques modernes: Cultes et usages chrétiens des corps saints des Réformes aux revolutions.* Paris: Éditions de l'École des hautes études en sciences sociales, 2009.

Brandmüller, Walter, ed. *Handbuch der Bayerischen Kirchengeschichte: Von der Glaubensspaltung bis zur Säkularisation.* Vol. 2. St. Ottilien, Germany: EOS Verlag, 1993.

Braun, Joseph. *Die Reliquiare des christlichen Kultes und ihre Entwicklung.* Freiburg im Breisgau, Germany: Herder, 1940.

Brossette, Ursula. "Die Einholung Gottes und der Heiligen. Zur Zeremonialisierung des transzendenten Geschehens bei Konsekrationen und Translationen des 17. Und 18. Jahrhunderts." In *Zeremoniell als höfische Ästhetik in Spätmittelalter und Früher Neuzeit,* edited by Jörg Jochen Berns and Thomas Rahn, 432–70. Tübingen, Germany: Max Niemeyer Verlag, 1995.

———. *Die Inszenierung des Sakralen: Das theatralische Raum- und Ausstattungsprogramm süddeutscher Barockkirchen in seinem liturgischen und zeremoniellen Kontext.* Weimar, Germany: VDG Weimar, 2002.

———. "Theatrum virtutis et gloriae: Barocke Freskenprogramme und Altargemälde im liturgischen Festkontext einer Säkularfeier." In *Mit Kalkül und Leidenschaft: Inszenierungen des Heiligen in der bayerischen Barockmalerei,* vol. 1, edited by Franz Niehoff, 124–61. Landshut, Germany: Museen der Stadt Landshut, 2003.

Brown, Peter. *The Cult of the Saints: Its Rise and Function in Latin Christianity.* Chicago: University of Chicago Press, 1981.

Brückner, Wolfgang. "Die Katakomben im Glaubensbewusstsein des katholischen Volkes: Geschichtsbilder und Frömmigkeitsformen." *Römische Quartalschrift für christliche Altertumskunde und Kirchengeschichte* 89 (1994): 287–307.

Buchner, Franz Xaver. *Das Bistum Eichstätt: historisch-statistische Beschreibung, auf Grund der Literatur, der Registratur des Bischöflichen Ordinariats Eichstätt sowie der pfarramtlichen Berichte.* Eichstätt, Germany: P. Brönner and M. Däntler, 1937.

Burkardt, Albrecht. "Les fêtes de translation des saints des catacombes en Bavière (XVII–XVIII siècles)." In *Les cérémonies extraordinaires du catholicisme baroque,* edited by Bernard Dompnier, 79–98. Clermont-Ferrand, France: Presses universitaires Blaise-Pascal, 2009.

———. "'Zur aller antiquitet lieb und naigung': La dynastie des Wittelsbach et les début du culte des saints des catacombes en Bavière." In *Reliques romaines: Invention et circulation des corps saints des catacombes à l'époque moderne,* edited by Stéphane Baciocchi and Christophe Duhamelle, 629–59. Rome: École française de Rome, 2016.

Burke, Peter. "How to Become a Counter-Reformation Saint." In *Religion and Society in Early Modern Europe, 1500–1800,* edited by Kaspar von Greyerz, 45–55. London: German Historical Institute, 1984.

Burschel, Peter. *Sterben und Unsterblichkeit: Zur Kultur des Martyriums in der frühen Neuzeit.* Munich: R. Oldenbourg, 2004.

Bynum, Caroline Walker. *The Resurrection of the Body in Western Christianity, 200–1336.* New York: Columbia University Press, 1995

Carell, Susanne. "Die Wallfahrt zu den sieben Hauptkirchen Roms: Aufkommen und Wandel im Spiegel der deutschen Pilgerführer." *Jahrbuch für Volkskunde* 9 (1986): 112–50.

Christian, William A. *Local Religion in Sixteenth-Century Spain.* Princeton, NJ: Princeton University Press, 1981.

Christl, Karl. *300 Jahre barocke Pfarrkirche Kühbach.* Kühbach, Germany: Kühbach Pfarrgemeinde, 1989.

Copeland, Clare. "Sanctity." In *The Ashgate Research Companion to the Counter-Reformation,* edited by Alexandra Bamji, Geert H. Janssen, and Mary Laven, 225–42. London: Routledge, 2013.

de Rossi, Giovanni Battista, and Antonio Ferrua. *Sulla questione del vaso di sangue: Memoria inedita con introduzione storica e appendici di documenti.* Rome: Pontificio Istituto di Archeologia Cristiana, 1944.

Delfosse, Annick. "Les reliques des catacombs de Rome aux Pays-Bas: Acteurs, réseaux, flux." In *Reliques romaines: Invention et circulation des corps saints des catacombes à l'époque moderne,* edited by Stéphane Baciocchi and Christophe Duhamelle, 263–86. Rome: École française de Rome, 2016.

Delooz, Pierre, "Towards a Sociological Study of Canonized Sainthood in the Catholic Church." In *Saints and Their Cults: Studies in Religious Sociology, Folklore and History,* edited by Stephen Wilson, 189–216. Cambridge, UK: Cambridge University Press, 1983.

Deutinger, Martin von, ed. *Die älteren Matrikeln des Bisthums Freysing.* 3 vols. Munich: Verlag der Erzbischöfl. Ordinariats-Kanzley, 1849.

Diedrichs, Christof L. *Vom Glauben zum Sehen: Die Sichtbarkeit der Reliquie im Reliquiar.* Berlin: Weißensee-Verlag, 2001.

Ditchfield, Simon, "How Not to Be a Counter-Reformation Saint: The Attempted Canonization of Pope Gregory X, 1622–45." *Papers of the British School at Rome* 60 (1992): 379–422.

———. *Liturgy, Sanctity and History in Tridentine Italy: Pietro Maria Campi and the Preservation of the Particular.* Cambridge, UK: Cambridge University Press, 2002.

———. "Martyrs on the Move: Relics as Vindicators of Local Diversity in the Tridentine Church." In *Martyrs and Martyrologies: Papers Read at the 1992 Summer Meeting and the 1993 Winter Meeting of the Ecclesiastical History Society,* edited by Diana Wood, 283–94. Oxford, UK: Blackwell, 1993.

———. "Reading Rome as a Sacred Landscape, c. 1586–1635." In *Sacred Space in Early Modern Europe,* edited by Will Coster and Andrew Spicer, 167–92. Cambridge, UK: Cambridge University Press, 2005.

———. "*Romanus* and *Catholicus:* Counter-Reformation Rome as *Caput Mundi.*" In *A Companion to Early Modern Rome, 1492–1692,* edited by Pamela Jones, Barbara Wisch, and Ditchfield, 131–47. Leiden, Netherlands: Brill, 2019.

———. “Text before Trowel: Antonio Bosio’s *Roma Sotterranea* Revisted.” In *The Church Retrospective: Papers Read at the 1995 Summer Meeting and the 1996 Winter Meeting of the Ecclesiastical History Society,* Studies in Church History 33, edited by Robert N. Swanson, 343–60. Woodbridge, UK: Boydell, 1997.

———. “Thinking with Saints: Sanctity and Society in the Early Modern World.” *Critical Inquiry* 35, no. 3 (2009): 552–84.

———. “Tridentine Worship and the Cult of Saints.” In *Cambridge History of Christianity: Reform and Expansion, 1500–1660,* edited by R. Po-chia Hsia, 201–24. Vol. 6 of *Cambridge History of Christianity*. Cambridge, UK: Cambridge University Press, 2007.

Dooley, Eugene A. *Church Law on Sacred Relics.* Washington, DC: Catholic University of America Press, 1931.

Dreher, Max. *Die Augustiner-Eremiten in München: Im Zeitalter der Reformation und des Barock (16. bis Mitte des 18. Jahrhunderts).* Hamburg: Kovač, 2003.

Duhamelle, Christophe, and Stéphane Baciocchi. “Des Guardes Suisses à las frontière confessionelle: Apothéose et banalization des corps saints des catacombes.” In *Reliques romaines: Invention et circulation des corps saints des catacombes à l’époque moderne,* edited by Baciocchi and Duhamelle, 371–411. Rome: École française de Rome, 2016.

———. “Les reliques romaines ‘hors la ville en quel lieu que ce soit du monde.’” In *Reliques romaines: Invention et circulation des corps saints des catacombes à l’époque moderne,* edited by Baciocchi and Duhamelle, 1–100. Rome: École française de Rome, 2016.

Ebermann, Bernhard P. “300 Jahrc St. Felix in Gars.” *Das Mühlrad: Blätter zur Geschichte des Inn- und Isengaues* 17 (1975): 69–81.

Erlmeier, Franz X. *Chronik von Frontenhausen und Umgebung: Die Übertragung der Gebeine des Hl. Amantinus nach Frontenhausen.* Frontenhausen, Germany: Lehner, 1928.

Evangelisti, Silvia. “Material Culture.” In *The Ashgate Research Companion to the Counter-Reformation,* edited by Alexandra Bamji, Geert H. Janssen, and Mary Laven, 395–416. London: Routledge, 2013.

Ferrua, Antonio. “Corpi Santi.” In *Enciclopedia Cattolica,* vol 4. Vatican City: Ente per l’Enciclopedia cattolica e per il libro cattolico, 1950.

Forster, Marc R. “Catholic Confessionalism in Germany after 1650.” In *Confessionalization in Europe, 1555–1700: Essays in Honor and Memory of Bodo Nischan,* edited by John Headley, Hans J. Hillerbrand, and Anthony J. Papalas, 227–43. Burlington, VT: Ashgate, 2004.

———. *Catholic Germany from the Reformation to the Enlightenment.* European History in Perspective. Basingstoke, UK: Palgrave Macmillan, 2007.

———. *Catholic Revival in the Age of the Baroque: Religious Identity in Southwest Germany, 1550–1750.* New Studies in European History. Cambridge, UK: Cambridge University Press, 2001.

———. *The Counter-Reformation in the Villages: Religion and Reform in the Bishopric of Speyer, 1560–1720*. Ithaca, NY: Cornell University Press, 1992.

———. "With and without Confessionalization: Varieties of Early Modern German Catholicism." *Journal of Early Modern History* 1, no. 4 (1997): 315–43.

François, Etienne. *Die unsichtbare Grenze: Protestanten und Katholiken in Augsburg, 1648–1806*. Stuttgart: Jan Thorbecke Verlag, 2002.

Freitag, Werner. *Die Reformation in Westfalen: Regionale Vielfalt, Bekenntniskonflikt und Koexistenz*. Münster: Aschendorff, 2016.

———. *Volks- und Elitenfrömmigkeit in der frühen Neuzeit: Marienwallfahrten im Fürstbistum Münster*. Paderborn, Germany: Schöningh, 1991.

Geary, Patrick J. *Furta Sacra: Thefts of Relics in the Central Middle Ages*. Princeton, NJ: Princeton University Press, 1978.

———. "Sacred Commodities: The Circulation of Medieval Relics." In *The Social Life of Things: Commodities in Cultural Perspective*, edited by Arjun Appadurai, 169–94. Cambridge, UK: Cambridge University Press, 1986.

Gentilcore, David. *From Bishop to Witch: The System of the Sacred in Early Modern Terra D'Otranto*. Manchester, UK: Manchester University Press, 1992.

Geraerts, Jaap. "Early Modern Catholicism and Its Historiography: Innovation, Revitalization, and Integration." *Church History and Religious Culture* 97, no. 3/4 (2017): 381–92.

Ghilardi, Massimiliano. "'Auertendo, che per l'osseruanza si caminarà con ogni rigore': Editti seicenteschi contro l'estrazione delle reliquie dalle catacombe romane." *Sanctorum* 2 (2005): 121–37.

———. "Il Custode delle Reliquie e dei Cimiteri." *Studi Romani* 1, no. 1 (2019): 175–210.

———. "Quae signa erant illa, quibus putabant esse significativa Martyrii? Note sul riconoscimento ed authenticazione delle reliquie delle catacombe romane nella prima etá moderna." *MEFRIM: Mélanges de l'École française de Rome—Italie et mediterranée* 122, no. 1 (2010): 86–104.

———. *Il santo con due piedi sinistri. Appunti sulla genesi dei corpisanti in ceroplastica*. Città di Castello, Italy: LuoghInteriori, 2019.

Gläßel, Adolf, *Adalbert Eder: Barocke Klosterarbeiten*. Waldsassen, Germany: Stadt Waldsassen, 1999.

Gotor, Miguel. *I Beati del papa: Santità, inquisizione e obbedienza in età moderna*. Florence: L. S. Olschki, 2002.

Grafton, Anthony. "Church History in Early Modern Europe: Tradition and Innovation." In *Sacred History: Uses of the Christian Past in the Renaissance World*, edited by Simon Ditchfield, Katherine van Liere, and Howard Louthan, 3–36. Oxford, UK: Oxford University Press, 2012.

Gregory, Brad S. "Persecutions and Martyrdom." In *Reform and Expansion, 1500–1660*, edited by R. Po-chia Hsia, 261–82. Vol. 6 of *The Cambridge History of Christianity*. Cambridge, UK: Cambridge University Press, 2007.

———. *Salvation at Stake: Christian Martyrdom in Early Modern Europe.* Cambridge, MA: Harvard University Press, 1999.

Guazzelli, Giuseppe Antonio. "Antiquarianism and Christian Archaeology (ca.1450–1650)." In *The Eerdmans Encyclopedia of Early Christian Art and Archaeology,* vol. 3, edited by Paul Corby Finney. Grand Rapids, MI: William B. Eerdmans, 2017.

———. "Cesare Baronio and the Roman Catholic Vision of the Early Church." In *Sacred History: Uses of the Christian Past in the Renaissance World,* edited by Simon Ditchfield, Katherine van Liere, and Howard Louthan, 52–71. Oxford, UK: Oxford University Press, 2012.

———. "Roman Antiquities and Christian Archaeology." In *A Companion to Early Modern Rome, 1492–1692,* edited by Simon Ditchfield, Pamela M. Jones, and Barbara Wisch, 530–45. Leiden, Netherlands: Brill, 2019.

Guazzelli, Giuseppe, Raimondo Michetti, and Francesco Scorza Barcellona, eds. *Cesare Baronio tra santità e scrittura storica.* Rome: Viella, 2012.

Hahn, Cynthia. *The Reliquary Effect: Enshrining the Sacred Object.* London: Reaktion, 2017.

———. *Strange Beauty: Issues in the Making and Meaning of Reliquaries, 400–circa 1204.* University Park: Penn State University Press, 2013.

———. "The Voices of Saints: Speaking Reliquaries." *Gesta* 36 (1997): 20–31.

———. "What Do Reliquaries Do for Relics?" *Numen* 57 (2010): 284–316.

Haliczer, Stephen. *Between Exaltation and Infamy: Female Mystics in the Golden Age of Spain.* Oxford, UK: Oxford University Press, 2002.

Hamm, Johannes. *Barocke Altertabernakel in Süddeutschland.* Petersburg, Germany: Imhof, 2010.

Harries, Karsten. *The Bavarian Rococo Church.* New Haven, CT: Yale University Press, 1983.

Harris, A. Katie. "Gift, Sale, and Theft: Juan de Ribera and the Sacred Economy of Relics in the Early Modern Mediterranean." *Journal of Early Modern History* 18 (2014): 1–34.

———. "'A Known Holy Body, with an Inscription and a Name': Bishop Sancho Dávila y Toledo and the Creation of St. Vitalis." *Archiv für Reformationsgeschichte* 104 (2013): 245–71.

Hartig, Michael. *Die Errichtung des Bistums Freising im Jahre 739.* Munich: Pfeiffer, 1939.

Harvolk, Edgar. "Die Translation eines Katakombenheiligen im Jahre 1825: Ein Beitrag zur Geschichte der Volksfrömmigkeit und der Säkularisation in Bayern." In *Dona Ethnologica Monacensia: Leopold Kretzenbacher zum 70. Geburtstag,* edited by Helge Gerndt, Klaus Roth, and Georg Schroubek, 83–96. Munich: Bayerisches Nationalmuseum, 1983.

Heidtmann, Bernhard. "Der Heilige mit dem zuckenden Fuß." *Der Stadtturm: Heimatkundlicher und Historischer Arbeitskreis Pfreimd* 22 (2006): 49–50.

Heinzelmann, Martin. *Translationsberichte und andere Quellen des Reliquienkultes.* Turnhout, Belgium: Brepols, 1979.

Hemmerle, Josef. *Die Benediktinerabtei Benediktbeuern.* Berlin: Walter de Gruyter, 1991.

Herklotz, Ingo. "Antonio Bosio und Carlo Bascapè: Reliquiensuche und Katakombenforschung im 17. Jahrhundert." In *Festschrift für Max Kunze: Der Blick auf die antike Kunst von der Renaissance bis heute,* edited by Stephanie-Gerrit Bruer, Detlef Rößler, and Max Kunze, 93–103. Ruhpolding, Germany: Verlag Franz Philipp Rutzen, 2011.

———. "Wie Jean Mabillon dem römischen Index entging: Reliquienkult und christliche Archäologie um 1700." *Römische Quartalschrift für christliche Altertumskunde und Kirchengeschichte* 106 (2011): 193–228.

Hernández, Montserrat A. Báez. "The *Corpi Santi* under the Government of Pius VI, Materiality as a Sign of Identity: First Approaches to Novohispanic Cases." In *Relics @ the Lab: An Analytical Approach to the Study of Relics,* edited by Mark Van Strydonck, Jeroen Reyniers, and Fanny Van Cleven, 21–42. Leuven, Netherlands: Peeters, 2018.

———. "El cuerpo relicario: Mártir, reliquia y simulacro como experiencia visual." In *Valor discursivo del cuerpo en el barroco hispánico,* edited by Rafael García Mahíques and Sergi Doménech García 323–33. Valencia, Spain: Universitat de Valencia, 2015.

Herrmann-Mascard, Nicole. *Les Reliques des saints: Formation coutumière d'un droit.* Paris: Klincksieck, 1975.

Herzig, Arno. *Der Zwang zum wahren Glauben: Rekatholisierung vom 16. bis zum 18. Jahrhundert.* Göttingen, Germany: Vandenhoeck and Ruprecht, 2000.

Hills, Helen. "How to Look Like a Counter-Reformation Saint." In *Exploring Cultural History: Essays in Honor of Peter Burke,* edited by Melissa Calaresu, Filippo de Vivo, and Joan-Pau Rubiés, 207–30, Farnham, UK: Ashgate, 2010.

———. *The Matter of Miracles: Neapolitan Baroque Architecture and Sanctity.* Rethinking Art's Histories. Manchester, UK: Manchester University Press, 2016.

———. "Nuns and Relics: Spiritual Authority in Post-Tridentine Naples." In *Female Monasticism in Early Modern Europe: An Interdisciplinary View,* edited by Cordula van Wyhe, 11–38. Aldershot, UK: Ashgate, 2008.

Holzem, Andreas. *Religion und Lebensformen: Katholische Konfessionalisierung im Sendgericht des Fürstbistums Münster 1570–1800.* Paderborn, Germany: Schöningh, 2000.

Hsia, R. Po-chia. *Social Discipline in the Reformation: Central Europe, 1550–1750.* Christianity and Society in the Modern World. London: Routledge, 1989.

Hubensteiner, Benno. *Vom Geist des Barock: Kultur und Frömmigkeit im alten Bayern.* Munich: Süddeutscher Verlag, 1967.

John, Sabine. "'. . . mit Behutsambkeit vnd Referentz zu tractieren': Die Katakombenheiligen im Münchner Pütrichkloster—Arbeit und Frömmigkeit." *Bayerisches Jahrbuch für Volkskunde* (1995): 1–34.

Johnson, Trevor. "Defining the Confessional Frontier: Bavaria and Counter-Reformation 'Historia Sacra.'" In *Frontiers and the Writing of History, 1500–1850,* edited by Steven G. Ellis and Raingard Esser, 151–66. Hannover-Laatzen, Germany: Wehrhahn, 2006.

———. "Holy Dynasts and Sacred Soil: Politics and Sanctity in Matthaeus Rader's *Bavaria Sancta* (1615–1628)," In *Europa sacra: Raccolte agiografiche e identità politiche in Europa fra Medioevo ed Età moderna,* edited by Sofia Boesch Gajano and Raimondo Michetti, 83–100. Rome: Carocci, 2002.

———. "Holy Fabrications: The Catacomb Saints and the Counter-Reformation in Bavaria." *Journal of Ecclesiastical History* 47, no. 2 (1996): 274–97.

———. *Magistrates, Madonnas and Miracles: The Counter Reformation in the Upper Palatinate.* St. Andrews Studies in Reformation History. Farnham, UK: Ashgate, 2009.

———. "*Trionfi* of the Holy Dead: The Relic Festivals of Baroque Bavaria." In *Festive Culture in Germany and Europe from the Sixteenth to the Twentieth Century,* edited by Karin Friedrich, 31–56. Lewiston, NY: Edwin Mellen, 2000.

Kamen, Henry. *The Phoenix and the Flame: Catalonia and the Counter Reformation.* New Haven, CT: Yale University Press, 1993.

Koudounaris, Paul. *The Empire of Death: A Cultural History of Ossuaries and Charnel Houses.* London: Thames & Hudson, 2011.

———. *Heavenly Bodies: Cult Treasures and Spectacular Saints from the Catacombs.* London: Thames & Hudson, 2013.

Krausen, Edgar. "Heilige 'zweiter Klasse' waren Namenspatrone lediger Kinder." *Charivari* 6 (1980): 3–9.

———. "Das heilbringende Öl des heiligen Antonius zu Landshut-Seligenthal." *Bayerisches Jahrbuch für Volkskunde* (1963): 58–70.

———. "Schicksale römischer Katakombenheiliger zwischen 1800 und 1980." *Jahrbuch für Volkskunde,* no. 4 (1981): 160–67.

———. "Die Verehrung römischer Katakombenheiliger in Altbayern im Zeitalter des Barock." *Bayerisches Jahrbuch für Volkskunde* (1966/67): 37–47.

Kühne, Hartmut. *Ostensio reliquiarum: Untersuchungen über Entstehung, Ausbreitung, Gestalt und Funktion der Heiltumsweisungen im römisch-deutschen Regnum.* Berlin: de Gruyter, 2000.

Laven, Mary. Introduction to *The Ashgate Research Companion to the Counter-Reformation,* edited by Alexandra Bamji, Geert H. Janssen, and Laven, 1–14. London: Routledge, 2013.

Lazure, Guy, "Possessing the Sacred: Monarchy and Identity in Philip II's Relic Collection at the Escorial." *Renaissance Quarterly* 60, no. 1 (2007): 58–93.

Lechner, Martin. "Der heilige Martyrer Lucius, der zweite Patron von Sankt Veit." *Heimat an Rott und Inn* (1968): 68–82.

Legner, Anton. *Reliquien in Kunst und Kult zwischen Antike und Aufklärung.* Darmstadt, Germany: Wissenschaftliche Buchgesellschaft, 1995.

———. "Vom Glanz und von der Präsenz des Heiltums—Bilder und Texte." In *Reliquien: Verehrung und Verklärung*, edited by Legner, 33–148. Cologne: Schnütgen Museum, 1989.

Lepage, Andrea. "Art and the Counter-Reformation." In *The Ashgate Research Companion to the Counter-Reformation*, edited by Alexandra Bamji, Geert H. Janssen, and Mary Laven, 373–94. London: Routledge, 2013.

Lewis, Nicola Denzey. *The Early Modern Invention of Late Antique Rome.* Cambridge, UK: Cambridge University Press, 2020.

Liebhart, Wilhelm. "'doch sagt mir her, seint eure Kinder Maryrer?' Katakombenheilige und ein geistliches Volksschauspiel aus dem Birgittenkloster Altomünster von 1694." *Schönere Heimat* 71 (1982): 489–94.

Lotz-Heumann, Ute. "Confessionalization." In *The Ashgate Research Companion to the Counter-Reformation*, edited by Alexandra Bamji, Geert H. Janssen, and Mary Laven, 33–55. London: Routledge, 2013.

Louthan, Howard. "Tongues, Toes, and Bones: Remembering Saints in Early Modern Bohemia." *Past & Present* 206, Supplement 5 (2010): 167–83.

Markmiller, Fritz, "Die Übertragung zweier Katakombenheiliger nach Niederbayern im 18. Jahrhundert." *Jahrbuch für Volkskunde* 4 (1981): 127–59.

Matrikel des Bisthums Regensburg nach der allgemeinen Pfarr- und Kirchen-Beschreibung von 1860 mit Rücksicht auf die älteren Bisthums-Matrikeln zusammengestellt. Regensburg, Germany: Bischöfliches Ordinariat, 1863.

Melion, Walter S. "Introduction: The Jesuit Engagement with the Status and Function of the Visual Image." In *Jesuit Image Theory*, edited by Wietse de Boer, Karl A. E. Enenkel, and Melion, 1–49. Leiden, Netherlands: Brill, 2016.

Mitterwieser, Alois. *Geschichte der Fronleichnamsprozession in Bayern.* 2nd ed. Munich: Weinmayer, 1949.

Mois, Jakob. "Reliquien und Verehrung der Heiligen Primus und Felicianus in Rottenbuch." *Lech-Isar-Land* (1978): 31–50.

Müller, Uwe. "Der Versuch Herzog Wilhelms V. von Bayern, das Reichsheiltum in seinen Besitz zu bringen." *Mitteilungen des Vereins für Geschichte der Stadt Nürnberg* 72 (1985): 117–35.

Nalle, Sara. *God in La Mancha: Religious Reform and the People of Cuenca, 1500–1650.* Baltimore, MD: Johns Hopkins University Press, 2008.

Olds, Katrina. "The Ambiguities of the Holy: Authenticating Relics in Seventeenth-Century Spain." *Renaissance Quarterly* 65, no. 1 (2012): 135–84.

———. "The 'False Chronicles,' Cardinal Baronio, and Sacred History in Counter-Reformation Spain." *Catholic Historical Review* 100, no. 1 (2014): 1–26.

Oryshkevich, Irina Taïssa. "The History of the Roman Catacombs from the Age of Constantine to the Renaissance." PhD diss., Columbia University, 2003.

Pentzlin, Nadja Irmgard. "The Cult of Corpus Christi in Early Modern Bavaria: Pilgrimages, Processions, and Confraternities between 1550 and 1750." PhD diss., University of St. Andrews, 2014.

Pfeiffer, Anna Caroline. "Auferweckt in Herrlichkeit! Barocke Heilige Leiber in Oberschwaben: Materialien, Fixierungstechniken, konservatorische Aspekte." Master's thesis, Fachhochschule Cologne, 2005.

Pötzl, Walter. "Bruderschaften, Wallfahrten und Katakombenheilige im Irseerherschaftsgebiet." In *Das Reichsstift Irsee: Vom Benediktinerkloster zum Bildungszentrum,* edited by Hans Frei, 112–32. Weißenhorn, Germany: Konrad, 1981.

———. "Katakombenheiliege als 'Attribute' von Gnadenbildern." *Jahrbuch für Volkskunde* 4 (1981): 168–84.

———. "Volksfrömmigkeit." In *Handbuch der Bayerischen Kirchengeschichte: Von der Glaubensspaltung bis zur Säkularisation,* edited by Walter Brandmüller, 859–964. Vol. 2 of *Handbuch der Bayerischen Kirchengeschichte.* St. Ottilien, Germany: EOS Verlag, 1991.

Reinhard, Wolfgang. "Pressures towards Confessionalization? Prolegomena to a Theory of the Confessional Age." In *The German Reformation: The Essential Readings,* edited by C. Scott Dixon, 169–92. Oxford, UK: Wiley-Blackwell, 1999.

———. "Reformation, Counter-Reformation, and the Early Modern State: A Reassessment." In *The Counter-Reformation: The Essential Readings,* edited by David Luebke, 105–28. Oxford, UK: Wiley-Blackwell, 1999.

———. "Was ist katholische Konfessionalisierung?" In *Die katholische Konfessionalisierung: Wissenschaftliches Symposion der Gesellschaft zur Herausgabe des Corpus Catholicorum und des Vereins für Reformationsgeschichte 1993,* edited by Heinz Schilling and Reinhard, 419–52. Münster: Aschendorff, 1995.

Reudenbach, Bruno. "Visualizing Holy Bodies: Observations on Body-Part Reliquaries." In *Romanesque Art and Thought in the Twelfth Century,* edited by Colum Hourihane, 95–135. State College, PA: Distributed by Penn State University for the Index of Christian Art, Princeton University, 2008.

Ritz, Gislind M. "Die Heiligen Leiber St. Stephanus und St. Benedictus und ihre Fassung." In *Heilig Kreuz in Donauwörth,* edited by Werner Schiedermair, 100–103. Donauwörth, Germany: Auer, 1987.

———. "Die Katakombenheiligen der Klosterkirche zu Altomünster." In *Festschrift Altomünster 1973,* edited by Toni Grad, 211–22. Aichach, Germany: Mayer und Söhne, 1973.

———. "Die Katakombenheiligen S. Sigismund und S. Ernest in der Pfarrkirche St. Jakob in Dachau." *Amperland* 28 (1992): 226–30.

Rubin, Miri. *Corpus Christi: The Eucharist in Late Medieval Culture.* Cambridge, UK: Cambridge University Press, 1991.

Rummel, Peter. "Jesuiten," In *Handbuch der Bayerischen Kirchengeschichte: Von der Glaubensspaltung bis zur Säkularisation,* edited by Walter Brandmüller, 842–70. Vol. 2 of *Handbuch der Bayerischen Kirchengeschichte.* St. Ottilien, Germany: EOS Verlag, 1991.

Schiedermair, Werner. "Klosterarbeiten: Hinweise zu Begriff, Wesen, Herkunft, Verwendung und Herstellern." In *Klosterarbeiten aus Schwaben,* edited by

Gislind M. Ritz and Schiedermair, 9–32. Gessertshausen, Germany: Museumsdirektion des Bezirkes Schwaben, 1990.

———. "Die Waldsassener Heiligen Leiber." In *Waldsassen: 300 Jahre Barockkirche,* edited by Paul Mai and Karl Hausberger, 357–68. Regensburg, Germany: Verlag des Vereins für Regensburger Bistumsgeschichte, 2004.

Schmid, Alois. "Altbayern 1648–1803." In *Handbuch der Bayerischen Kirchengeschichte: Von der Glaubensspaltung bis zur Säkularisation,* edited by Walter Brandmüller, 1–64. Vol. 2 of *Handbuch der Bayerischen Kirchengeschichte.* St. Ottilien, Germany: EOS Verlag, 1991.

———. "Die 'Bavaria Sancta et Pia' des P. Matthäus Rader SJ." In *Les princes et l'histoire du XIVe au XVIIIe siècle actes du colloque organisé par l'Université de Versailles—Saint-Quentin et l'Institut Historique Allemand, Paris/Versailles, 13–16 mars 1996,* edited by Chantal Grell, 499–522. Bonn: Bouvier, 1998.

Schmitz-Esser, Romedio. *Der Leichnam im Mittelalter: Einbalsamierung, Verbrennung und die kulturelle Konstruktion des toten Körpers.* Ostfildern, Germany: Thorbecke, 2014.

Schudt, Ludwig. *Le guide di Roma: Materialien zu einer Geschichte der römischen Topographie.* Westmead, UK: Gregg International, 1930.

Schutte, Anne Jacobson. *Aspiring Saints: Pretense of Holiness, Inquisition, and Gender in the Republic of Venice, 1618–1750.* Baltimore, MD: Johns Hopkins University Press, 2001.

Seelig, Lorenz. "Dieweil wir dann nach dergleichen Heiltumb und edlen Clainod sonder Begirde tragen: Der von Herzog Wilhelm V. begründete Reliquienschatz der Jesuitenkirche St. Michael in München." In *Rom in Bayern: Kunst und Spiritualität der ersten Jesuiten,* edited by Reinhold Baumstark, 199–262. Munich: Hirmer, 1997.

Smith, Jeffrey Chipps. "Repatriating Sanctity, or How the Dukes of Bavaria Rescued Saints during the Reformation." In *Crossing Cultures: Conflict, Migration and Convergence,* edited by Jaynie Anderson, 1084–89. Carlton, Australia: Melbourne University Publishing, 2009.

———. "Salvaging Saints: The Rescue and Display of Relics in Munich during the Early Catholic Reformation." In *Art, Piety and Destruction in the Christian West, 1500–1700,* edited by Virginia Chieffo Raguin, 23–44. Burlington, VT: Ashgate, 2010.

———. *Sensuous Worship: Jesuits and the Art of the Early Catholic Reformation in Germany.* Princeton, NJ: Princeton University Press, 2002.

Smith, Julia M. H. "Portable Christianity: Relics in the Medieval West (c.700–c.1200)." *Proceedings of the British Academy* 181 (2012): 143–67.

———. "Saints and Their Cults." In *Early Medieval Christianities, c. 600–c.1100,* edited by T. F. X. Noble and Smith, 581–605. Vol. 3 of *The Cambridge History of Christianity.* Cambridge, UK: Cambridge University Press, 2008.

Snoek, Godefridus J. C. *Medieval Piety from Relics to the Eucharist: A Process of Mutual Interaction.* Leiden, Netherlands: Brill, 1995.

Soergel, Philip. *Wondrous in His Saints: Counter-Reformation Propaganda in Bavaria.* Berkeley: University of California Press, 1993.

Spindler, Max, ed. *Handbuch der bayerischen Geschichte: Das alte Bayern,* vol. 2. Munich: Beck, 1977.

Sprinkart, Alfons. "Kapuziner." In *Von der Glaubensspaltung bis zur Säkularisation,* edited by Walter Brandmüller, 795–824. Vol. 2 of *Handbuch der Bayerischen Kirchengeschichte.* St. Ottilien, Germany: EOS Verlag, 1998.

Steiner, Peter Bernhard. "Der gottselige Fürst und die Konfessionalisierung Altbayerns." In *Um Glauben und Reich: Kurfürst Maximilian I,* edited by Hubert Glaser, 252–63. Vol. 2.1 of *Wittelsbach und Bayern.* Munich: Hirmer, 1980.

Strasser, Ulrike. "Bones of Contention: Catholic Nuns Resist Their Enclosure." In *Unspoken Worlds: Women's Religious Lives,* edited by Nancy Auer Falk and Rita M. Gross, 255–88. Belmont, CA: Wadsworth, 2001.

———. *State of Virginity: Gender, Religion, and Politics in an Early Modern Catholic State.* Social History, Popular Culture, and Politics in Germany. Ann Arbor: University of Michigan Press, 2004.

Ticchi, Jean-Marc. "Mgr Sacriste et la distribution des reliques des catacombes dans l'espace Italien." In *Reliques romaines: Invention et circulation des corps saints des catacombes à l'époque moderne,* edited by Stéphane Baciocchi and Christophe Duhamelle, 175–223. Rome: École française de Rome, 2016.

Touber, Jetze. *Law, Medicine and Engineering in the Cult of the Saints in Counter-Reformation Rome: The Hagiographical Works of Antonio Gallonio, 1556–1605.* Leiden, Netherlands: Brill, 2014.

Toussaint, Gia. *Kreuz und Knochen: Reliquien zur Zeit der Kreuzzüge.* Berlin: Dietrich Reimer Verlag, 2011.

———. "Die Sichtbarkeit des Gebeins im Reliquiar—eine Folge der Plünderung Konstantinopels?" In *Reliquiare im Mittelalter,* edited by Gia Toussaint and Bruno Reudenbach, 89–106. Berlin: Akademie Verlag, 2005.

Ulčar, Milena. "Saints in Parts: Image of the Sacred Body in an Early Modern Venetian Town." *Sixteenth Century Journal* 48, no. 1 (Spring 2017): 67–86.

van Os, Henk. "Seeing Is Believing." In *The Way to Heaven: Relic Veneration in the Middle Ages,* edited by van Os, 103–62. Baarn, Netherlands: De Prom, 2000.

Veit, Ludwig, and Ludwig Lenhart. *Kirche und Volksfrömmigkeit im Zeitalter des Barock.* Freiburg, Germany: Herder, 1956.

Walsham, Alexandra. "Introduction: Relics and Remains." *Past & Present* 206, Supplement 5 (2010): 9–36.

———. "Skeletons in the Cupboard: Relics after the English Reformation." *Past & Present* 206, Supplement 5 (2010): 121–43.

Wandel, Lee Palmer. *The Eucharist in the Reformation: Incarnation and Liturgy.* Cambridge, UK: Cambridge University Press, 2006.

Weis, Eberhard. *Die Säkularisation der bayerischen Klöster 1802/03: Neue Forschungen zu Vorgeschichte und Ergebnissen.* Munich: Verlag der Bayerischen Akademie der Wissenschaften, 1982.

Wenhardt, Franz. "Felix-Wallfahrt und Radegundis-Verehrung in Gars." In *Zeit-FlussLäufe: Säkularisation der Klöster Au und Gars am Inn—1803–2003*, 44–53. Gars am Inn, Germany: Bibliothek der Redemptoristen, 2003.

Woeckel, Gerhard. *Pietas Bavarica: Wallfahrt, Prozession und Ex voto-Gabe im Hause Wittelsbach in Ettal, Wessobrunn, Altötting und der Landeshauptstadt München von der Gegenreformation bis zur Säkularisation und der "Renovatio Ecclesiae."* Weißenhorn, Germany: A. H. Konrad, 1992.

Worcester, Thomas. "Saints and Baroque Piety." In *The Oxford Handbook of the Baroque*, edited by John D. Lyons. Oxford, UK: Oxford University Press, 2019.

Zarri, Gabriella. "Living Saints: A Typology of Female Sanctity in the Early Sixteenth Century." In *Women and Religion in Medieval and Renaissance Italy*, edited by Daniel Bornstein and Roberto Rusconi, 219–303. Chicago: University of Chicago Press, 1996.

Ziegler, Walter. "Bayern." In *Land und Konfession 1500–1650: Der Südosten*, edited by Anton Schindling and Ziegler, 56–71. Vol. 1 of *Die Territorien des Reichs im Zeitalter der Reformation und Konfessionalisierung*. Münster: Aschendorff, 1989.

———. "Reformation und Gegenreformation 1517–1648: Altbayern." In *Von der Glaubensspaltung bis zur Säkularisation*, edited by Walter Brandmüller, 1–64. Vol. 2 of *Handbuch der Bayerischen Kirchengeschichte*. St. Ottilien, Germany: EOS Verlag, 1998.

Zwingler, Irmgard. *Das Klarissenkloster bei St. Jakob am Anger zu München: Das Angerkloster unter der Reform des Franziskanerordens im Zeitalter des Dreißigjährigen Krieges*. Munich: Verlag des Verein für Diözesangeschichte von München und Freising, 2009.

INDEX

Italicized page numbers refer to figures and maps; page numbers followed by a t *refer to tables.*

Studies in Early Modern German History

Music and Urban Life in Baroque Germany
Tanya Kevorkian

Strange Brethren: Refugees, Religious Bonds, and Reformation in Frankfurt, 1554–1608
Maximilian Miguel Scholz

A German Barber-Surgeon in the Atlantic Slave Trade: The Seventeenth-Century Journal of Johann Peter Oettinger
Edited and translated by Craig M. Koslofsky and Roberto Zaugg

Furnace and Fugue: A Digital Edition of Michael Maier's "Atalanta fugiens" (1618) with Scholarly Commentary
Edited by Donna Bilak and Tara Nummedal

The Devil's Art: Divination and Discipline in Early Modern Germany
Jason Philip Coy

Four Fools in the Age of Reason: Laughter, Cruelty, and Power in Early Modern Germany
Dorinda Outram

The Executioner's Journal: Meister Frantz Schmidt of the Imperial City of Nuremberg
Translated by Joel F. Harrington

Hometown Religion: Regimes of Coexistence in Early Modern Westphalia
David M. Luebke

Enlightenment Underground: Radical Germany, 1680–1720
Martin Mulsow, translated by H. C. Erik Midelfort

Crossing the Boundaries of Belief: Geographies of Religious Conversion in Southern Germany, 1648–1800
Duane J. Corpis

Crime and Culture in Early Modern Germany
Joy Wiltenburg

The Witch in the Western Imagination
Lyndal Roper

The Fuggers of Augsburg: Pursuing Wealth and Honor in Renaissance Germany
Mark Häberlein

"Evil People": A Comparative Study of Witch Hunts in Swabian Austria and the Electorate of Trier
Johannes Dillinger, translated by Laura Stokes

Witchcraft and the Papacy: An Account Drawing on the Formerly Secret Records of the Roman Inquisition
Rainer Decker, translated by H. C. Erik Midelfort

The German Discovery of the World: Renaissance Encounters with the Strange and Marvelous
Christine R. Johnson

Cautio Criminalis, or a Book on Witch Trials
Friedrich Spee von Langenfeld, translated by Marcus Hellyer

Bacchus and Civic Order: The Culture of Drink in Early Modern Germany
B. Ann Tlusty

Shaman of Oberstdorf: Chonrad Stoeckhlin and the Phantoms of the Night
Wolfgang Behringer, translated by H. C. Erik Midelfort

Obedient Germans? A Rebuttal: A New View of German History
Peter Blickle, translated by Thomas A. Brady Jr.

Lost Worlds: How Our European Ancestors Coped with Everyday Life and Why Life Is So Hard Today
Arthur E. Imhof, translated by Thomas Robisheaux

Mad Princes of Renaissance Germany
H. C. Erik Midelfort